# After the Restoration

MICHIO UMEGAKI

# AFTER THE RESTORATION

## The Beginning
## of Japan's Modern State

NEW YORK UNIVERSITY PRESS
NEW YORK AND LONDON

**Library of Congress Cataloging-in-Publication Data**

Umegaki, Michio.
  After the Restoration.

  Bibliography: p.
  Includes index.
  1. Japan—Politics and government—1868-1912.
I. Title.
DS822.U43   1988        952.03        88-1614
ISBN 0-8147-8552-2 (alk. paper)

*New York University Press books are Smyth-sewn
and printed on permanent and durable acid-free paper.*

———

*To my parents*
*Yoshiharu and Etsuko Umegaki*
*and to my wife*
*Lynn J. Thiesmeyer*

———

# Contents

# Notes on Dates and Japanese Names

DATES IN the old Japanese calendar are converted to the Western calendar according to *Kindai inyōreki taishōhyō* (Tokyo, 1910). In the footnotes and the tables, I use a simplified date, for example, 1/3/1868, in which the numbers represent the month, day, and year, respectively.

Japanese names are given in Japanese order, that is, the family name comes before the first name. The Hepburn system of romanization has been followed throughout to maintain consistency with earlier transcriptions of proper nouns.

# Preface

TWICE IN the history of Japan's prewar political system — at its inception and toward its collapse — the emperor emerged as the pivot of profound political change. During the 1850s and the 1860s, the emperor became the ultimate source of legitimacy. All partisan political forces sought his sanction in their efforts to either challenge or defend the existing Tokugawa political order. In the 1920s and the 1930s, as the Great Depression deepened, the emperor again emerged as the key symbol of political legitimacy for many partisan groups. Included among them were moderate as well as expansionist military leaders, party politicians, academics, and government officials.

It is easy to dismiss these unusual instances of the political primacy of the emperor simply as symptomatic of a society, threatened by imminent crises, in need of a rallying symbol. However, there are several intriguing similarities between these two periods of imperial influence. First is the fact that the emperor was, on both occasions, *outside* of the formal political framework which these partisan political forces tried to either reform or displace. Second, a general expansion of the basis for political participation — the rise of the so-called low- and middle-rank samurai in the 1840s and the 1850s, and the manhood suffrage act of 1926 — preceded each of these instances, respectively. The effects of the emperor's rise to political primacy were also strikingly similar: the replacement of the intense partisan differences by an equally intense competition for the *same* claim that each was more loyal to the emperor than the others among the partisan forces, which in turn led to a political equilibrium among the contestants for the emperor's sanction.

This issue of why the emperor had been entrusted with this peculiar role in times of crisis initially inspired me to write this book. Soon I began to recognize more patterns: that the intense competition for the same object resulted in a tendency toward its moderation among the contestants; and that arrogance and insecurity coexisted in each of the contestants for the emperor's sanction. In order to pursue this initial inspiration I decided to examine, first, the politics and histories of the Meiji Restoration. This study began with the hope of establishing what amounted to an archetypal authority relationship involving the prewar emperor. I started reading the biographies, autobiographies, and diaries of the key activists of the Restoration with a fairly clear sense of what to look for — not the signs of self-confident revolutionaries or of arrogant nation-builders, but the signs of their uncertain forays into the uncharted terrain of a new order.

Such a reading, however, inevitably placed the basic thrust of this study at odds with my own past training as a political scientist preoccupied with "macro" trends. Then I came across a powerful appeal to reconsider, or at least suspend, such a preoccupation:

> One of the constant temptations of the intellectual historian is to see pattern or unity where once there was chaos or opposition. As the near past recedes from us, its quarrels, once sculpted in high relief, flatten out; we discover an overarching unity in its diversity; we invent the generalizations by which we characterize a decade, an age, and finally a civilization. (Alex Zwerdling, *Orwell and the Left* [New Haven: Yale University Press, 1974], p. 3).

In this volume, I am still concerned with macro trends or issues — tracing the collapse of the prewar Japanese state to its very beginning. But I am also concerned with the fine contours of the terrain in which the formidable political change of the Restoration was carried out by individuals who were more insecure than arrogant, more deeply jealous of each other than united, and far more tentative than convinced.

There are many individuals who have offered me precious advice and encouragement throughout the preparation of this volume. I would like to express my gratitude to Professors Marius Jansen and Harry Eckstein, not only because they were my mentors at Princeton, but also because of something more. Professor Jansen convinced me that it was all right for a political scientist to study events before World War II, while Professor Eckstein reminded me that there is always politics regardless of time. Had it not been for this encouragement from them, I might have not taken the first steps in writing this book.

The support from Professors Harry Harootunian of the University of Chicago and Ronald Toby of the University of Illinois at Champaign Urbana came at later stages, when I was revising the manuscript. The timing was perfect. It was at the point when I was beginning to develop the suspicion that perhaps too many Restoration histories might already have been written, and growing impatient with myself because the manuscript still seemed far from what I had wished it to be.

At Georgetown University, where I have been teaching since 1979, I have received invaluable support. My colleagues in the Department of Government have been extremely patient with me while I refused to stop revising the book manuscript to meet my own goals. My friends in the Asian Studies Program have never ceased to amaze me for their unwavering support for me throughout. Let me mention a few of these colleagues and friends at Georgetown in token of my appreciation: Karl Cerny, Steve Gibert, Marshall Goodman, and Eusebio Mujal-Leon (Government Department); Matthew Gardner, Helen Chauncey, George (Sam) Crane, James Reardon-Anderson, Howard Spendelow and John Witek, S.J. (Asian Studies Program). This list of Georgetown colleagues, however, would be incomplete without Professor Avner Yaniv of Haifa University. As a visiting professor to Georgetown on several different occasions, he has understood my struggle to complete this volume. His advice and encouragement could not have been better timed.

I also owe a profound debt of gratitude to two Japanese scholars whose influence goes far beyond the scope of this book. The late Professor Hashikawa Bunsō used to tell me that the Meiji Restoration was one issue that one ought to keep going back to, whether as a political scientist, a political theorist, or an intellectual historian of Japan, for it was there that the basic political ideas of modern Japan were condensed. He also loved to warn me that the Restoration would keep coming back to me as long as I stayed in the field of modern Japanese politics. Professor Uchiyama Hideo of Keio University has been with me every step of the way, first, when I was a student of comparative politics and international relations at Keio, and later as I began expanding my study to include political theory and contemporary history upon leaving Keio in the early 1970s. Most of all, Professor Uchiyama has been the best critic, listener, and friend any student of politics could ask for.

Finally, I would like to thank Colin Jones of New York University Press and R. Miriam Brokaw, formerly of Princeton University Press, for keeping this publication project afloat. Without these two sympathetic professionals at the receiving end of the manuscript, I might not have taken the final steps to complete this volume.

# After the Restoration

# Introduction

JAPAN IN 1868 was far from the modern state it was to become by the beginning of the twentieth century. The leaders of the Restoration marking the beginning of modern Japan would have been the first to be astounded by its growth. Profound doubts about the gains to be made from the restoration of Imperial rule in 1868 beset Japan's leaders for much of the next decade. One of them was Kido Kōin, an activist-turned-government official from Chōshū, who by 1870 had resigned himself to the belief that the foundation of the Imperial government would have to be limited to the territories it had inherited from the Tokugawa and their supporters. Sasaki Takayuki, a Tosa activist, was also rudely awakened to the resistance to the rise of the Imperial government when he encountered indifference and even hostility from his fellow Tosa samurai toward his efforts to recruit them as officials for central offices. And Ōkubo Toshimichi, from Satsuma, was convinced that the emperor's government was precariously placed on a tripod of politically unseasoned Court nobles, a mere handful of samurai officials willing to forgo their domain loyalty, and the great mass of Japanese indifferent to its existence. In short, the Restoration leaders were deeply troubled by uncertainties about whether the closing of the Tokugawa shogunate might itself have helped displace the old political order, about the form in which a new system of rule was to emerge, and about what actions might be necessary to stabilize the new system.

The great transformation of the Tokugawa decentralized order into the Meiji centralized order has inspired large numbers of biographical, institutional, and political histories. However, the uncertainties faced by the key Restoration leaders have largely eluded these historical writings. As will be discussed shortly, the failure to capture or address these uncertainties stems from a variety of causes, and its effect is to overlook the significance of the critical decade immediately following the Restoration to the rise of Japan's modern state.

This book is about these uncertainties, their sources, and their consequences. From 1868 to 1878, these uncertainties were intricately woven into the changing central-local government relationship, the shifting alignment among the Restoration leaders, and the widening basis for popular political participation. The two simultaneous dynamics of dispersion and concentration of political power, which had been at work since the middle decades of the nineteenth century, intensified these changes at the end of the Tokugawa shogunate. Thus, this book is also about the leaders' growing awareness of, and adaptations to, these political dynamics.

In a reversal of the usual perspective of the Meiji Restoration, the present study seeks to understand its achievements and limits by probing the significance primarily of the immediate consequences of the restoration of Imperial rule. The reversed perspective shows the uncertainties of the Restoration leaders no longer to be inevitable reactions to any radical transformation of society. Nor does it let the critical decade pass as simply harboring the potential for modern nation-building. Looking through and across the formative years of Japan's modern state, this volume seeks in their uncertainties, and the ways the architects of the Restoration dealt with them, the foundations of Japan's prewar political system: one which came to derive its legitimacy from, ironically, the politically irresponsible sovereign, the emperor.[1]

## The Politics of the Critical Decade

The politics of this critical decade has its roots in the opening of the central arena of politics in the old system of rule in the mid–1850s. The old system of rule, often called "centralized feudalism," was a unique but stable blend of central control by the Tokugawa shogunate (the bakufu) and extensive local autonomy in the 270 feudal domains (the han).[2] However, by the mid–1850s, the system had failed to adjust effectively to the developing market economy and to the increasing demands by the Western powers to end the nation's self-seclusion policy. Fear of financial bankruptcy and of Western encroachment awakened critics to the deficiencies of the existing system of rule and inspired fiscal and administrative reforms in the bakufu and in some domains. More importantly, the reform efforts drew diverse political actors into the administrative processes, destabilizing the central arenas of politics both in the bakufu and in the reforming domains, and eventually ending the hereditary monopoly of the governing power by the few privileged samurai. At the same time, both the critics and the defenders of the old system began seeking sanction for their positions and actions from the one source of legitimacy higher than themselves: the emperor. Resorting to this higher source of legitimacy further facilitated the collapse of the old system of rule. Thus, both the pressures for and resistance to change propelled the emperor into the position that had eluded him for several centuries. In the wake of the emperor's ascendancy emerged the key political issues — political participation and legitimacy — of the critical decade in particular and of Japan's prewar political development in general.

As presented in many histories, the restoration of Imperial rule in January of 1868 and the ensuing decade of consolidation and expansion of Imperial rule followed a linear progression. The late 1867 decision to abdicate by the last of the Tokugawa shoguns, Tokugawa Yoshinobu, led to the removal in January of 1868 of all the previous institutions that had rendered the emperor and the Court politically insignificant. The newly created Imperial government in Kyoto then launched an eighteen-month military campaign — the Boshin War — against the Tokugawa family and their loyal supporters. The petition by four of the key pro-Restoration domains in the spring of 1869 to "return the fiefs and the peoples" to the emperor prompted most of the other feudal domains to follow suit by the summer of the same year. Many historians view this petition, called the *Hanseki hōkan*, as the preliminary step toward another, more direct measure for expanding the Imperial rule. In the summer of 1871, the Imperial government abolished all feudal domains and created in their place the prefectures, which were to be its local administrative arms. Contact thereby became more direct between the central governing authority and the local populace, who had previously been divided into jurisdictions of the feudal authorities of the domains. The reduction in the number of prefectures in the following months then provided significant momentum toward the transformation of the populace into a national "constituency"[3] for the new government.

Placed in this linear evolutionary construct were also the reforms of the critical decade. With the local government institutions in place, the Imperial government embarked on a number of reform policies. Some, such as the abolition of samurai privileges and the creation of a nationwide school system, sought to bring social institutions into harmony with the new, more open and active society. The Land Reform, launched in 1873, provided the impetus for commercial agriculture and consequently turned rural areas into arenas for political aspirants seeking national representation. Other reforms, such as the creation of a modern conscript army and the establishment of a modern judicial system, were designed to gain political and military credibility with the West.

The restoration of Imperial rule, however, came at a time when only a few had foreseen the passing of the Tokugawa monopoly of the governing power, much less the consequences enumerated above. Likewise, little thought had been given to what the restored Imperial rule might entail. In fact, it was not until the 1880s that the trend toward wider political participation finally reached a substantial portion of the commoners, and the emperor was fully restored as the ultimate arbiter of political competition. Preceding this constitutional development of the 1880s was the critical post-Restoration decade, during which these two issues of political participation and legitimacy produced unpredictable turns of politics. On the one hand, the basic agreement that the emperor was the ultimate source of legitimacy for the government engaged the new leaders themselves in a divisive competition for power as they all claimed their proximity to the emperor. On the other hand, the participation of new actors in politics generated two new problems: how to regulate the relationship among them, and how to adapt the emerging system of rule to the continued pressure for even wider political participation.

From the very beginning, in fact, the progression toward the consolidation and expansion of Imperial rule was complex and haphazard. The victory by the Imperial forces over the pro-Tokugawa domains in the Boshin War did not produce a corresponding realization that the feudal domains would be incompatible with the new Imperial government. For many in both the new government and the feudal domains, the petitions to "return the fiefs and the peoples" appeared to be no more than the act of making the Imperial government the recreator of the feudal domains. An intriguing question, then, is why the same feudal domains showed no resistance to the Imperial decision in the summer of 1871 to liquidate them. Furthermore, the changes in the system of rule, coupled with the reform policies, greatly destabilized the relationship among the new leaders in the Imperial government and left the vast majority of the commoners to seek ways in which the new system of rule could be made accountable to them. The strains led to a wave of samurai rebellions culminating in 1877 in the Satsuma War, waged by some of the same Satsuma samurai who once had been the core of the Imperial forces. The local populace, the majority of whom had viewed the Restoration as a remote political phenomenon, ceased to be mere passive observers of the emerging new rule.

In short, the whole process unveiled complex and unstable interactions among the various actors supporting or resisting the changes of the decade. The chief destabilizing forces were the changes in the system of rule themselves, as they determined who was to be enfranchised in or disenfranchised from the developing political system. The widely held belief that the Imperial rule was to be responsive to the entire "nation" only intensified the pressure upon all to gain or maintain a voice in the new government.

Among the various actors supporting or resisting change were the daimyo and their loyal samurai retainers, who had constituted the foundation of the feudal domains. How did they react to the demise of the Tokugawa bakufu, which had sanctioned the feudal domains and provided political stability to the feudal divisions in the nation? Did these members of the passing order now see their end as being determined by the end of the bakufu? In fact, they did not. The feudal domains had begun distancing themselves from the Tokugawa bakufu long before the restoration of the Imperial rule, letting their domain interests prevail over loyalty to the Tokugawa family. Harold Bolitho convincingly documents this tendency toward self-interest even among the *fudai*, the vassal daimyo, who were supposed to be particularly loyal to the Tokugawa.[4] What, then, did these feudal actors think would result from the creation of the Imperial government and the progression toward centralized political control, and how did they respond?

Similarly, the emergence of the new system of rule did not make the key members of the new "central" government equal participants in its process, nor did it promote cohesion among them. On the contrary, the changes in the system of rule engaged the members of the new leadership in an unstable framework of interaction which constantly threatened to divide them. This unstable relationship among the new leaders originated in their years as Restoration activists. The key members came from the four most prominent domains that supported the Restoration, led by Saigō Takamori and Ōkubo Toshimichi from Satsuma, Kido Kōin and Itō Hirobumi from Chōshū, Itagaki Taisuke from Tosa, and Ōkuma Shigenobu and Etō Shimpei from Saga. They all rose to national prominence from the rank of retainers in these powerful southwestern domains. Their protracted and difficult efforts in the anti-bakufu movement eventually led to their forging the core of the Imperial forces. However, their common experience did not free these samurai activists from mutual suspicion, largely based on jealousy and rival domain affiliations. Furthermore, their successful campaign to end the bakufu naturally reinforced in each of these men his conviction of being the emperor's sole proxy, thereby increasing the competition among them.

The continued existence of the feudal domains after the Restoration only complicated the competitive dynamics among the new leaders. First, though now the emperor's officials, they were still also retainers of the key domains. The problem of loyalty to both their emperor and their daimyo impeded their acting as a cohesive group of leaders for the new government. Second, the fact that the new government relied for its very existence on the support of these key Restoration domains made these former activists particularly crucial to the Imperial rule and, in turn, aggravated their rivalry. Third, despite the reinforced credibility of these men as the emperor's proxies following the Restoration, the sphere of action for them as a group was still narrowly limited to the territories that the Imperial government had inherited from the Tokugawa family and its supporters. Such an external limitation further intensified their internal rivalry. The changes in the system of rule did eventually displace these domains. However, they also unveiled an irony: they cumulatively improved the limited status of the Imperial government, yet at the same time amplified the divisive competition among the new leaders. The ambitions of these self-styled proxies of the emperor rose proportionately.

Finally, there were those at the boundary of the expanding Imperial rule whose most effective means of "political participation" under the old system of rule had been violent uprisings. To these commoners, the emerging new system of rule should have meant primarily a local shift from the "benevolence" of individual rulers under the disparate feudal authorities to the "fairness" of a uniform, single system of local governance under the new prefectures. But the expansion of the new Imperial rule meant the sudden intrusion of alien political institutions into their local communities; the policies the new central government launched often threatened to undermine their familiar mode of community management. For some of them, however, this intrusion also meant an opportunity to enter the central arena of the emerging system

of rule themselves. The commoners' reactions to the expansion
of Imperial rule thus ranged from outright rejection to further
violent uprisings to political apathy. To manage the boundary of
the expanding Imperial rule, the Imperial government needed to
accommodate the demands of the local populace which had to
moderate its resistance and shake off its indifference to constitutional means of political participation.

In short, there is a discrepancy between the apparent linear
progression toward the consolidation of Imperial rule and actual
events. These events are indicative of resistance to the progression
from within the government, of a lack of foresight among the
leaders, and of the absence of a broad framework for the new
system of rule. It is not enough to conclude merely that the process of expansion and consolidation was haphazard. It is important
to examine how the key actors struggled to make the process
accountable to them, and what costs this haphazard process ex-
tracted from them. These questions and their broader implications merit a closer observation of the politics of the decade
following the Restoration.

## Problems in Meiji Histories

The critical decade after the Restoration occupies a neglected
place in the literature of the Meiji Restoration. This is despite
the fact that Japanese and Western scholars have carefully documented the institutional changes and developments in early
Meiji politics.[5] Yet such documentation has not dislodged the
period from the dominant views that the politics of the years
following the Restoration simply form an epilogue to the preceding decades of revolutionary turbulence, or a prologue to the more
systematic opening of the central political arena. The decade, in
other words, has up to now been viewed as a passing phase brack-
eted by two eras of politics whose characteristics may be more
readily discernible.

To a large extent, the prevalent concern with the socioeconomic
origins of the Restoration movement accounts for this perspective. Beginning with E. H. Norman's *Japan's Emergence as a Mod-*

*ern State* (1942), and Tōyama Shigeki's *Meiji ishin* (1951 and 1972),[6] historians have commonly identified the decades of fiscal and administrative reform in the 1830s and 1840s as the crucial period. The attempts at reform resulted in both criticism of and demands for further reform. This reform process subsequently produced those samurai of middle and lower rank who were to become the major activists in the Restoration movement. Norman's and Tōyama's pioneering works have since been modified and refined by other historians. However, their basic evolutionary views have remained intact. Among the Japanese, Tanaka Akira and Shibahara Takuji place these activists in the context of their changing political orientations, goals, and modes of action. All recognize that the course of the Restoration movement in the end allowed only some of these activists to survive. But the survival itself, often the result of individual ability, is seen as less important than the emergence and the strengthening of a core political orientation among them. In this view, the progression from the phase of separate domain reforms, through the anti-West phase, to the anti-bakufu phase awakened the activists to two things: the need for a unified government in the face of Western encroachment and the possibilities of the developing market economy. The corresponding realization that the bakufu was the obstacle to attaining either or both prompted them to exploit the emperor as the symbol of legitimacy and to monopolize the means for change. The surviving activists, or the "absolutist officials" as these historians call them, are portrayed as bent on making Japan an aggressive modern state and determined to subject all other social and political priorities to that ultimate goal. There are differences among these historians, but they lie primarily in their attribution of different time frames for, and relative significance of, the shifting phases in the Restoration movement.[7]

What is still wanting, however, is an examination of the new leaders in the context of the politics of the critical decade. The "absolutist officials" are viewed as exploiting the emperor in their efforts to strengthen the new governing authority over the feudal domain governments before 1871 and over any forces outside of their own nexus, including the rebellious peasants. They are depicted as particularly hostile to the demand for wider political

participation out of fear that their power base would be undermined and their policy priorities contradicted. The critical years
following the Restoration are thus viewed as the period when the
"absolutist" state, the instrument of the survivors of the Restoration movement, refined its method of procuring and exploiting
the necessary resources for its growth and when the survivors
themselves grew more unified. Few questions are raised as to the
nature of the political competition among them and the significance of the particular kind of political insecurity to which their
competition exposed them. Western scholars, generally unsympathetic to the Japanese historians' "absolutist" perspective, still
adopt a similar perspective for the new leaders during these crucial
years and characterize them, instead, as being broadly motivated
and united by a "nationalist resolution."[8]

Along with the historians' focus on the origin and nature of the
leadership, another broad consensus has obscured the significance
of the politics during this critical decade. Once again following
Norman and Tōyama, most historians recognize the 1830s and
1840s as the period that marked the division between the winners
and the losers in pre-Restoration politics, a few of the southwestern domains being the winners, and the bakufu and its supporters being the losers.[9] The anticipated profits of a developing
market economy as well as the fear of its corrosive effect on the
existing order, they argue, led the southwestern domains to devise
mercantilist policies to exploit that development. These policies
necessitated the promotion of the previously neglected managerial talent of those soon to become the "absolutist officials." The
mercantilist trend set them on a collision course with the bakufu,
which methodically applied conservative measures to arrest the
development of a market economy. The bakufu's more innovative
policies came too late, well into the 1860s, and had too little
effect to stabilize the economy. The political alignment worked
out among the southwestern domain leaders (the entrepreneurial
daimyo, their innovative retainers, and their financial backers),
then, placed Japan at the stage typical of a late feudal society ripe
for the emergence of an absolutist state. Ōe Shinobu, sharing this
basic evolutionary view with Norman and Tōyama, observes:

Generally, the political development of absolutism is shaped through attacks by a monarchical power against feudal barons or their alliances. But in Japan's anti-bakufu drive, it was the alliance of the feudal domains that challenged the bakufu's despotism, albeit the fact that the substantial power of the alliance was in the hands of influential samurai activists acting in the name of their lords. In essence . . . the absence of the corresponding monarchical center made it necessary for that alliance to become a surrogate monarchy as the foundation of absolute power in the place of the bakufu which had lost the basis to grow to be the monarchical center itself.[10]

According to this view, once the anti-bakufu alignment was forged, the emergence of an aggressive Imperial government was a foregone conclusion. Such an Imperial government would have been unsympathetic both to those outside that alignment and to those actively conspiring against it. The new government is seen as being shrewd both in guarding against threats from these forces and in promoting itself with the Western powers, who were formidable threats themselves as well as being Japan's models of aggressive modern states. This selective sensitivity of the new government prompted E. H. Norman and others to call Japan's first modern state an "enlightened absolutism."[11] Even those who do not share the critical language of this absolutism thesis still agree with the basic scheme of the mechanism and development of the Restoration coalition. They usually use the scheme to emphasize both the skills of the Restoration leaders in maintaining the coalition and their innovativeness in keeping government and society free from disruptions after the end of the coalition in 1871.

The differences among the historians lie primarily in the dates they assign to the transformation of the anti-bakufu coalition into the coalition for the Imperial government and the eventual disappearance of the coalition. They also interpret the turning points in that transformation differently. Haraguchi Kiyoshi and Inoue Kiyoshi emphasize the Boshin War as the first of the new government's steps that eventually broke up its coalition; it was the first sign that the feudal domains and the absolutist Meiji government were incompatible.[12] Shimoyama Saburō, whose concern has been the documentation of the institutional development of a modern, absolutist emperor system, the *tennōsei*, gives more credit to the removal of the old offices of the Court and that of shogun (January 3, 1868) for beginning the process leading to the Imperial "absolutist" state.[13] Shimoyama's view is surprisingly consistent with that of Western scholars who refuse to accept the absolutism thesis. The latter view as linear and cumulative all the major events in early Meiji politics — the declaration of the Imperial restoration (January 3, 1868), the promulgation of the Oath (April 6, 1868), the *Hanseki hōkan* (the Return of the Fiefs to the Court, July 25, 1869), and the *Haihan chiken* (the Abolition of the Feudal Domains and the Creation of the Prefectures, August 29, 1871). The difference is that the Western scholars rely on the seemingly less loaded term "rational" to characterize the process sustained by the leaders' commitment to streamline the old system of rule.[14]

A problem with this broad consensus on the coalition basis of the Restoration is a sort of determinism that allows the events during the decade to carry only certain prescribed meanings. Furthermore, each meaning is held to be consistent with the others in the unfolding of the rational construction of a Meiji government far more centralized than the old bakufu, far more conducive to producing innovative policies, and far more firmly imbued with the unified goal of placing Japan on an equal footing with the West. Thus in this scheme, too, the critical decade is a passing phase of political development whose course had been already set at the forging of the anti-bakufu coalition.

Finally, the existing literature on the subsequent constitutional debate in the 1880s, known as the period of the *minken* (the people's rights movement), requires a further and closer examination of the actual changes and the significance of the decade. For some historians, the measures for constitutional development demanded by the *minken* activists and delivered by the Imperial government are signs that there was nothing especially authoritarian in the efforts of the new Imperial government to stabilize its rule.[15] Critical historians, by contrast, see the decade after 1868 as a key era in creating an authoritarian regime. This view gives the *minken* movement most of the credit for bringing a government opposition to bear in early Meiji politics, a perspective based on the earlier interpretation by E. H. Norman. According to Norman, the aggressive and authoritarian bent in the Imperial government during this first critical decade led to the militancy of the people's rights activists in the following decade.[16] The preoccupation with this militancy in and of itself is by no means misplaced, in view of the several organized uprisings in the 1880s by the *minken* activists and the use of violence by the government to quell them. But it does tend to depreciate the significance of the various ways by which the *minken* activists came to recognize the gradual opening of the central arena of politics during the critical decade. The demand for political participation was by no means the desperate cry only of those who had been denied access to the emerging new system of rule during this decade. In fact, it was also the voice of those who had gained the initial entry to politics, especially at local levels, as the scope of the Imperial government had begun to expand — a voice demanding more of what had already been achieved.

## The Politics of Participation and the New Leadership

In view of these problems in the broader perspectives on the Meiji Restoration, there is an evident need to isolate the politics of the critical decade from the events leading up to and following it. The first major task of this study is to examine two key developments during the crucial years following the Restoration: the changing relationship between central and local governments and the making of the new and long-lasting political leadership. Each of these changes profoundly influenced the other. The new system of rule created by the Restoration activists constantly influenced the struggles among them and threatened to divide them long before it finally shaped them into the new leadership that was to persist for decades to come.

In an analysis of the changing relationship between the central (bakufu and Imperial government) and local (feudal domain and prefectural) governments, three basic processes in the politics of the decade may be identified. The first is the one in which the feudal domains initially survived both the demise of the Tokugawa bakufu and the political ascendancy of the emperor and the Court. In the next, the Imperial government outlived all the feudal domains and especially its reliance on the four southwestern domains of Satsuma, Chōshū, Tosa, and Saga. The abolition of the feudal domains and the establishment of the prefectures marked the beginning of the third and final process. Through these processes the central governing authority finally reached the populace, from whom it and the Restoration had been so remote.

In tandem, the analysis of the making of the new system of rule must call attention to two types of political dynamics: the simultaneous dispersion and consolidation of political power. These two aspects of change were at work throughout all phases leading to the Restoration and subsequent political development. As noted earlier, the reform attempts since the 1840s had generally weakened the hereditary monopoly of the governing powers by the few privileged samurai and had left the future activists to seek the consolidation of their power at a new, higher level. In other words, the Restoration movement was essentially an unstable process during which the activists first consolidated their power within their respective domains and then sought to disperse the bakufu's monopoly of the governing powers within the nation. The dislocation of the Tokugawa bakufu was the culmination of this process.[17]

The restoration of Imperial rule did not put an end to the operation of these two dynamics among the activists, now the central leaders. The simultaneous dispersion and consolidation of political power continued to influence the leaders in their efforts to stabilize and solidify the new Imperial rule. Before 1871, the dispersion-consolidation dynamics dictated the leaders' efforts to anchor the new Imperial government in the collective support, and not the exclusion, of the feudal domains. After 1871, with the feudal domains gone, the leaders' efforts to stabilize the new rule led to limited but expanding popular participation at the local level. Thus, the efforts after the Restoration to strengthen the legitimacy of the new government at its center were usually balanced by the efforts to keep the central arena of politics open.

The two dynamics continued to influence the actions of the Restoration leaders in another way. Within the new government, the simultaneous dispersion and consolidation of power was manifested in two conflicting ways. Each leader sought to reinforce his sense of proximity to the emperor and at the same time had to prevent anyone else from becoming more powerful at the cost of the others. The year 1868 was thus only the beginning of the deepening competition among them. By the summer of 1871, the competition had at times reached a point of nearly paralyzing the Imperial government. A complete breakdown was avoided largely because of the acute awareness among the leaders that the very Imperial government that ensured their political power precariously depended upon the support of each one's feudal domain. By the same token, the liquidation of the domains removed this most powerful constraint on internal competition among the individual leaders. With the domains gone, the two types of political dynamics, having earlier projected the samurai activists to national prominence, now began to produce significantly different consequences. On the one hand, the continued working of the dispersion and consolidation of political power could only mean the inclusion of new political actors from outside the original nexus of Restoration activists. On the other hand, the former samurai activists also needed to face the effect these political dynamics had upon their *internal* relationship — the intensified competitive politics among themselves. The winners and losers of this competition constantly changed places. But they leveled the same allegation against one another — the "evil subject adjacent to the throne." The emerging new system of rule in these crucial years thus did not uniformly benefit the Restoration activists; it exposed them to further complexities in the simultaneous dispersion and consolidation of political power and, in the end, even deprived some of them of access to the central arena of politics.

This analysis of the making of the new leadership offers two new observations. First, the leaders in the new government were by no means unsympathetic to the widening of political participation per se. After all, it was the thrust toward wider political participation that they had tried to sustain as activists. Now they were primarily concerned about its unsettling impact upon the central arena of politics. It is this ambivalence that greatly circumscribed their response to the demands for a more open political system.

Second, an equally significant consideration influenced the efforts of the samurai leaders to codify the new political order into a constitution. The most significant of these codifications concerned the place of the emperor in the new system of rule. The elevation of the emperor to his "rightful" place, perhaps the least partisan issue throughout the first decade, was eventually written into the Meiji Constitution of 1889. It is important to note, however, that every one of the key Restoration leaders had all along claimed to be the proxy of the emperor, which engaged all of them in an almost anarchical competition for his sanction as they drove toward further consolidation and dispersion of political power. The eventual political detachment of the emperor, as defined unequivocally in the Constitution of 1889, reflected the national consensus that his rightful place was above the formal structure of rule. Yet, more importantly, this constitutional definition of the emperor also reflected the need both to protect him from too much exposure to such competition and to moderate that debilitating competition itself. In other words, the political detachment of the emperor was a subtle expression of the collective insecurity of the new leaders, who found themselves trapped by their very efforts to strengthen the power base for the new government as much as for themselves. However, separating the emperor, the ultimate source of legitimacy for government, from the formal system of rule also removed the constitutional checks against the abuse of the emperor by whoever might claim to have his sanction. It was the political competition for this elusive Imperial sanction that would weaken the stability of Japan's political system during much of the period before World War II.

The first half of this study examines the political changes that occurred between the fall of the Tokugawa bakufu and the dismantling of the feudal domains. As pointed out earlier, the linkage between these two events was not direct. Some of the feudal domains themselves had provided the Court with much of its strength in its anti-bakufu campaign and were thus the Court's allies. Therefore, it is not surprising that the majority of the feudal domains foresaw no threat to their continued existence from the political ascendancy of the emperor and the Court. In the eyes of the feudal domains, the real threat could come only from their association with the Tokugawa mainhouse, once the house of the shogun and now the enemy of the emperor. As a result, once the domains had successfully severed their former ties with the Tokugawa family in the early stages of the Boshin War, they believed they had removed the threat to their continuation as well (Chapter 1). The domains' indifference to the implications of the political ascendancy of the emperor also subtly inhibited the ways in which the new Imperial government tried to break with the past (Chapter 2). The causes of the dismantling of the feudal domains lie both in the fact that the majority of the daimyō houses maintained the pre-Restoration management of their domain affairs and in the ways that the new central government disengaged itself from these domain affairs in the first few years of its existence (Chapter 3).

The second half of the book is concerned with the political consequences of dismantling the feudal domains and of expanding the Imperial rule which was allowed by this process. A discussion of the power relations among key members of the central government in its most unstable years until the abolition of the feudal domains (Chapter 4) is followed by an examination of how the commoners' response to the intrusion of Imperial institutions into their political life resulted in a broadening of the basis for their political participation (Chapter 5). The consequences of the disappearance of the feudal domains for the power relations among the proxies of the emperor in the Restoration government is then examined (Chapter 6). The final chapter investigates the ways in which the new government responded with constitutional measures to the demands to increase its political accountability to the populace. It analyzes the spread of these demands among two distinct groups of political actors: the newly enfranchised among the commoners and another group of former samurai, many of whom had been in effect disenfranchised from local and, in some cases, national politics by the expansion of Imperial rule. The final chapter concludes with the observations on how the Restoration limited Japan's prewar constitutional development as evidenced by the politics of the post-Restoration decade.

# 1

# Restoration

THE BEGINNING of the great transformation from the Tokugawa order to the Meiji order was muddled by the changing partisan divisions of the bakumatsu (end of the bakufu) politics. The shifting positions on the West, the bakufu, and the emperor gave rise to unstable coalitions among the critics and defenders of the existing order, often across partisan lines. The rise of such partisan divisions was the hallmark of bakumatsu politics. It did not, however, indicate the ultimate demise of the existing political order. At best, it spread the notion that the Tokugawa monopoly of the governing powers was gradually coming to an end. Further, neither the winners nor the losers of the bakumatsu political struggles were convinced that the end of the Tokugawa bakufu meant the eventual liquidation of the feudal domains.

The origins of the conviction that the Tokugawa monopoly was ending can be traced to the earlier decades of the nineteenth century. The increasing rural and urban disruptions testified to the fact that the mechanisms for production and distribution of the nation's wealth had largely become antiquated.[1] Furthermore, the approaching West made it apparent that Japan was hopelessly behind the "civilized" world. Because of Japan's great distance from Europe, the chances of colonization by the West might have been slim in reality. But increasing exposure to the West left the idea among the better-informed Japanese that the bakufu's self-seclusion policy had turned Japan into an "ignorant" nation, badly prepared to meet the Western challenge. As a sense of crisis took hold of an increasing number of Japanese, it prompted doubts about the bakufu's ability to govern.

However, the belief that the Tokugawa order had weathered long periods of difficulties in the past often counteracted any effective plans for a new political order. Thus, it was only gradually that the partisans of bakumatsu politics began to turn to the emperor, the authority higher than all of them, to legitimize their positions and actions. Yet, they were preoccupied more with adapting to the declining primacy of the bakufu in national politics than with speculating about the consequences of the political ascendancy of the emperor.

As suggested in the Introduction, this is the area of the greatest richness and strength of most of the writings on the Restoration, especially in English. Among the more recent writers, Thomas Huber describes the period leading up to the Restoration as one in which the Chōshū samurai activists challenged the hereditary monopoly of government by the privileged few in Chōshū, and in which their conviction of the need for a more open society was tested as they brought their struggle for power into the national context. Huber's treatment of the lower-ranking samurai from Chōshū as radical inevitably casts the bakufu leaders in the opposing role of conservatives busy defending the decaying political order. The politics of the closing of Tokugawa rule thus hinge upon the unstable interactions that the equally unstable alliances among the radicals and the conservatives brought about.[2] By contrast, Conrad Totman differs from Huber, most other Western writers on the Restoration, and many Japanese historians who view bakumatsu politics as the testing ground for the anti-bakufu coalition and the breeding ground for the future "absolutist officials." Totman's exclusive focus on bakumatsu politics after 1862 directs attention more to the bakufu's ability to renovate its administrative structure, modernize its army, and even shape the course of bakumatsu political development to a significant degree. In Totman's view, the Tokugawa leaders actively engaged in remodeling their political order right until the very end of their rule.[3] The value of his observation to this study may lie in its implication that the bakumatsu partisan divisions were not as distinct or as firm as many of the "absolutist" historians have made them out to be.

These and other works on bakumatsu politics cited in the Introduction usually identify a range of partisan positions on the West, the bakufu, and the emperor. Through various combinations of these positions, the historians distinguish the conflicting parties in bakumatsu politics and illuminate the shifting coalitions among them. The Restoration, in these writings, came upon the parties involved as the balance of power shifted slowly and irrevocably toward the anti-bakufu camp, until the last of the Tokugawa shoguns finally capitulated. This chapter, too, focuses on the political competition created by bakumatsu partisan politics. But its major purpose is to direct attention to two consequences of the competition: that the political ascendancy of the emperor made all feudal houses equal before him, and that the closing of the Tokugawa bakufu by no means presumed the demise of the feudal domains.

## Toward a Restoration: The Tokugawa Abdication

No historical writing is guilty of overdramatizing the end of what appeared, only a few decades before, to be a perpetual rule by the Tokugawa. The argument this study follows, however, emphasizes the Tokugawa's survival as a military house like those of Satsuma, Chōshū, Tosa, and Saga, and the broader significance of this survival to the rest of the military houses.

At the core of the old political system was the Tokugawa bakufu. This military government, exercising direct control over one-quarter of the agricultural land of Japan, had perfected the balance of power among the other 270 military houses of the daimyo (the han), which in turn held considerable local hegemony over the rest. Within this system was another balance among a smaller number of less powerful but more loyal vassal daimyo and the Tokugawa's direct vassals (the *hatamoto*), who constituted the core of the bakufu's bureaucracy.[4] A highly complicated system of checks and balances had thus kept the potentially divisive forces of the military houses from venturing to challenge the monopoly of the governing power by the bakufu for most of the Tokugawa period.

The system also had created a long-standing tradition in which neither the unbroken line of succession of each of the daimyo houses nor its territorial autonomy was threatened by the bakufu. To be sure, there were differences in standing among the daimyo on the bases of their familial relations to the Tokugawa mainhouse, their geographic locations, and the military potentials of their domains. All of these were of some consequence in the bakufu's political control, especially during its formative years. However, the basis of the authority relationship in this political order was that neither the bakufu nor the feudal domains, regardless of the daimyo's particular relationship with the Tokugawa family, would attempt any action to incur a fundamental redefinition of its role at the expense of the other.

The stability of this authority relationship hinged upon the degree of what one might call calculated indifference on the part of the bakufu and the feudal domains toward each other. For the Tokugawa family, having survived the battles for national hegemony with ambitious daimyo at the beginning of the seventeenth century, there were two inseparable assumptions about their own power which prompted them to observe this calculated indifference. The first assumption was that no daimyo or their alliances would become powerful to the extent of rivaling the Tokugawa bakufu; and the second, its counterpart, was that the Tokugawa bakufu itself would not pose a threat to the feudal domains. Thus, the transfer of daimyo from one locality to another or the outright confiscation of their fiefs by the bakufu, which served as demonstrations of the bakufu's power in the earlier Tokugawa period, were rooted in these assumptions and not meant to remove categorically the daimyo's claim to local autonomy.[5] In other words, the exercise of shogunal power vis-à-vis any particular daimyo was more demonstrative and specific than systemic: it was used to remind the other daimyo that the shogunal indifference was a calculated one.

The system of checks and balances that had kept the feudal domains at bay was also consistent with these assumptions by the shogunal power. It was a mixed expression of both the insecurity and the arrogance attendant upon the Tokugawa leaders, who had abandoned the unification process before its completion. On the one hand, they had earlier instituted alternating residence requirements, the *sankin kōtai*, for the daimyo. The requirements forced the daimyo to reside in the shogunal capital of Edo (Tokyo) every other year and leave their heirs apparent behind them as tokens of loyalty to the Tokugawa bakufu.[6] The *sankin kōtai* system, which was to be scrupulously observed by the daimyo, drained the feudal domains financially and thus weakened their military potential. The adherence to these requirements forced the daimyo to finance expensive trips between their domains and Edo and to maintain extravagant mansions in Edo with sizable numbers of retainers. On the other hand, the apportioning of weaker but loyal daimyo (the *fudai*) houses around Edo and along the eastern corridor between Edo and Kyoto contrasted with the settling of powerful and more ambitious daimyo in the distant regions. This arrangement betrays the cautious, almost timid, geopolitical minds of the earlier shoguns and their ministers, based on their awareness of the limits upon the shogunal power imposed by its own reliance on the loyalty of the daimyo. For their part, the daimyo, whether they were ambitious or simply powerful, saw no point in challenging the shogunal indifference either. The cost to them would have been a protracted civil war, at best. The Tokugawa bakufu, in short, carefully limited its insistence upon being the "central" government; and the military houses of the daimyo followed suit by restricting their autonomy to the established confines of their domains.

This insular state of the domains greatly helped the transformation of samurai as a social class.[7] As the daimyo's retainers, comprising approximately 3 to 5 percent of the population, they constituted the inner circle of the daimyo's government. Once the basic balance of power between the Tokugawa family and the other military houses was established at the beginning of the seventeenth century, each domain began its own internal unification by removing the samurai vassals from their lands. The relocation of the samurai to the castle towns of the daimyo precipitated their transformation from a half-agrarian and half-military class into a stable, distinctly urban, administrative class. Since then, the perpetual peace within the domains as well as the nation had helped this most literate sector of the populace develop a great deal of administrative skill in finance, education, policing, and other services. The samurai's transformation left their military skills as an emblem of cultural refinement and the symbol of ruling privilege. Their feudalistic loyalty in the absence of external threats gradually became less personal and more "public": it was directed no longer toward the person of the daimyo but toward the continuity of the houses of daimyo. Samurai were rewarded with stipends in kind for their administration of public services for their domains. They held a secure position as the superior class in society in exchange for feudalistic loyalty to the daimyo houses they served, which they protected from any threat of discontinuity by the bakufu in the case of, for example, the death of a daimyo without an heir. The stability of this political order thus generated a complex network of interdependence among its major beneficiaries, including the shogun and his officials, and the daimyo and their retainers, all of whom had long ago given up estimating the costs of changing it.

The voices that began to question this political order came, however, from precisely those who were among its "beneficiaries." The catalyst for their criticism was the realization of the innate inflexibility that some 200 years of internal peace had instilled in the political institutions and in those who managed them, an unresponsiveness especially evident in this time of crisis. The dissenters in the political order included those samurai of low and middle rank whose skills were increasingly, though unsystematically, called upon for the handling of rural and financial crisis management for the domains. Grouped together broadly, these samurai were what Thomas Huber termed the "service intelligentsia,"[8] men who came to recognize their importance to their domain administration but remained without commensurate institutional recognition. Along with their underlying frustration, the threat of Western encroachment also prompted these men to see in the unresponsive political institutions something of larger concern. Witnessing the bakufu's in-ability to curtail the Western powers' open transgressions against Japan's old self-seclusion policy, they began to anticipate further and more profound crises, like the Taiping Rebellion or the Sepoy Rebellion in the western reaches of Japan.[9] They deduced from these instances of the bakufu's vulnerability a more general weak-ening of its ability to govern the nation. Yet because the bakufu still appeared capable of inflicting reprisals on any challenge from within to *its* calculated indifference, the majority of the daimyo and their retainers preferred to remain largely oblivious to the sense of emergency that the skeptical activists tried to project. Quite often, their indifference to the impending crises even re-sulted in outright suppression of the critical voices within the samurai ranks.

It was from these two classes — some dissatisfied samurai and some even among the daimyo — that the challenge to the bakufu finally came. Styling themselves the "men of high purpose," or *shishi*, scores of samurai dissenters first began to take more direct action to disassociate themselves from the existing political order. Leaving the confines of their own domains in search of the like-minded elsewhere was one such action. Reprisals by the alarmed bakufu and insecure domain authorities limited these actions both in scope and in consequence. It was in this adverse envi-ronment that the *shishi* found themselves in desperate need of giving their actions at least the appearance of a higher sanction. Accordingly, they began to publicize their claim, however ima-ginary, to being the emperor's proxies. In addition, such a claim had the significant effect, within their minds at least, of reducing the bakufu's invincible position as the governing authority to one stripped of the emperor's sanction. After invoking the name of the emperor, these activists next had to involve their own do-mains, which after all possessed the material resources necessary for contesting the Tokugawa monopoly of the governing powers.

The rejection of the bakufu's calculated indifference, which the *shishi*'s flights from their domains symbolized, next began to spread even among the daimyo. Some of the daimyo were at the very core of the existing political order, serving at times as advisors to the Tokugawa shogun in different capacities. Among them, Matsudaira Yoshinaga, the lord of Fukui, was one of the earliest to question the rationale behind this calculated indifference. As early as the 1850s he had proposed the relaxation of the *sankin kōtai* for the sake of relieving the financial burden of the domains, whose treasuries had been seriously depleted. Matsudaira Yoshinaga's proposal fell only one step short of presenting the more general verdict that the Tokugawa monopoly of the governing powers had ceased to serve the nation's interest and thus no longer could receive the support of the "realm" (the *tenka*).[10] Coming from one of the central beneficiaries of the existing political order, his criticism was especially potent. The deepening sense of crisis finally reached even some in the inner core of the existing political order, making them, to borrow an apt expression of Conrad Totman's, "functionally 'lower samurai' "[11] in terms of their political orientation toward bakumatsu politics.

The incessant rural and urban unrest helped spread Matsudaira Yoshinaga's position slowly but progressively among men even of this daimyo rank. In addition, the relentless pressure from the Western powers to open the country hastened the diminishing of confidence in the bakufu. In the face of the Western threat, the bakufu issued a series of reactive and inconsistent policies that lacked any consensus about either preserving or changing the self-seclusion policy. For the rest of the population, the bakufu's inconsistency only deepened the fear that the nation would capitulate to the aggressive West. It was this diminishing confidence in the bakufu that, with increasing momentum, promoted the tendency among some of the daimyo to ignore the calculated indifference of the shogunate.[12] Such a tendency came close to challenging the Tokugawa monopoly of the governing powers. More importantly, it motivated the search for a source of legitimization for an alternative to the bakufu monopoly in national politics, such as a framework for a *collective* effort by leading daimyo from a selected few domains to govern the nation.[13] These daimyo, in a similar manner to the samurai activists, sought the sanction for their alternative in an authority higher than the ba-

kufu—the emperor. In this way, the skeptics of the existing political order among the ranks of the daimyo, like the samurai
*shishi*, began to style themselves the proxies of the emperor.

Were the Tokugawa and their supporters, then, left isolated
amid the increase of the emperor's proxies critical of the Tokugawa monopoly of the governing powers? Through their shifting
positions toward the anti-West cause, the bakufu in fact itself
went through adjustments that led the Tokugawa and their sympathizers to declare themselves the emperor's proxies. Furthermore, the Tokugawa's ultimate survival as a military house
hinged upon these adjustments despite the demise of the bakufu.

One crucial opportunity for the Tokugawa leaders to make their
status as the emperor's proxies explicit came when they confronted the rebellious Chōshū in the mid–1860s. Chōshū had been
known for producing scores of *shishi* from the ranks of its retainers. Furthermore, the Chōshū activists in the mid–1860s had
succeeded in generating an internal consensus strong enough to
launch their domain-backed campaign against the West in direct
defiance of the bakufu's primacy in national politics. In the summer of 1864, Chōshū moved its forces to Kyoto in the attempt to
involve the Imperial Court directly in its "Expel the Barbarians"
campaign. Confronted with this direct challenge by Chōshū, however, the Tokugawa leaders successfully forged an alliance with
three other feudal domains to defend the Imperial Palace and
claimed that this alliance had the emperor's sanction. As a result,
the summer of 1864 proved doubly disastrous for the rebellious
Chōshū. Its forces were dealt a decisive blow when defeated at
the Palace gates by the combined forces of the bakufu, Satsuma,
Aizu, and Kuwana. In quick succession, at the end of the summer,
Chōshū was again defeated on its home territory by a punitive
expedition of bakufu-domain forces. The confrontation between
two parties claiming to be the proxies of the emperor resulted in
the bakufu's irrefutable victory, thereby strengthening the latter's
position as one in the service of the emperor.

However, the Tokugawa joined the ranks of the proxies of the
emperor by virtue not of the successful campaign against the
rebellious domain but of its reliance on Imperial sanction. The
invoking of the emperor's sanction, previously a practice among

only those who were challenging the existing order, clearly marked the end of the bakufu's uncontested authority and its ability to maintain the calculated indifference by example. Subsequently, in order to survive, Chōshū was forced in 1864 to temporarily drop its "anti-barbarian" crusade. The bakufu, on the other hand, no longer invincible, had to prepare for the likelihood of more challenges to its primacy in national politics. The bakufu leaders were compelled to maintain constant combat readiness in order to protect their position in national politics. The practicalities of maintaining a standing army in turn kept many goods, especially rice, from the markets, drove their prices up, and thus intensified the urban and rural unrest. The second punitive expedition to Chōshū in 1866, again justified as being at the command of the emperor, turned out to be a military disaster for the bakufu forces. The key consequences of this venture were, first, an impression of the ineptitude of the bakufu in the face of both domestic turmoil and the encroachment of the ambitious West, and second, the bakufu's own belief that it could no longer sustain its invincible governing authority. Ironically, therefore, it was the irreparable damage to the bakufu's authority that gave credibility to the Tokugawa's claim to be the emperor's proxy.

Accordingly, the final days of the bakufu were marked by the Tokugawa's efforts to make their primacy in national politics compatible with the elevated status of the emperor. These efforts were also intended to defuse the explosive partisan politics generated by the dissenters' *sonnō jōi*, or the "Revere the Emperor and Expel the Barbarians" cause. The Tokugawa leaders asserted that they and their sympathizers had never been strangers to the *sonnō* movement. They insisted that the Tokugawa family was the house of the shogun, an office that was after all formally legitimized by the emperor to be the overlord of all military houses. The Tokugawa leaders thus began far more explicitly than before to exploit the *sonnō* cause, partly to shore up the damaged status of the bakufu and partly to prevent the anti-West hysteria from developing irreversibly into an anti-bakufu movement. But the major function of this espousal of *sonnō* was to protect the bakufu's new claim that the Tokugawa was the emperor's proxy. The Tokugawa family wanted to show that it would cause no polarization in the system of rule: the two recently emerged political poles of rule, the bakufu and the Court, could be readily integrated in such a way that the latter, as it had done in the past, would delegate the governing powers to the former.

Accompanying these developments in bakumatsu politics was a significant change also in the meaning of the *jōi*, the "Expel the Barbarians" cause. Reflecting the growing fear of Western encroachment, the change in fact helped the bakufu leaders blunt that partisan edge critical of them. The repeated appearances of Western boats demanding the opening of the country had eliminated the possibility of self-seclusion for all practical purposes within a few years after Commodore Perry's "black ships" arrived in 1853. Even Chōshū had been rudely awakened to the immense technological gap separating Japan and the West by the tremendous firepower of the allied fleet of the United States, Great Britain, France, and the Netherlands in 1864 during the bombardment of Shimonoseki. By the mid–1860s, then, the initial repugnance toward things Western had begun shifting to fear. As a result, a few prominent activists began to separate the *jōi* cause from the *sonnō* movement as entailing two different sets of tasks, and then turned the *jōi* into a euphemism for a broader national preparedness to face the powerful West. They also recognized that this preparedness would require internal unity rather than the dissension stimulated earlier by the "Expel the Barbarians" cause. Nakaoka Shintarō of Tosa, for example, cited the American Declaration of Independence and the Seven Years' War between a weaker United States and a more powerful Great Britain as an example of successful *jōi* on the part of the former, the threatened but unified colonies.[14] Implicit in this change in the *jōi* cause was therefore the suspension of the partisan politics of pro-emperor versus pro-Tokugawa.

This change in the meaning of the *jōi* cause also offered a political opportunity for the Tokugawa leaders: the need for national consensus placed *all* the emperor's proxies in a uniquely competitive context instead of serving as the catalyst for unification from which the Tokugawa family could have been alienated. It engaged the Tokugawa loyalists and their critics alike in a contest in which each tried to prove its stronger commitment to "protecting the honor of the Imperial house and projecting its power abroad," as Ōkubo Toshimichi of Satsuma phrased the prevailing sentiment. Against this background, a unique term, *kakkyo*, literally the "independent campaigns for national hegemony," began to dominate the political vocabulary of the contestants.[15] Taken from the civil war period in Japan prior to the establishment of the Tokugawa bakufu some 250 years before, the term *kakkyo* was now revived to imply the competitive politics among the military houses vying for national authority and for recognition of such authority by the emperor and his Court. Thus, though antithetical to national unification, *kakkyo* provided an opportune framework for all contestants in which the supremacy of the Imperial house was ultimately protected while they competed among themselves for proximity to the emperor.

Perhaps the most crucial development at this juncture of the bakumatsu politics was the adjustment that the Tokugawa leaders made in order to exploit this logic of the *kakkyo* themselves. The equality among *all* military houses, as implied by "independent campaigns for national hegemony," irrevocably convinced the bakufu leaders of the decline of the Tokugawa's primacy in national politics. At the same time, nothing could prevent the Tokugawa family and their supporters from fully participating in the *kakkyo* competition for national primacy themselves as their founders had once done, provided that they could be rid of their privileged status as the current house of the shogun. Thus, the Tokugawa leaders did not try to reverse the course of political events that had quickly diminished the opportunities for them to survive as the house of the shogun. Instead, they took steps that were extraordinary for the house of the shogun but perfectly logical for *a* military house: they abdicated, demoting themselves to the same rank as all the other military houses. Tokugawa Yoshinobu, the fifteenth and last shogun, took a series of actions late in 1867 ending the 250 years of Tokugawa rule. This self-demotion, at the same time, formally qualified the Tokugawa house to enter the *kakkyo* contest on a par with the other military houses.

On November 11, 1867, after months of internal debate among his own ministers and a few allies among the ranks of daimyo,

Yoshinobu submitted a letter to the Court proposing that he return the governing powers to the emperor. Ten days later another letter followed, this time announcing his resignation from the office of shogun. By vacating the highest military office legitimized by the emperor, the last Tokugawa shogun himself lifted the emperor from nearly seven centuries of political oblivion. The immediate result was particularly gratifying to the Tokugawa leaders, who were now intent on surviving the *kakkyo* contest and unifying Japan under *their* renewed leadership. Two days after the letter of Yoshinobu's resignation, an Imperial order was issued commanding the attendance of all the daimyo at Kyoto. However, most of the daimyo refused this order. Loyal to the Tokugawa house, these daimyo stressed their allegiance to the shogun's command only and the observance of their *"on,"* their houses' private obligation, owed to the head of all military houses, the Tokugawa. To emphasize their status as "vassals" of the Tokugawa house, their letters of refusal were addressed not to the Court, but to the outgoing shogun.[16] Thus, the Tokugawa's move to participate in, and survive, the *kakkyo* contest on an equal basis with the anti-Tokugawa forces brought about exactly the result that justified their decision. It was against this uniquely competitive background that Imperial rule was restored.

## The Kogosho Decision: Partisan Politics and the Making of the War

On January 3, 1868, the restoration of Imperial rule was formally announced from the Imperial Palace in Kyoto, which was heavily guarded by troops from Satsuma, Tosa, Aki (Hiroshima), Fukui, and Owari (Nagoya). Present were the young emperor, the son of that Komei who had earlier driven many *shishi* into the fanaticism of *sonnō jōi*, a score of Court nobles, and several daimyo and their leading retainers. Tokugawa Yoshinobu was locked in place at his Kyoto residence, the Nijō Castle, surrounded by his own troops and unable to take part in the meeting.

The domains represented by these daimyo included some that

provided the troops: Satsuma, Tosa, Fukui, and Owari, all of them powerful at this point. The first two, Satsuma and Tosa, the great southwestern domains, had been influential for quite some time, having produced many activists from the ranks of their retainers since the beginning of the anti-West campaign. Their particularly opportune presence in Kyoto was a result of their shrewd exploitation of the decline of the Tokugawa in order to increase their own political influence. They had accomplished this by leading the weakening bakufu to rely on them at some times and undermining the efforts of the anti bakufu forces at others. The other two domains, Fukui and Owari, had expanded their significance in national politics as Yoshinobu himself increased his reliance upon the counsel of their daimyo in the efforts to bolster the diminishing confidence in the bakufu in its closing years. By contrast, Chōshū was conspicuous by its absence from Kyoto. Its more steadfast anti-Tokugawa and anti-West positions had previously made the domain especially vulnerable to the vacillations of the Court, which had hardly been consistent with regard to the West and no more so toward the bakufu. The result for Chōshū had been the 1864 and 1866 punitive expeditions of the bakufu, who had managed to gain support for them from the Court. In fact, Chōshū's status had been only recently reinstated through the restoring of Court titles to its lord and his father.

The restoration of Imperial rule, however, did not end the divisive bakumatsu politics. The announcement of the Restoration was quickly followed by another decision, on the same day at the adjacent Small Imperial Palace (the Kogosho), demanding that Tokugawa Yoshinobu return his Court title and fief to the emperor. This decision, however, came after the anti-Tokugawa momentum had largely dissipated, as the Tokugawa had already successfully disengaged themselves from the responsibilities of the shogun's office. Thus, to the Tokugawa and their supporters, this additional decision against them seemed unduly partisan. They suspected an ulterior motive on the part of the southwestern domains, especially Satsuma, which seemed to them to be ambitious to replace the Tokugawa house. When Matsudaira Yoshinaga of Fukui and Tokugawa Yoshikatsu of Owari brought the

decision the next day to Yoshinobu at the Nijō Castle, the Tokugawa loyalists angrily received the two daimyo as no more than
couriers performing at Satsuma's pleasure.

Fearing this hostility would break into violence, Yoshinobu
immediately decided to retreat to Osaka, southwest of Kyoto,
with his own troops. In so doing, he ignored his obligation to
respond to the Kogosho decision, to accept or reject its ruling
concerning his title and fief. Thus, Yoshinobu's retreat from Kyoto
was as inconclusive as the Kogosho decision that prompted it.
More significantly, Yoshinobu's departure from Kyoto left those
responsible for the Kogosho decision divided in a new phase of
partisan politics.

The key participants in the Kogosho decision were divided into
two groups: the moderates and the militants.[17] For the moderates
such as Matsudaira Yoshinaga, Tokugawa Yoshikatsu, and Yamanouchi Toyoshige (Yodo), father of the current lord of Tosa,
the "return of his court title and his fief" was an undue punishment of Yoshinobu for what was, after all, a voluntary move to
restore the emperor to his rightful place. For them, the Kogosho
decision bordered on a denial of feudal justice, since the other
daimyo houses escaped such punishment. Yoshinobu's departure
for Osaka thus left time for them to reverse their initial concurrence with the decision.

The second group, the militants who promoted the decision,
included men such as Ōkubo Toshimichi of Satsuma and Iwakura
Tomomi, a Court noble. For them, the crux of the matter lay in
the evidence — growing at an alarming pace since the closing
months of 1867 — of the Tokugawa's ability to command the
allegiance of the vast majority of the feudal domains, which belied
the true motive behind the former shogun house's demotion of
its status to one equal to Satsuma, Chōshū, or Tosa. To the militants, the Tokugawa leaders, in their new-found position as proxies of the emperor, appeared to be well on their way to regaining
the national primacy that had been slipping away from them
throughout most of the bakumatsu political development. For
these militants, therefore, the *kakkyo* contest had already been
reduced to a single issue by the time of the announcement of the

Imperial restoration: how to discredit the Tokugawa's claim that they, too, were the proxies of the emperor.

It is in this context of the militants' increasing uneasiness that, even before the successful closing of the bakufu, these men began referring to the emperor by the peculiar metaphor of *gyoku*, literally "jewel": the person of the emperor was stripped of its infallible divinity and made an "object" that could be easily won or lost.[18] The militants had begun to hope that the "jewel," once in their possession, would deny the Tokugawa leaders the very basis for their participation in the *kukkyo* contest on an equal footing with the other military houses. For the militants at the Kogosho Conference, therefore, whether the emperor's concurrence in the decision on Yoshinobu's title and fief was positive or passive mattered little. What was important was only, first, the emperor's mere presence, which could in effect sanction any decision *they* made, and second, a clear rejection of such a decision by its recipient, the former shogun. Thus, the ultimate significance of the Kogosho decision demanding the return of Yoshinobu's court title and fief lay in its anticipated refusal by Yoshinobu. The militants could have then used the rejection to deny Yoshinobu's claim to be the emperor's proxy. Therefore, when Yoshinobu left Kyoto without making any reply to the Kogosho decision, the militants' "possession" of the "jewel" proved tenuous at best.

Yoshinobu's inconclusive departure for Osaka thus left both the moderates and the militants in Kyoto trying desperately to reinforce their positions. Matsudaira Yoshinaga and the other moderates were concerned primarily with stabilizing the relationship between the Court and all the military houses in general, now that the emperor had been restored to his "rightful" place. They therefore insisted on retaining for the ruling the kind of language that would emphasize the *formal* equality among the military houses before the Court: the contribution of the Tokugawa's services to the restoration of the Imperial rule was to be derived from the house's capacity, that is, the size of the Tokugawa's fief; and the head of the house was to be allowed, in much the same way as a few other daimyo like the moderates themselves, to participate in the new and broadened framework for national policy-making.[19]

The militants, by contrast, needed more than ever to reinforce their tenuous "possession" of the emperor. They pressed to make the wording of the Kogosho decision even stronger, demanding the "confiscation" and "deprivation," instead of "return" and "surrender," of the court title and fief of Yoshinobu. Such militancy, they hoped, would preempt even the remotest possibility of the Tokugawa's acceptance of the decision. Only then could the militants count on Yoshinobu's refusal, the surest sign of his slighting the "will" of the emperor, and thus disprove the Tokugawa leaders' claim to being the emperor's proxies, thereby also disqualifying the Tokugawa house from the *kakkyo* contest.

Finally, there was Tokugawa Yoshinobu himself, no longer shogun yet commanding a vast majority of daimyo and loyal vassals of the house. While he was in Osaka, his position was becoming stronger as the moderates in Kyoto continued to resist the militants. Moreover, he was acutely aware that any shift in the critical balance among the contending parties, including himself, would easily affect access to the emperor and the sanction that went with it. Therefore, his relocation to Osaka was actually as positive an act as the militants' efforts to strengthen their possession of the "jewel." Yoshinobu was fully convinced that Satsuma had masterminded the plan to have him separated from the emperor. He admitted later that he had every intention of removing the Satsuma leaders, if necessary by force, from the Imperial Palace in order to possess the "jewel" himself.[20] The move to Osaka was nothing less than a means to regroup his forces. Thus, at the very point when the emperor was declared the pivot for the new political order, his presence precipitated the last phase of the bakumatsu political competition.

During the three weeks following Yoshinobu's sudden departure from Kyoto, the moderates gained further strength because, apprehensive of the undue "punishment" implied in the Kogosho decision, they refused to support it. Moreover, the Court nobles also began to show their innate conservativism in the face of such a disruptive change. To a large extent, the reluctance of the Court nobles and the moderate daimyo to face any drastic action at this point reinforced Ōkubo's and the other militants' conviction that an even more extreme measure might be necessary to break with the past. One result of this conviction was Ōkubo's proposal on February 18, 1868, to move the capital from Kyoto to Osaka in order to isolate the emperor from the conservative atmosphere of Kyoto;[21] another result was the eventual transfer of the capital to Tokyo on April 5, 1869. At any rate, the absence of action during this period began to work in the Tokugawa's favor simply by prolonging the debate between the conflicting camps in Kyoto.[22]

Finally, on January 25, 1868, Yoshinobu decided to move his forces in Osaka toward Kyoto with the intent of ending the debate by removing the "evil" Satsuma from the circle adjacent to the throne.[23] Yoshinobu's forces met those of Satsuma, Tosa, and others halfway to Kyoto, at Toba and Fushimi. But the battle was surprisingly brief. The Tokugawa forces were resoundingly defeated. Yoshinobu then retreated to Edo where he finally acknowledged that further action to recover the "jewel" would be of no avail. The militants' original design was now realized: the denunciation of the Tokugawa and the confiscation of his fief were finally announced shortly thereafter. Several missions, headed nominally by the Court nobles and escorted by the troops of Satsuma and others, were sent to "pacify" the regions where Tokugawa diehards were trying to salvage what was left of their cause after the emperor was permanently lost to them. The War of the Restoration thus began, ending a year and a half later on the northernmost island of Hokkaido.[24]

## The War: Adaptation by the Feudal Domains and the Tokugawa

In view of these developments leading to the Tokugawa's demise, it is clear that the War of the Restoration was not a struggle against all the feudal houses. The daimyo did not necessarily see any conflict between the continuation of their domains and the new Imperial government's claim to be representative of the nation at large. The threat they felt arose primarily from the Court's

condemnation of the Tokugawa family as the enemy of the emperor, an action that justified the use of arms against them by the
few domains supporting the emperor. For the other daimyo, there
was only "guilt by association." Nonetheless, the threat could be
real. Thus, the daimyo and their retainers responded to the war
by minimizing their association with the Tokugawa to avoid
being condemned by the Court and punished militarily.

Some daimyo disassociated themselves from the Tokugawa
family simply by stressing that they had no intention of siding
with the enemy of the emperor. Others downplayed their status
as vassals of the Tokugawa mainhouse by arguing that such a
relationship was of a private nature. Such a position allowed them
both to minimize their houses' own obligation to the Tokugawa
and to appeal to the Court for leniency toward the Tokugawa
family, which had already borne the indignity of descending to
the status of the other military houses. The distinctions among
these responses were not clear, but behind them all was a similar
desire: the need of the daimyo and their retainers to adapt, with
a minimum of real change but a variety of tactics, to the restoration of Imperial rule.

Many feudal domains now began scrambling to present signs
of their allegiance to the emperor in Kyoto. After the battle of
Toba and Fushimi, the Imperial troops were sent out to demand
allegiance from various domains. In response, the domains tried
to confirm this allegiance before the arrival of the Imperial forces.
Hotta Masatomo, lord of the Sakura han, east of Edo, and one of
the many daimyo previously loyal to the shogun, had disobeyed
the Imperial order demanding his attendance at Kyoto following
Yoshinobu's resignation from the office of shogun. He left for
Kyoto with his domain troops on April 1 and offered an apology
to the advancing Imperial forces for his previous neglect and for
the hostilities waged by his overlord, Tokugawa Yoshinobu. When
his apology did not prevent his house arrest in Kyoto, his domain
officials were left with no choice but to join Satsuma and the
other Imperial forces in the war against the Tokugawa.[25] Similarly, Matsudaira Sadayasu of Matsue tried to reach Kyoto to
apologize for his earlier disregard of the November order. But by
the time he arrived in Kyoto, the Imperial troops had reached the

domain neighboring his and demanded proof of Sadayasu's loyalty to the Court. The remaining retainers of Sadayasu had to choose one of the following of proofs: the surrender of half of his fief, the lives of the ranking vassals of his house, or the surrender to Kyoto of his heir. Refusal to choose one would have brought about a direct confrontation with the emperor's forces. The ranking vassals of the house chose the second option and prepared themselves for the death that would spare the house from total condemnation and demolition.[26]

Any direct involvement of the feudal domains against the emperor's forces made it harder for them to escape denunciation by the new government. One convoluted example involved the lord of Takamatsu, who tried to excuse his troops' participation in the battle of Toba and Fushimi by insisting that they had been unable to take the proper course of action because they unfortunately had marched next to the troops of Aizu,[27] the last domain to stay in the war against the new Imperial government.

Perhaps the most unusual fate was that which befell the Hamada han retainers. Matsudaira Takesato, who was the son of the Mito lord Tokugawa Nariaki and also the younger brother of Tokugawa Yoshinobu, came to the ill-fated Matsudaira house in Hamada at a young age to succeed to its lordship. The domain began to falter when the bakufu's second punitive expedition in 1866 to Chōshū cost Takesato and his retainers the Hamada domain itself at the hands of the Chōshū irregular troops. Due, perhaps, to shogunal sympathy, however, Takesato was allowed to remain a lord in exile. He and his retainers drifted from one locality to another until they finally reached one of the small detached territories of his own fief. Their next setback came when some of his retainers were found participating in the battle of Toba and Fushimi against the emperor. After their defeat at the battle, apparently aware that the very house of Matsudaira was threatened and that their lord's mental and physical condition might be less than normal, the ranking vassals of the house frantically prepared a series of explanatory letters to the Court in his name. The first, on February 8, insisted that the house's allegiance to the emperor had never been obscured by the lord's being a brother of Yoshinobu.[28] Another, following on February 11, pleaded ignorance of any rebellious action that might have been committed at Toba and Fushimi and attempted to isolate those delinquent retainers from their Hamada daimyo who personified the domain:

> Those retainers whom I had sent to Osaka fell under the command of the Tokugawa, became the vanguard [of Yoshinobu's forces] and were involved unexpectedly in the battle at Toba and Fushimi. Unaware of the presence of the Imperial forces, it was a total surprise to them to learn of Yoshinobu's rebellious act.... Henceforth, I shall await punishment while I confine myself to my residence. The [lives of the] retainers [who were at the battle scene] shall be placed at your disposal.[29]

Finally, still another letter was devised a week later in an explicit attempt to disassociate the retainers' act from the daimyo who, it insisted, had been seriously ill.[30] Their attempt to prove their allegiance to the emperor was a dramatic example of what many of the domains found themselves obliged to do.

The domains' efforts to disassociate their retainers from their daimyo also often entailed more than rhetoric: there were always other loyal retainers whose deaths could rectify the "crime" committed in the name of the domain, thereby keeping the daimyo's house intact. Takesato's retainers were no exception, and neither were those of the lord of Takamatsu. A ranking retainer of Takesato eventually committed suicide, and the domain authority decided to send some one hundred troops to join the Imperial forces following the acceptance by the Court of their daimyo's apology. Similarly, the Takamatsu domain officials surrendered to the Court the heads of two high-ranking retainers whom they held to be responsible for the domain troops' involvement in the battle at Toba and Fushimi.[31]

The advance of the war thus engaged many domains in the effort to demonstrate their loyalty to the new Imperial government. What was once a question of either breaching or defending the feudalistic code of honor between the Tokugawa and the daimyo quickly became a question of the survival or extinction of the daimyo houses. However, this development did not render feudalistic loyalism completely obsolete, nor did it allow the rational calculations only for survival by the domains to prevail entirely over the old code of honor. Debates arising within the daimyo houses about which code to honor — that of the emperor or that of the shogun — still involved the issue of feudalistic loyalism. The only difference concerned to whom the loyalty should be shown. Therefore, the shift toward the new government in the domains' allegiance was prompted by the domain officials' commitment to protecting their daimyo's houses, to whom they owed loyalty as vassals, in much the same way as the earlier support of the Tokugawa had followed from the daimyo's being the vassals of the Tokugawa shogun.

Timing of the shift in allegiance varied. The few domains in the north were slower to recognize that the daimyo houses' preservation was at stake, and only did so after direct confrontation with the growing Imperial forces. Consequently, they could preserve the daimyo houses only at the cost of a great deal of the territory of their fiefs. For the last domain to resist the Imperial forces, the Aizu han, the shift came after its military defeat. Their loss was thus considerably higher, as it involved the relocation of their entire fief to the northern tip of Honshu, where the agricultural productivity was dismally poor.

Along with these adjustments by the military houses to the Restoration, there was also that of the Tokugawa mainhouse, whose lord, Yoshinobu, now ceased to be the pivot for internal consensus even in his own house. The debate on loyalism among its retainers did not easily distinguish one type of loyalist from the other, for the Tokugawa was at once the house of the shogun, which had incurred Imperial condemnation, *and* one of the 270 military houses. But like the other daimyo's retainers, they all demonstrated some form of continued feudalistic loyalty. Some devised a new cause to save the old one: the attempt to undo the "unjust" condemnation of the Tokugawa mainhouse led these men to fight a war first in the city of Edo against the forces of the new regime and then to drift farther northward to join the pro-Tokugawa domain forces for some time. In the meantime, the continuation of the mainhouse was also granted on July 13, under a new lordship (Tokugawa Kamenosuke from a related

house), with a greatly reduced fief of 700,000 *koku* — less than
one-tenth of what the house had once held — and with the additional condition of the transfer of the fief to Shizuoka.[32] This
development provided the other retainers with yet another cause,
no less consistent with their familiar feudalistic loyalty, of protecting the house with whatever resources were available. The
majority of the Tokugawa retainers, perhaps less actively involved
with either of these two causes, nonetheless exhibited a reminder
of feudalistic loyalism. The provisional government established
by the Imperial forces in Edo had proposed that they be given the
choice of leaving the Tokugawa vassalage, thereby becoming the
"subjects" of the emperor; yet only a few complied until their
new lord encouraged them to do so.[33]

Contrary to the initial expectation among the Restoration leaders, the military houses including the Tokugawa house quickly
adapted to the ascendance of the emperor and the Court as the
new center of the political order. The inclusion of the military
houses in making the Imperial government a new "central" government was indeed progressive. It is equally important to note
that essentially their inclusion was dependent upon the ability
of the military houses to generate an internal consensus for shifting their allegiance to the Court. Thus, the recognition of such a
shift by the Court inevitably implied the recognition also of the
intrinsic linkage between the continuation of the military houses
and the resurrected feudalistic loyalism of the houses' retainers.

In contrast to the domains' shift in loyalty, the repossession of
the Tokugawa territories by the Imperial forces was an easier task.
The main factor in this process was not so much the usual working of feudalistic loyalism as the unique manner in which the
Tokugawa had administered their fief, the largest of all the military houses. Their lands were scattered all over Japan, collectively
yielding one-quarter of the nation's agricultural wealth. Yet, fewer
than sixty local bakufu offices governed the scattered lands. The
regulations of 1725 for the management of the entire Tokugawa
territories ruled also that there be only about thirty officials
(mostly clerical) in one office per land producing 50,000 *koku*,[34]
which was the equivalent of the size of a feudal fief for a daimyo
house normally managed by some 500 samurai officials or more.

The thirty functionaries, recruited from the house's direct vassals, the *hatamoto*, were usually of only low- or middle-level prestige; the expenses for each office, remarkably small, were appropriated from the treasury of the bakufu. The result, as Conrad Totman estimated, was that "at a cost to the central treasury of about 1,000 *koku*, the bakufu could expect to receive the produce of a 50,000 *koku* domain. . . . "[35]

This reliance of the Tokugawa house upon the lower echelons of the shogunal bureaucracy for the management of their entire territories had in fact been a point of recurrent concern.[36] Katsu Kaishū, himself a Tokugawa retainer of low origin and later pivotal in minimizing the Tokugawa loyalists' resistance to the Court, made a curiously penetrating observation before the Restoration. Katsu argued that such reliance was a weakness in the foundation of the Tokugawa mainhouse that could cause most of the territories to be lost to the other military houses once the Tokugawa's primacy declined. Katsu, however, also wondered whether such an arrangement might also indicate the "Tokugawa's lack of self-interest" for the sake of the nation, implying that the founders of the Tokugawa bakufu had disinterestedly constructed its system of rule in such a way as to minimize the impact on the nation of its own eventual fall, thereby making later unification easier.[37]

Indeed, at the time of the Restoration, these bakufu functionaries in the local outposts of the Tokugawa territories, the *daikan*, *gundai*, and *bugyō*, were isolated and easy targets for the Imperial pacification missions. One such mission was spearheaded by Ayakōji (Ōhara) Toshizane, an Imperial court noble. He had slipped out of Kyoto before the confiscation of the Tokugawa territories was announced, and was joined later by another Court noble at the northeastern border of Kyoto for a thrust toward the shogun's local office in Kasamatsu farther north.[38] These mavericks were joined by still another group of men, led by Sagara Sōzō, who had previously engaged in insurrection in Edo as a part of the anti-Tokugawa agitation plotted by Satsuma. They quickly became a self-styled pacification mission devising and offering their own version of what the Restoration stood for, notably a 50 percent tax cut for the local populace along the way.[39] Not surprisingly, then, the lands studded by the fiefs of the Tokugawa retainers immediately fell under the command of these men. And the fall of the Kasamatsu office "recovered," for the Court, land worth 120,000 *koku* with remarkable ease.

A similar recovery of administrative power for the Court also occurred without resistance in the Tokugawa territory of Nagasaki. A large port on the island of Kyūshū, Nagasaki had been known as the exception to the shogun's self-seclusion policy and for its strategic importance to the shogun in keeping an eye on ambitious Kyūshū domains such as Satsuma. However, the political instability of the final years of the Tokugawa had already engulfed the port city of Nagasaki and its bakufu office. An open trading city of a sort, Nagasaki had harbored many clandestine meetings for Restoration activists who were eager to obtain modern weapons from the West. The bakufu's Nagasaki office had been primarily a supervisory body, coordinating the security functions performed by local samurai and representatives of some fifteen domains from the adjacent areas, including the powerful Satsuma, Saga, Chōshū, and Tosa.[40] But the significance of this office as a bakufu outpost, by the same token, diminished quickly as the Tokugawa's primacy declined, prompting more autonomous action by men from these domains. The office lost both the shogun's otherwise unwavering protection and its prestige, in fact, as early as 1866 during the bakufu's second and unsuccessful military expedition against Chōshū.[41]

The last official from Edo for the Nagasaki office, Kawazu Sukekuni, was appointed on the eve of the Restoration. His arrival at the office on November 8, 1867, was followed immediately by one report of the restoration of Imperial rule and by another of the battle of Toba and Fushimi. Kawazu's subsequent flight from office immediately turned Nagasaki into a stage on which retainers from the adjacent domains competed for prominence as Restoration activists. They reinstated the government of Nagasaki as a body of representatives from these domains, and clarification of their allegiance to the emperor was deemed as urgent a matter as recovery of the security and other functions abandoned by the last of the shogun's officials.[42] A pledge was drafted by a Chōshū retainer and approved by Sasaki Takayuki of Tosa and

Matsukata Masayoshi of Satsuma[43] to the effect that a concerted effort by the representatives of the three domains should be promoted in Nagasaki to maintain order, to ward off the foreign powers, and to enhance the honor of the emperor's nation. The victory of the Imperial forces at the battle of Toba and Fushimi further bolstered these men's convictions and prompted them to declare that these aims be extended to the "entire island of Kyūshū,"[44] although the Imperial mission itself did not arrive there until early March of 1868. The return of the Tokugawa lands to the Court thus proceeded virtually unchecked.

The progressive inclusion of the daimyo houses in the making of the new government resulted in the preservation of their domain governments, but the repossession by the Court of the Tokugawa territories was modeled on a different administrative plan. The Imperial government promptly instituted in these territories its provisional governing machines, variously called *chindai* or *shichū torishimari*, at first, and later *saibansho*. These were soon renamed fu and ken, the names that eventually were to be employed for the local government units, the prefectures, following the liquidation of the domains in 1871.[45] Usually Court nobles were chosen to head the territorial offices, flanked by samurai deputies from Satsuma, Chōshū, Tosa, or other domains with records of action in the anti-Tokugawa campaigns. The fact that these men occupied what had been the lower tiers of the Tokugawa government, however, did not mean that they formally became "local" officials of "local" offices, a hierarchical relationship not likely to be appealing to these spirited men. Nor was the central-local division of government a suitable framework for the expression of resurrected Imperial rule by these men. The actual administration of the repossessed Tokugawa lands was left to the former employees of the bakufu and local recruits, while the samurai deputies often simultaneously held territorial assignments and positions in the new "central" government, or else frequently moved from one locality to another or back to the central offices. They became, in effect, the extended "center," and the fu and ken the stations along their route.

The question remains as to whether or not the creation of fu and ken in the former territories of the Tokugawa was any indication of a greater change that would alter the relationship between the new government and the feudal domains. Robert Wilson, in one of the very few writings on the Meiji government at this stage, seems to argue in the affirmative. He notes, in support of his point, that the names fu and ken were used both for the former Tokugawa territories under Imperial rule before the abolition of the domains in 1871 and for the prefectures after 1871.[46]

On the whole, however, the initial reactions to the creation of the fu and ken indicated the prevailing belief that it was no more than a provisional means of adjustment to the dislocation of the Tokugawa from his own territories. Since some of these former Tokugawa territories included open port cities and exposed their new samurai deputies to close contact with the West, these offices occupied unique places in the infant Imperial government. They also provided some necessary information on how the new government was received by the foreign powers. Ōkuma Shigenobu of Saga, Terajima Munenori of Satsuma, and Inoue Kaoru of Chō-shū were some of the former anti-Tokugawa activists sent to these offices, taking upon themselves the taxing job of defending the new central government against the suspicious Western powers. The experience was to provide invaluable political expertise for their later significant roles in managing the Imperial government. However, it is one thing to recognize these men's experience as meaningful to their own political careers and to the new central government; and it is another to derive from, and read into, their experience a hint of an alternative, specifically for the central-local government relationship of the future.

Katsu Kaishū's observation indeed had been correct, but only partially: the displacement of the Tokugawa was quick. But the displacement neither induced much momentum for unification nor did it pose a threat to the collective lives of the other daimyo houses. For them the most important adjustment to the demise of the Tokugawa bakufu was completed when they shifted their allegiance from the shogun to the emperor. In fact, the *gunken*, an ancient system of central control now revived as a collective term for the fu- and ken-based centralized control of local government, turned out to be no more than a metaphor for the po-

litical ascendancy of the emperor and his Court. As such, the
frequent use of the terms fu and ken, or *gunken*, in government
documents and in private and public debates indicated no more
than a limited adjustment of the Imperial government to acquiring
the Tokugawa territories. Nothing in the references to the *gunken*
system was threatening to the continuation of the feudal domains.

### After the Restoration: The Gunken-Hōken Debate

A decree issued by the Imperial government on May 4, 1868,
revealed the discrepancy between the Court's claim of creating a
new political order and the unchanged behavior of the daimyo
houses:

> The sacred enterprise of the Restoration will be realized only when
> those laws and regulations [which had existed since fiefdom was
> established] that do not fit the present day situation are unhesitat-
> ingly abandoned, thereby founding the bases for reforms; and when
> concerted efforts are made between the Court and the domains. . . .
> It is beyond belief to learn that, nonetheless, there are some who
> think the Restoration means only matters of the Court. For each
> han, the foundation for reforms realizing the emperor's will lies in
> removing the inertia of the old customs, in promoting men of ability,
> and in renovating the han administration. Yet, . . . many of the han
> . . . leave the affairs of administration to the privileged vassals, mak-
> ing reforms of the old customs unlikely. . . . Now that [the privileged
> groups] are removed from the Court, each han must remove theirs
> who are unable to adapt to the present-day circumstances and . . .
> promote men of talent and advance the reforms of the han
> administration.[47]

The decree expressed the government's frustration that the Restoration had not actively involved the majority of the feudal domains, and that nothing had changed beyond the displacement of
the Tokugawa family from the shogun's office. In other words, it
was evident that the majority of the daimyo houses had been
returning to their long-accustomed "calculated indifference." The
*gunken* system, if instituted, would have had no such room for

the feudal houses' noninvolvement and, on the contrary, presumed that the daimyo houses would give up their local autonomy in the face of central control. Nonetheless, the fact that the
creation of fu and ken did not mean a step toward such a *gunken*
system was obvious even to the Restoration government itself.

A case in point is the *Seitaisho* Constitution of June 11, 1868.
The *Seitaisho* for the first time formally recognized fu and ken,
along with the domains (han), as comprising the three legs of a
tripod on which to found the new regime. However, in the actual
articles of the *Seitaisho* defining local governing institutions, the
fu and ken were virtually indistinguishable from the han. Article
V, for example, ruled that the fu and ken would furnish *kōshi*,
which had been a special category for retainers of the domains,
to be sent to a deliberative body in the central government, the
*kōgisho*. Another, Article XI, reinforcing the fact that there was
no clear distinction between fu, ken, and han, reads:

> The government in each fu, han, and ken must be conducted in
> accordance with the principles laid down in the Oath. The laws of
> one place must not be held binding to the others. No title must be
> bestowed, no money coined, and no foreigners employed arbitrarily.
> No coalitions may be formed between neighboring han, nor between
> a han and a foreign power. This is in order that there be no conflict
> of greater and lesser authority, no confusion in the Constitution.[48]

Fu and ken, conceived here as indistinguishable from han, were
the vehicles, at most, for prompting the domain officials to realize
that the reforms in the new central government were to be replicated by the domains as well.

Another case in point is the reaction to a daimyo's proposal to
restore the proper relationship between the feudal domains and
the emperor. The lord of the Himeji in late 1868 submitted a
letter to the emperor proposing that his fief be returned to the
Court.[49] Except for Itō Hirobumi from Chōshū, all the Restoration
leaders apparently ignored this proposal. Itō Hirobumi urged that
the other daimyo houses follow Himeji's example. He argued that,
despite the Restoration, so far only the Tokugawa's governing
powers had been returned to the emperor. The military houses

still maintained their own armed forces and were in constant rivalry among themselves. Laws and regulations in the feudal domains were written and enforced independently, and the government of the nation was hardly unitary. Itō Hirobumi concluded by insisting that the daimyos' domains all be governed in accordance with the "institutions of fu and ken."[50]

However, Ito's conclusion was hardly convincing as one pointing toward anything new in view of what he might have meant by the "institutions of fu and ken." Recalling later the "origin" of the *Haihan chiken* (the abolition of the domains), Itō Hirobumi cited a discussion prior to the Restoration between Iwakura Tomomi and Tamamatsu Misao, a noted scholar of "national learning" (*Kokugaku*), in which they insisted that the legendary Jimmu, the founding emperor of Japan, had instituted the *gunken* system as the basis of his nation.[51] But on another occasion, Itō himself identified, with little sense of self-contradiction, Jimmu's campaign for unifying the nation as, instead, the "beginning of the *hōken* [feudal] system."[52]

Thus, the references to the fu and ken in government documents and in public and private debates indicate that they, or the *gunken* in general, were given no consistent or established meaning. They even failed to distinguish the imperial territories from those under the rule of the feudal domains at times. The use of fu and ken derived mostly from nostalgia for the ancient system associated in the leaders' minds with the restoration of the Imperial rule.

Regardless of the implications drawn from its association with ancient Imperial rule, the *gunken* never became the intellectual basis for discontinuing the feudal domains. On the contrary, in fact, the *gunken* system posed an immediate problem to some of the members of the new government: how to reconcile themselves to the fact that it was only the Tokugawa mainhouse that had surrendered parts, if not all, of its fief to the Court. If the unequivocal principle of the ancient *gunken* system defined both the land and the people as belonging only to the emperor, that principle was being violated by the very domains that, having staged the restoration of the Imperial rule, continued to keep their lands. Furthermore, the *gunken* system remained obscure in the realm of practice, however vividly it had been resurrected in the realm of legend—thus providing a clear contrast to the *hōken* system, or feudalism, upon which some hundred years of internal peace and order had been founded. Matsudaira Yoshinaga, on the eve of the Restoration, openly admitted his anxiety over applying this previously untested practice of government; he felt that the Restoration could not mean the reintroduction of a *gunken* system that was, after all, only "a remote Imperial institution." [53]

Additional evidence exists that the references to the *gunken* system did not necessarily imply the conception of a new central-local government relationship distinctly different from the "centralized feudalism" under the Tokugawa shogun. An interesting debate took place among the representatives, or *kōshi*, from the domains over the two alternatives for "local" administration, *gunken* and *hōken*, at a meeting held by the new government in mid-June of 1869. By this time a substantial number of the domains had submitted letters proposing the return of their fiefs to the Court, following the example made by the four principal southwestern domains earlier in the same year. Even at this point, the *gunken* system still seemed harmless to the feudal domains, as well as largely indistinguishable from the *hōken* system.

Of the domain representatives at this meeting, about eighty supported the *gunken* and a little over 110 favored the *hōken*. One group of proponents of the *gunken*, including those from Kanazawa, Wakayama, and the aforementioned Himeji, urged that all lands be made public property under the emperor and that the laws and regulations "originate from one source." In order to achieve these aims, they proposed, among other things, that "there shall be fu in a large province, and smaller provinces shall be governed by the adjacent fu," and likewise that "there shall be ken for each land worth 100,000 *koku*...." The same group insisted that governors of fu and ken "shall be furnished from the former lords" or from the high-ranking officials of the domains. According to another group also supporting the *gunken*, including Fukui and Sakura, this ancient system of rule was to be almost identical with the *hōken* system in that the feudal lords were to become the governors of fu and ken, which were renamed han of large, medium, and small sizes. The fiefs of the lords were not to be taken away from or wholly given to them, but rather "entrusted" to them; and, in keeping with the persistent *hōken* notions, the offices of the governors were to be "hereditary." Those in favor of the *hōken* system based their argument on such merits of that time-honored system as the "life-long bond between the lord and his vassals." They argued that such a bond would be indispensable in maintaining the cohesion of the nation in times of crisis, and that the presence of lords in every locality could promote a reciprocity of obligations and duties. Neither of these two virtues, the group asserted, could be brought about by "government officials" who were merely functionaries under the *gunken* system. Finally, there was one more group of feudal representatives. To them, neither the *gunken* nor the *hōken* system seemed an inspired alternative. The choice would not have to be either one or the other, but a combination of the two. They maintained that Japan could be governed best by a harmonious division, with one-third of the country designated for Imperial rule and governed under the *gunken* system and the rest brought under the *hōken* system.[54]

In the end, the notion of the *gunken* system was a measure of the extent to which the Imperial decree of May 4, 1868, was honored by the individual domains. One lord, Tokugawa Mochitsugu of Wakayama, actually received Imperial recognition for active reforms carried out in his domain government in accordance with the "form of *gunken*."[55] However, the reforms of his domain, such as modernization of his troops, promotion of samurai officials on the basis of merit, and removal of some of the institutionalized privileges of the samurai stratum, were merely internal domain affairs.[56] In other words, the *gunken* had become a code word or idea for the receptivity of the daimyo houses to the language of the "Restoration," a token of their acceptance of the symbolic hegemony of the new central government that had ended the old bakufu. For the time being, the Restoration had accomplished no more than the fall of the Tokugawa from the house of shogun.

# 2

# The Constitutional Politics of the Restoration: From the Oath to the *Haihan Chiken*

HOW TO END the war as promptly as possible became the primary concern of the Restoration leaders soon after its beginning, a concern that preoccupied them as much as the codification of the restored Imperial rule. One reason was the overall political instability caused by the war. The regions north of Edo, where some of the Tokugawa retainers demonstrated a disorganized yet stubborn resistance, began to show signs of protracted civil war. By the beginning of the summer, the Aizu han and a score of its neighboring domains had also forged an alliance against the forces of Satsuma and others. The Court's concession granting the continuation of the Tokugawa mainhouse under a new lord on July 13, 1868, seemed to have little effect in weakening this resistance. In addition, the prolonged war was weakening security in these regions and depriving them of the manpower to tend the rice fields and plant the rice seedlings. Hence, the War of the Restoration exacerbated the widespread rural unrest that had prevailed during the closing decades of the bakufu.[1] For the Restoration leaders, mindful of how the watchful Western powers would accept the new Imperial government, the prolonged war was exacting both financially and militarily a "tremendous drain upon the nation, which could inevitably lead to its collapse."[2]

A deeper concern was how the war was affecting the Restoration leaders' efforts to codify the Imperial rule. The war was reinforcing a particular development in bakumatsu politics that all feudal houses had become equal before the emperor. As seen in the previous chapter, the successful military campaigns of the Boshin War left in their wake a growing number of daimyo and their retainers who shifted their allegiance from the former house of the shogun to the emperor. The shifts were taking place in exchange for assurances that the feudal houses would be given places in the new Court-centered order. These assurances were, in effect, Imperial recognition of the retainers' efforts to attenuate their daimyo's previous association with the emperor's "enemy," the Tokugawa. This conversion of the feudal houses, however, added an ironical twist to the war—its continuation both diminished the number of pro-Tokugawa houses *and* increased the pressure on the Imperial government to offer similar opportunities to the remaining feudal houses to shift their allegiance in order to survive. A petition attributed to the lord of Chōshū spoke of the wisdom of not forcing an enemy at bay. But sympathy for the last of the feudal domains still resisting the emperor's political ascendancy was evident.[3] Another petition by nearly forty daimyo also exerted this unexpected pressure and requested a cease-fire with Aizu han and its allies.[4]

These petitions enumerated similar reasons to pardon Aizu. They emphasized Aizu's devoted loyalty to the Imperial house as exhibited in its service as a security force in Kyoto before the Restoration; explained its initial siding with Yoshinobu as its daimyo's private obligation to the outgoing shogun; and insisted that its current resistance to the Imperial forces resulted from ignorance of the Court's benevolent decision to preserve the Tokugawa mainhouse. Yet within these petitions was a message far more significant than sympathy for the besieged Aizu han and its allied domains: even these very last of the pro-Tokugawa domains were no different from the rest and thus, like the others, should be allowed to reverse their initial pro-Tokugawa position before their complete extinction. These petitions prevailed, allowing even Aizu to be preserved, though at the cost of a great deal of its fief, with Imperial recognition. In other words, in the conversion of the pro-Tokugawa domains, all feudal domains could find places in the new Imperial rule under the formal equality that was to be assured by the Court, regardless of prior status or loyalty. The leaders in the new government, who hoped to codify in constitutional terms both the restoration of the emperor to his rightful place and a break from the past, could not ignore the significance of this process.

Many historians, particularly in Japan, stress the beginning of the war itself as the irreversible first step leading to a centralized political order that offered no place for the feudal houses. Likewise, William Beasley sees in the conception of the Return of the Fiefs to the Court (the *Hanseki hōkan*), as the Boshin War was winding down in 1869, the initial step toward the *Haihan chiken*, which institutionally ensured the emperor's "direct" rule.[5] Attention to these concerns—the need to end the war and the growing notion of equality among the domains before the Court—casts in a new light the Restoration leaders' constitutional efforts in the following several years. The interpretation of this study—that these efforts were designed primarily to reconcile the emperor's political ascendancy with the continuation of the feudal domains—is at odds with that of many histories of early Meiji politics. This viewpoint also raises important questions: for example, where then did the idea of terminating the feudal domains come from and how did it gain the support of the Restoration leaders who were initially committed to preserving the feudal domains?

## *Setting Things Right: From the Oath to the Return of the Fiefs*

The Oath, promulgated on April 6, 1868, was the first constitutional document to follow the formal declaration of restored Imperial rule. The Oath was a remarkable document in its own right, addressing itself to some of the key strains on society accompanying nation-building, and has won much praise from constitutional historians and theorists. Its emphasis upon broader political participation reflects the recognition of two problems: that of making the new political system accountable to society, and that of regulating the relationships among the dominant political forces in society. The need to protect social stability in these times of radical transformation was acutely perceived—hence the Oath's emphasis on unity within as well as on society's adjustment to its new exposure to the West from without. However, this capacity of the Oath to embrace a broad range of problems in developing polities should not overshadow the immediate tasks with which its writers were confronted, as well as their acute awareness of the limited capacity and resources upon which the Restoration government could rely. Moreover, the careful wording of the Oath still honored the continuation of the feudal domains.

In order to understand the significance of the Oath to the new central government, society at large, and the domains, it is necessary to look at the Oath closely, that is, to examine the stages it went through in preparation. What follows are two preliminary drafts of the Oath, one prepared by Yuri Kimimasa of Fukui and the other by Fukuoka Takachika of Tosa. These drafts are followed by the final version of the Oath, as revised by Kido Kōin.[6] (I have emphasized significant points.)

### Giji no taii (The *Outline of the Constitution*)

1. It is expected that every commoner shall pursue his own calling so that there shall be no stagnation of spirit.

2. Upper and lower orders shall unite in the active conduct of the affairs of state.

3. Knowledge shall be sought throughout the world in order to strengthen the foundations of the Imperial rule.

4. *Kōshi* [the representatives to be sent to the Court by the domains] shall be subject to replacement after a certain tenure by *men of ability*.

5. All matters shall be decided by *public discussion*, and shall not be subject to private deliberations.

### Kaimei (The United *Pledge*)

1. *A deliberative assembly of the feudal lords* shall be established so that all matters may be decided by *public discussion*.

2. Men of all classes, including the nobility and the military, shall each be expected to pursue his own calling so that there shall be no stagnation of spirit.

3. Upper and lower orders shall unite in vigorous conduct of the affairs of state.

4. Knowledge shall be sought throughout the world in order to strengthen the foundations of the Imperial rule.

5. *Chōshi* [the Court appointees from the rank of domain retainers for the new government] shall be subject to replacement, after their tenure, by *men of ability*.

### Sei (The *Oath*)

1. *Deliberative assemblies* shall be widely convoked and all matters shall be decided by *public discussion*.

2. Upper and lower orders shall unite in active conduct of the affairs of state.

3. Men of all classes, including the nobility and the military, shall each pursue his calling so that there shall be no stagnation of spirit.

4. Evil customs of the past shall be broken off and everything shall be based upon the universal law.

5. Knowledge shall be sought throughout the world in order to strengthen the foundations of the Imperial rule.

Of interest in these drafts of the Oath are the repeated use of the term "public discussion" and the changes made between the preliminary and final drafts: the shift of the title, in increasingly committed terms, from the "Outline" to the "Pledge" to the "Oath"; the insertion of the "assembly of the feudal lords" and its replacement by the more general "deliberative assemblies"; and the shift first from *kōshi* to *chōshi* and finally to "men of ability" generally. These changes illustrate the workings of the writers' minds as woven into the constitutional documents. One point must be emphasized: the final Oath is not necessarily the most refined version resulting from careful revision of the preliminary drafts or from a consensus among the central leaders of what the Oath was meant to be. What disappeared from the preliminary drafts tells as much about the background of the writing as what was retained in the final Oath.

The exigencies of time under which the Oath was prepared offer a convenient start for this analysis. First, there was the urgent problem of securing financial resources for the new government in Kyoto in order to sustain the war against the Tokugawa and their allies. When the battle of Toba and Fushimi broke out, there was virtually no cash at the disposal of the Court. In soliciting material support, the Court was thus impelled to stress that the current struggle between it and the forces of the Tokugawa was not of a private nature and to emphasize the uncontested sovereign whom the local financiers were asked to serve.[7]

The increased encounters between foreigners and the Japanese brought about a similar but even more pressing need to clarify the locus of the legitimate governing authority of the nation. Some of the encounters with the West were violent, such as those at Kōbe and Sakai on February 14 and March 18, 1868, respectively, between the domain troops on guard at these port cities and the foreign troops and nationals. Costing a score of lives on both sides, these incidents raised serious questions about the authority of the new central government at a critical time. Coming under scrutiny was its ability to maintain internal order, to protect foreign interests, and, most of all, to override the domain governments in deciding the fate of those retainers involved in the incidents. The execution of those samurai involved eventually followed, but not without considerable political bargaining by members of the Restoration government with the foreign powers, who demanded severe punishment *and* with the feudal domains, which resisted the primacy of the new central government over their own retainers.[8] The writing of the Oath took into account these contingencies, which alerted the Restoration leaders to the pressing need for signaling internally and externally the uncontested authority of the emperor and his Court.

Furthermore, the elevation of the authority of the Court, however symbolically, above that of the feudal domains uncovered a special issue critical to the authority relationship between the Court and the feudal domains. The Court was in effect powerless without the allegiance of the military houses—particularly those few, such as Chōshū and Satsuma, that by means of their military support had lifted it from political oblivion. A suspicion thus quickly arose within the Restoration camp that "either Chōshū or Satsuma might put forward a new shogun."[9] Likewise, a Tosa official detected a prevailing "air of suspicion" during the writing of the Oath regarding the possible "consequences of the displacement of the Tokugawa at the hands of Satsuma and Chōshū."[10] This increasing anxiety over the possibility that the Tokugawa monopoly might be replaced by that of another military house underscored the use in the Oath of the term "public discussion," with a definite stress upon the first word. First and foremost, this emphasis was intended to defuse the suspicion that the emperor's ascendancy was merely fictitious in the face of the apparent primacy of Chōshū and Satsuma in the new central government.

In this context, one should note that the Oath also partially originated in response to the division in the Restoration camp at the Kogosho Conference between moderates, such as Tosa's Yamanouchi Yōdō, and militants, such as Satsuma's Ōkubo Toshimichi; that is, between those who would have been satisfied with the Tokugawa's self-demotion alone and those who demanded more from the former house of the shogun.[11] To the moderates, who had gained strength prior to the battle of Toba and Fushimi, the stress upon "public discussion" was intended to demonstrate the constitutional expression of the formal equality of all daimyo houses before the Court, an equality that was becoming established in fact as the War of the Restoration advanced. The emphasis upon "public" indicates the strength of the moderates' position in the Court, even though the denunciation of the Tokugawa family appeared to conform to the militants' demand.

The unstated aim of expressing this formal equality underlay the two stages of revision. From the Outline to the Pledge, this goal meant that the constitutional document was to concern itself broadly with the general authority relationship between the Court and the military houses, instead of narrowly with procedural matters internal to the new central government. From the Pledge to the Oath, it further dictated that the act of the pledge was to be undertaken not only by the Court before the military houses but by a real union between the Court and the military houses. The disappearance of the explicit term "assembly of the feudal lords" from the Oath, too, was highly consistent with this aim. The omission certainly did not mean the removal of this specific group in preference to a broader one. The writers had simply assumed in the beginning that the deliberative assembly would consist of the daimyo. Therefore, by dropping the explicit mention of the daimyo, they could seem to expand, symbolically, the Court's sanction of more general "assemblies" without sacrificing its actual reliance for its authority on the domains. This wording signaled yet another attempt, by way of the more general notion of "deliberative assemblies," to emphasize the symbolic primacy of the Restoration government on which the union of the Court and the military houses could be expressed constitutionally. Indeed, the line "deliberative assemblies shall be widely convoked and all matters shall be decided by public discussion" was repeated elsewhere proclaiming the restored Imperial rule. The original reference group of the feudal daimyo was not lost. One such announcement, addressed to the populace of northern Japan in mid-September of 1868, reads in part: "Government and laws shall be vigorously reformed; *the Court nobles, feudal lords and men of samurai rank* from all localities shall be widely convoked to the deliberative assemblies so that all matters shall be decided by public discussion"[12] (my emphasis).

There was one curious aberration in these documents of otherwise uniformly decorative, abstract constitutional language: the shift from *kōshi* in Yuri's draft to *chōshi* in Fukuoka's draft. This aberration, as well as the stress upon the more general "men of ability," too, however, tells us something about the psychological makeup of the Restoration leaders: the mixture of insecurity, arrogance, pride, and fear in men whose actions fell short of conviction. Appointed by the daimyo from among their high-ranking retainers for services in the Court, the *kōshi* represented the domains' and the daimyo's interests in the new government; an observer went so far as to call them "emissaries."[13] The *kōshi* existed as long as the feudal domains lasted after the Restoration. The *chōshi* category, on the other hand, indicated those daimyo's retainers who were recruited and appointed by Imperial order to join the new government and whose allegiance to the Court was expected to supersede that to their daimyo. The two terms thus illustrate a peculiar mixture of the continuity and discontinuity of the feudalistic political norm within exactly that document in which discontinuity was most conspicuously presented.

Of particular importance here is the *chōshi* status. If the Restoration had symbolically made the daimyo of all standings equal among themselves, the *chōshi* status now had the effect of symbolically elevating the recruited retainers to the rank equal to their own daimyo's before the Court. Kido Kōin, Ōkubo Toshimichi, and Yuri Kimimasa were some of the few prominent activists who gained the *chōshi* status. Not surprisingly, such elevation was not without its price. Their fellow retainers at home often were suspicious of the *chōshi* for placing their loyalty to the new central government before that to their own domains.[14] *Chōshi* officials were also characterized condescendingly as "men of questionable origins."[15] Behind these signs of displeasure expressed by the majority of samurai lay something much more serious—namely, a distrust of the new government itself, which sanctioned the *chōshi*. Thus in shifting from *kōshi* to *chōshi*, and then to their replacement by "men of ability," the writers of the Oath had a dual purpose in mind. First, they were attempting to diffuse the visibility of specifically designated categories of men; at the same time, they were expressing their desire to multiply *their* type of men for the new era. Hence, the cautious language of the Oath indeed showed some hope for discontinuing the old political order. Yet, in practice, the effect was mainly to confirm a formal change consisting primarily of the displacement of the Tokugawa. Beyond that, the writers' efforts continued to be subtly constrained by the tenacious past.

The Petition for the Return of the Fiefs to the Court, the *Hanseki hōkan*, followed the basic concern dictating the writing of the Oath. The Petition was one more effort to complete what the Oath appeared to leave only implicit: the clarification of the feudal domains' status in the new Court-centered order. Shortly before the Oath reached its final draft, Kido Kōin prepared a petition pleading that the land and the people be returned from the daimyo to the emperor. Typical of his writings, the petition resorted to highly abstract language. It proclaimed that the "fundamental principle and cause" (*taigi meibun*) of the Restoration rested with the new method of political recruitment on the basis of merit, with the removal of antiquated practices of government, and with the restoration of the emperor, to whom the people and the land belonged. But the part that follows shows Kido's uneasiness about the state of affairs:

> The Imperial Court relies on Satsuma and Chōshū; Satsuma and Chōshū in their turn rely on their military strength; and the other domains by and large follow suit.... Where the Sovereign rests is, therefore, ambiguous. [Under these circumstances, once the war ends, and] the troops of the daimyo return to their homes, reinforce their defenses and resume the conduct of government as well as the maintenance of public order within each, the removal of the harm they thus create will become impossible.[16]

In other words, the steps toward the *Hanseki hōkan* were prompted by an increasing concern among the Restoration leaders that every one of the feudal domains was becoming and acting like a "miniature bakufu," with little or no sense of the significant change in the central government.[17] These steps by no means predestined the ultimate attack on the feudal domains; they were intended, rather, to impress the feudal domains with the emergence of the Court-centered order.

## *Return of the Fiefs:* Hanseki Hōkan

Kido Kōin's campaign for the *Hanseki hōkan* was at first an indirect one. In order to seek an initial endorsement for the effort in his own domain, Kido returned to Chōshū in the early summer of 1868. Yet his return did not elicit any particular response among his fellow retainers. His insistence upon the necessity of unified support for the Court among the daimyo houses remained too vaguely or too generally stated to receive any tangible reactions. His domain instead first responded to his return with the allegation that he was oblivious to its internal affairs. Such a reaction and the suggestion that he immediately join the Chōshū contingents in the battleground of northern Japan only demoralized him and further hampered his efforts.[18] Not until late in the summer of 1868 did Kido finally seize upon the opportunity to suggest to his daimyo the idea of the return of the fief to the Court. Even then, his arguments were as contrived as they were indirect. Kido made a reference to Ōe Hiromoto, founder of the Mōri house, which had headed Chōshū 700 years earlier, as an example of a loyalist inspired by the need for restoring civil order through national unification by the direct rule of the Court. Citing the founding and consolidation of the Mōri, one of the oldest military houses, Kido argued that Ōe Hiromoto had also taken significant steps toward national unification, yet his mission was only half-finished.[19] The choice that was opening up 700 years later before the head of the same house, his rhetoric seemed to suggest, was either to complete the mission or compensate for the founder's failure to produce the other half[20] by offering the house's territory itself to the Court.

The daimyo endorsed Kido's proposal couched in this euphemistic language, though at the same time he expressed his fear of the divisive impact of the idea of *Hanseki hōkan* upon his own Chōshū.[21] With this basic approval, however, Kido further sought and won the support of two other powerful southwestern domains, Satsuma and Tosa, through their retainers in the new government, Ōkubo Toshimichi and Gotō Shōjirō. By the beginning of 1869, the return of the fiefs to the Court no longer seemed to arouse even the slightest signs of debate among these leading figures. Later joined by another southwestern domain, Saga, the Petition for the Return of the Fiefs to the Court was submitted on March 2, 1869.

The absence of overt disagreement or even debate among these four domains on the Petition prior to this date is itself a significant clue to understanding the way the remaining domains viewed the Petition. The fact that the four major domains behind the Restoration engineered the Petition is also at least as important as the content of the Petition itself. Samurai from the Tanakura han in the North circulated a memo:

Even those southwestern domains with such distinguished Restoration records presented a righteous proposal of returning their fiefs to the Court. Should it not be us, [those] guilty [of siding once with the Imperial enemy], who need to return our fiefs before anybody else?[22]

The point here is not so much their seeming enthusiasm for the Petition, prompted by guilt, but rather their sense of competition with the southwestern domains, reminiscent of the *kakkyo*, the "independent campaigns" on the eve of the Restoration, or the show of loyalism toward the Court when the feudal domains attempted to escape Imperial denunciation during the Boshin War. In other words, the majority of the feudal domains responded to the four-domain Petition in much the same way as they had done earlier when confronted by the demand of allegiance to the emperor during the war: their reaction was dictated by the fear of becoming the last to endorse the action of the four key domains. Okayama han, the first to follow the four-domain Petition, was almost blatantly competitive in insisting that it had always entertained the aims of the Petition and that its own efforts had been unexpectedly outrun by the four domains.[23] Likewise, when news of the four-domain Petition began to spread among the rest of the domains, a rush of similar petitions followed. By July, the majority of the domains had turned in their own petitions to the Court, and the original four-domain Petition and the others were formally accepted by the Court on July 25, 1869.

The Petition itself also allowed a degree of ambiguity that made it much less threatening to the feudal domains and thus more easily replicated by them. It states that "hereby we humbly return our fiefs" but follows with the controversial passage stating that the Court "should give what should be given and take [what] should be taken" to and from the daimyo houses.[24] In Satsuma and Tosa as well as at the Court, the dominant view of the Petition by the four domains seemed to be that it was more of a preparatory step toward Imperial support of the domains' right to their own fiefs than an outright displacement of the feudal domains.[25] Wakayama han's petition, for example, indicates no fundamental change in the Court-military relationship, with the exception of its own proposal that the feudal domains voluntarily contribute 10 to 20 percent of their lands to the Court.[26] Even Kido Kōin had recorded in his diary back on March 11, 1869, that the everlasting assurance of continuation was now achieved for the "three hundred daimyo houses" as a result of the four-domain Petition.[27] The most conspicuous result of the *Hanseki hōkan*, as seen in its edict that the daimyo were to be official governors of their own domains, was that the daimyo were once again the rulers of their own fiefs. The Court thus reconciled itself with the feudal domains by becoming their recreator.

Not surprisingly, this Imperial sanction of the feudal domains did little in terms of the problems plaguing the new government: the financial difficulties of the central treasury, the domains' general indifference to the central government and what its creation meant, and the unpredictability of the provincial samurai. Neither did the end of the Boshin War, with the surrender in Hokkaidō of the last of the Tokugawa loyalists on June 27, 1869, ease the burden of these problems upon the Restoration government and its leading members.

The financial difficulties were alarming to both the Restoration government and the domains. The war itself had resulted in a general increase in the size of the standing armies to be sustained by the domain treasuries. For those domains that had been active in the Restoration movement longer than others, the increase had reached the point of far exceeding financial capacity. The end of the war simply made this expensive superfluity of fighting forces even more apparent.[28] Anticipating that a greater harmony between the Court and the domains would follow from the *Hanseki hōkan*, Iwakura Tomomi proposed a solution to lessen the financial burden of at least the central treasury: a contribution from each domain of 10 percent of its income to the Restoration government. However, because such a solution for the new government could only worsen the financial problems of the domains, Iwakura quickly conceded that even this 10 percent should be waived for at least five years or so, given the depleted coffers of the military houses. Furthermore, the new government would have neither the will nor the power to enforce such a solution, should collection prove difficult.[29] Kido Kōin felt a resignation even a year after the *Hanseki hōkan*: " ... for the time being, the Court should establish itself independently within the resources of the 8,000,000 *koku* [of its recently confiscated lands]...." By "for the time being," Kido meant "ten, fifteen, or twenty years."[30]

Such resignation illuminates another issue, which was more central to the authority relationship between the new government and the feudal domains: namely, the continued indifference of the military houses upon which the existence of the new government precariously depended. In fact, whenever the presence of the new government was felt beyond its own boundary, it was only seen as introducing alien ideas into the political life of the domains, ideas especially threatening to the feudal loyalism that had seemed to revitalize the internal relationships of the domains. Sasaki Takayuki's vain effort around the time of the *Hanseki hōkan* to recruit his fellow retainers in Tosa to a central office, the Justice Department, illustrates the isolation of the new central government:

> [Men] of samurai rank tend to detest the idea [of sending our retainers to the central government], believing that working in the Imperial government means serving more than one overlord. They, accordingly, despise us exceedingly.... It is in the very interest of our lord and the honor of the Yamanouchi house to furnish as many men as possible to the important offices in the Imperial government.... It would beyond the shadow of a doubt be in the interest of our domain as well as that of the Court to establish cooperation between those inside and outside the domain.... My plea, however, receives no sympathy.[31]

Almost a year later, Sasaki expressed his frustration more bluntly: "It just does not please the men at home to argue for the strengthening of the Court these days."[32]

Samurai presented a problem in themselves. They saw no reason to change their feudalistic orientation with the change in the "central" government from the Tokugawa bakufu to the Court. The War of the Restoration and its end likewise did not deter them from their provincial commitments. On the contrary, they saw in the new situation the imperial recognition of their defense of their daimyo when confronted by the earlier choice of supporting the Tokugawa family or the emperor. Kido and others in the new government detected in these provincial samurai a renewed indifference blinding them to the ascendancy of the Court. Furthermore, some saw in them an explosive unpredictability that could easily be ignited by any challenge to their existence: "You need two battalions to keep an eye on one,"[33] said Ōmura Masujirō of his own creation, Chōshū's powerful army. Ōmura himself became a victim of samurai assassins from Chōshū soon after, and he died in November 1869 while serving in the Army Department of the new government. Worse yet, some 1,000 of the Chōshū irregular troops rebelled early in 1870 against the measures by the Chōshū authority to streamline its own armed forces, drawing the domain's leaders in the central government into nearly a year of cumbersome efforts to disband them; they eventually fled to Kyūshū and capitulated.

Finally, the new government did not present itself as a united front to facilitate the removal of the old political order and norms. The inter-domain rivalry was not arrested but intensified within the new government. Sasaki Takayuki attributed the Satsuma-Chōshū rivalry in the Imperial government to mutual suspicion and jealousy originating in the pre-Restoration years when the two domains' activists competed for the dominant role in bakumatsu politics.[34] The continued rivalry was a telling indication that something fundamental from the past had remained intact behind the facade of change since the Restoration. Neither was the new government resistant to the resurgence of feudal practices; far from it, the Court even appeared to be catering to it. Following the end of the Boshin War, some in the new government even entertained a proposal that the contributions of the domains and samurai activists to the Imperial cause be rewarded with new fiefs, and some one million *koku* worth of lands from the northern region may have been set aside for that purpose. This reminder of the aborted Kemmu Restoration some 500 years earlier did not escape the notice of some of the alarmed members of the new government, and a similar failure was thus averted.[35] Still, the proposal, though never implemented, was an indication of the deep-seatedness of feudal political practices even within an Imperial government professing to depart from them.

Thus, from within and without, the new government faced many problems challenging its very existence or discrediting its new approach. To a large extent, these problems set before the Restoration leaders were of their own making, arising out of their efforts to establish the primacy of the new government in constitutional terms. Their efforts had been tailored primarily to the fashioning of one theme—equality among the military houses before the Court—that had begun to emerge toward the closing moments of the Restoration movement and continued to gain momentum throughout the War of the Restoration. However, once realized, this theme had only disappointing consequences. When expressed formally, it did not make the governing authority of the new central government any higher or broader than that of the bakufu. In practice, too, the inability of the new government to solve these problems was the most telling evidence that its constitutional primacy was no more than symbolic. "The threats to the foundation of the Imperial state are more pressing now than a year ago"[36] was the bitter lament of Ōkubo Toshimichi, whose efforts to replace the bakufu with the new central government had led to little real change in the political order.

## The Haihan Chiken Decision

The liquidation of the feudal domains in the summer of 1871 directly contradicted previous developments. Therefore, the thinking of the central leaders must have shifted fundamentally at some point during the months preceding the *Haihan chiken*. The timing itself was significant: the decision came after the continuation of the feudal domains seemed to have gained formal recognition, namely, when the military houses were least prepared for such a drastic turn of events. No less important was the growing sense among some of the Restoration leaders that their constitutional efforts had done little to bolster the authority of the new central government. As a result of this constitutional failure, the leaders were left with no choice but to devise an entirely different alternative, culminating in the final dissolution of the feudal domains.

The central leaders were acutely aware that their new system of rule lacked a firm basis for its own governing power. After an Imperial review on October 2, 1870, of the troops of Satsuma, Chōshū, Tosa, and Saga, the Satsuma troops left Tokyo, and the Restoration leaders felt more than a simple drain on the coalition foundation of the new government. The intention behind the Satsuma troops' departure remains a mystery, but the central leaders immediately suspected a renewal of Satsuma's hegemonial ambitions.[37] The constitutional recognition of the feudal domains, moreover, had made the presence of these forces in the service of the Court even more contingent upon the will of the individual domains than on the ability of the new government to command.

Given the continued existence of the feudal domains, however, the central leaders' first inclination was to see the weak foundation of the new government as an internal problem. The fact that the new "central" government was easily shaken by one domain's suspicious moves and unable to transcend divisive rivalries among its members, they believed, betrayed a lack of leadership among those who supposedly had devoted themselves to the Imperial cause.[38] This sense of powerlessness plaguing the central leaders was indicative of a more complex psychological phenomenon as well. At its core was their awareness that, given its coalition basis, the strengthening of the new government—and thereby its ability to command—might produce a "boomerang" effect: a further increase in its reliance upon a few of the domains. Then, too, there was a reasonable fear that the increased importance of the few domains would only deepen their mutual distrust. Finally, nothing would have been more demoralizing for the leaders of the new government than convincing themselves that they had little power without the support of their none-too-friendly feudal forces at home for these least desirable reasons.

The behavior of Ōkubo Toshimichi in the months following the *Hanseki hōkan* is indicative of these problems. He shuttled back and forth among the key central leaders, and between the Imperial government and the domains, in an attempt to clear himself and his domain of suspicion.[39] Being from Satsuma, he was identified with lingering allegations of his domain's hegemonial ambition; he also faced a considerable lack of popularity at home among his fellow retainers because of his service in the Imperial government. Ōkubo's diary reflects his difficult position as he sought ways in which the Imperial government could strengthen its foundation. In one entry, he recorded his plea for the kind of unwavering commitment to action in the interest of the new government once known among the activists—a commitment to come, if necessary, from the Satsuma han alone.[40] At the same time, Ōkubo was also wary of the deepening mistrust of Satsuma attendant upon any such commitment, particularly among those in the central government's Chōshū contingent. Accordingly, his determination was carefully combined with deference to Kido Kōin, the man through whom Chōshū's dissatisfaction as well as suspicion had often been expressed.[41] Yet Ōkubo also had to deal with the withholding of support from him and other Satsuma men in the new government by retainers in his own domain. One cause of the absence of support was Shimazu Hisamitsu, father of the Satsuma lord-governor and *de facto* ruler of the domain since the closing years of the bakufu, who had demanded undivided loyalty from the Satsuma samurai. Since the *Hanseki hōkan*, Shimazu Hisamitsu had intensified this demand as his importance in national politics declined. This double concern, with Kido Kōin and Chōshū and with Hisamitsu and Satsuma, dictated much of Ōkubo's behavior. Finally, Ōkubo was still preoccupied with the protection of constitutional equality among the feudal domains. This equality of the feudal domains before the Court, Ōkubo reasoned, would ideally have prevented the dependence upon only a few specific domains, such as Satsuma and Chōshū, from becoming a habit of the new central government "whenever it faces difficulties."[42]

Ōkubo's quest to strengthen the new government thus had to rest on the support of one domain, a few domains, or all the domains, now formally equal. Mostly by default, Ōkubo was inclined to emphasize the middle course, that of reliance on the few key domains. The first alternative, of relying solely on Satsuma, was much too risky and costly, and the last had so far proved ineffective. In addition, historical precedent provided one positive reason for choosing the middle course: a few domains, such as Satsuma, Chōshū, and Tosa, had always set things in motion before, leaving the rest of the houses to follow suit.[43]

The result of this reasoning was what is known as the *sampan kempei*, the decision to contribute to the Court some of the domain troops from Satsuma, Chōshū, and Tosa. Orchestrated by the leading members in the new government from these domains, this action was meant to reestablish the harmony that had existed among them during the overthrow of the Tokugawa bakufu. Furthermore, the combined forces of Satsuma, Chōshū, and Tosa, the architects of the decision reasoned, would strengthen the credibility of the Imperial government. At the same time, as long as the Imperial government continued to rely on these domains, its increased authority would still not threaten the existence of the other domains. In other words, the decision and its implementation would stop safely short of challenging the constitutional continuation of the feudal domains in general.

Ōkubo engineered the mobilization of the Satsuma troops through complicated maneuvers that would agitate neither Kido Kōin of Chōshū nor his own Satsuma retainers at home. The pivotal figure of the actual mobilization was Saigō Takamori, who had as much popularity and allegiance from the Satsuma retainers at home as Shimazu Hisamitsu. Saigō's support of the *sampan kempei* had one thing in common with that of Ōkubo. "The Court tends to resort to authority without having substance, allowing itself to be shaken by threats of physical force by the military houses," Saigō declared in his twenty-one-point petition to the Court, believed to have been written in early 1871. The alternative Saigō had in mind was the creation of a "national" army of some 10,000 strong from some of these major domains, whose own as well as their families' allegiance would rest with the Court.[44] The creation of such an army would facilitate, in effect, the transformation of the Court into a powerful "military" house, but again it did not presume the liquidation of the existing military houses.

Though still disquieted by his suspicion that Satsuma had outmaneuvered both him and Chōshū, Kido Kōin had no objection in principle to such a show of unity in the Court. In fact, when the three domains of Satsuma, Chōshū, and Tosa agreed on the decision, Kido resorted, as usual, to highly emotional language in his diary entry of March 29, 1871, to describe how deeply he was moved in witnessing this token of concord overcoming the rivalries among the ambitious domains.[45]

The third of the three domains, Tosa, did not join in this decision to mobilize the domain troops until January 17, 1871, when Saigō Takamori, Ōkubo Toshimichi, and Kido Kōin visited Tosa after reaching an agreement between the first two domains on the contribution of troops. In part, Tosa's delay was due to the fact that certain powerful Tosa figures, Itagaki Taisuke in particular, were now absent from the central government while occupying high offices at home. In part, Tosa had been devising its own political strategem all along, with Yamanouchi Toyonori, its lord-governor, having paid a visit to Satsuma early in 1870, ostensibly to promote a joint contribution to the new government.[46] One important reason behind this separate action of Tosa in 1870 is suggested by the reaction of one of Yamanouchi Toyonori's retainers to the visit to Satsuma. His comments revealed, perhaps inadvertently, the dominant sentiment of his fellow retainers— or for that matter, of many samurai elsewhere—that they had always been outmaneuvered in the conduct of national affairs by the Satsuma and Chōshū activists now in the new government.

[In the early days of the Restoration] everything was constantly changing; the minds of the people were still unstable; the Imperial government was occupied by men of unidentifiable background and was increasingly vacillating. As things stood then, chaos seemed imminent again. Satsuma and Chōshū seemed incompatible and conflict between them appeared unavoidable. Facing these circumstances, if Tosa had rushed then to the military subjugation of Shikoku Island as the Chōsokabe [unifiers of the Island before the Yamanouchi] did long ago, the control of the Island would have been easy, but we would have missed the moment to advance to supremacy [in Japan]. . . .

[Given this understanding], there was a grand design behind our Shikoku Conference [of the representatives from thirteen Shikoku domains in the spring of 1869 and fall of 1870]. Through this Conference, the coalition of the Shikoku domains was to be strengthened. Then, on the arrival of the right time, Tosa, without fear of disturbances in the Island, was to form a fleet to transport the entire

Tosa force to the coast of Osaka, defend the Imperial flag, guard the
Imperial house, and then advance to pacify the discontented domains
in northern Japan as well as in the areas adjacent to Kyoto. . . . It was
in this context that our lord paid a visit to Satsuma to investigate
the situation therein and perhaps also to solidify the relationship
with them.[47]

Tosa's commitment to the *sampan kempei* thus was not without its own motives. Having remained aware all along of what
sort of rivalries and coalitions might result from the political
fluidity following the Restoration, Tosa's late decision to support
the *sampan kempei* was an attempt at the very least not to afford
Satsuma and Chōshū another occasion for political monopoly.

This analysis of the underlying suspicion and competitiveness
among the representatives of the key domains suggests that the
*sampan kempei*, like the other changes, was not meant to be an
integral step toward the *Haihan chiken*, which proceeded in the
months following the implementation of the *sampan kempei*. In
fact, during the months between *Hanseki hōkan* and the *Haihan
chiken*, not once did "Haihan" or any other word hinting at the
liquidation of the domains appear in the many letters exchanged
among the central leaders. Instead, they were usually full of ambiguous and diffuse references to, for example, "great reforms in
accordance with the spirit of the Restoration," "the achievements
of the Restoration," and the like, perhaps because of conscious
attempts on the part of the leaders to avoid any premature, violent
repercussions from the other feudal forces. However, the preoccupation of the central leaders such as Ōkubo, Kido, and certainly
Saigō with strengthening the coalition basis of the Imperial government is a more plausible explanation for their behavior.

The successful concerted effort by the three domains was accompanied, however, by unsettling feelings. Those outside the
three-domain nexus, men from the ranks of the Court nobility in
particular, felt that their presence, as in the past, would prove
inconsequential without Ōkubo, Kido, Saigō, or Itagaki. This anxiety increased in proportion to the progress of accord among the
two and then the three domains: "The three houses seem to
become more and more powerful while the other houses are be-

coming increasingly meaningless," wrote Iwakura Tomomi to another Court noble, Sanjō Sanetomi, on May 23, 1871. "Would this not turn to great harm someday?"[48] While these leaders from the ranks of the nobility began to reiterate their argument that all the feudal domains were equal before the Court,[49] some of the architects of *sampan kempei* were having to cope with their own kind of anxiety: the realization that the long-sought unity among these principal domains would leave the central government no alternative recourse to safeguard its stability if their three key domains failed to sustain it.[50]

It was at this juncture that a previously uncharted course of action offered itself: the strengthening of the new government *not* on a coalition basis but on one that rendered the coalition altogether unnecessary. It is conceivable that this option began to occur to the architects of the *sampan kempei*, such as Kido and Ōkubo, some time after the troops from the three domains had begun to arrive in Tokyo in mid-April of 1871. The last of the domain troops are believed to have arrived by the end of June; all these troops were soon to become the core of the royal army. Even with this evidence of the three-domain cooperation, the architects of the *sampan kempei* as a group still seemed to entertain no further thoughts of action. But, at least the division among the central leaders, as indicated by Iwakura Tomomi's critical stance toward the *sampan kempei*, had begun to fade by this point. Iwakura had earlier objected to the three key domains' dictating the decision of national consequence. By July, his criticism had subsided, perhaps because all the actions defined by the *sampan kempei* had been completed, or far more importantly, because some views on terminating the existence of the domains had begun to occupy the minds of some, if not all, of the key members of the Restoration government. Thus, Iwakura's criticism was eventually replaced by a general plea to give the other domains some share of responsibility in decisions affecting the governing of Japan.[51]

The phase preceding the decision to terminate the domains was somewhat anticlimactic, as the final impulse for the decision did not come from Kido Kōin or Ōkubo Toshimichi, and certainly not from Saigō Takamori or Itagaki Taisuke. It came, rather, from

Yamagata Aritomo, Inoue Kaoru, and a few other men from Chō-shū. The origins of these lieutenants of Kido Kōin were crucial in their push for the abandonment of formal equality of the feudal domains, a process that would necessarily end with their liquidation: all of them had risen to their current prominence from utter obscurity in the feudal political organization. Bakumatsu politics had disrupted Chōshū earlier than most domains, and some of these men originally were in the *Kiheitai*, one of Chōshū's irregular armies in which social origins played a markedly limited role and which had come into existence amid crises atypical of the other feudal houses. Furthermore, Chōshū had had the longest period of constant military alert and engagement of any domain since its confrontation with the forces of the bakufu, Satsuma, Aizu, and a few others in Kyoto in the summer of 1864. These extraordinary activities in bakumatsu politics caused the growth of Chōshū's standing army—and hence its expense—to far exceed those of the other houses. Inoue Kaoru, for example, recognized early on that this militarization would drain the domain treasury.[52] Less of a beneficiary of the old order than many retainers, Inoue could see more clearly the problem of financial management and harbor far less resistance to the demise of the domains. Earlier, he had kept this managerial judgment to himself for fear of reprisals by Chōshū troops. However, with the creation of the royal army under the command of the Imperial government, the situation appeared favorable for the exercise of Inoue's managerial sense. For Yamagata Aritomo,[53] a similar sense of managerial realism had been sharpened by constant involvement in military operations first in Chōshū and later in the new government. Yamagata had become acutely aware of the difficulty involved in the simultaneous but separate maintenance of military forces by both the new government and the feudal domains. Now, with the central treasury depleted and the forces of the three key domains uprooted from their own territories, Inoue, Yamagata, and the others had little hesitation in proposing the termination of all the feudal domains in order to end the precarious coalition basis of the Restoration government. The termination would also remove the costly armed forces sustained by the feudal domains and neutralize the innate hostility toward the new government demonstrated by provincial samurai who continued to honor their obligation to their daimyo and domains.[54]

This managerial realism and, perhaps, the weaker sense of feudalistic loyalism among these men led them to reach their conclusion in a crucial discussion on August 20, 1871, and to communicate their agreement on the need to liquidate the domains shortly thereafter to Kido, Ōkubo, and Saigō. However, it seems that even at this late point, only a little over a week before the formal announcement of the *Huihun chiken*, the notion of terminating the domains had hardly been discussed formally among the key leaders in the Restoration government. In fact, Yamagata, Inoue, and the others from Chōshū suspected that even their own senior, Kido Kōin, might not go along with their idea. Such a suspicion prompted one of them, Torio Koyata, to suggest assassinating Kido Kōin, if necessary, in the event that he disagreed with them. Also, Saigō Takamori's quick support of the idea, which surprised many, was qualified by his demand that the idea first receive Kido Kōin's endorsement.[55] One important assumption for all these leaders at this crucial moment must have been, again, that no single domain could resist a decision backed by the allied forces of Satsuma, Chōshū, and Tosa.

Initially, Iwakura Tomomi was not even informed of the decision to terminate the domains because of his earlier insistence upon honoring the basic tenet of formal equality among the feudal domains. He was told of the final decision only two days before it was to be implemented.[56] Facing the declaration of the *Haihan*, to be made on August 29, 1871, Iwakura's own final act was to treat Owari, Fukui, and Kumamoto as having been as instrumental as Satsuma, Chōshū, and Tosa in the decision, in the "Procedure for the Announcement of the Termination of the Feudal Domains."[57] He thus attempted, in the very last days of the military houses, to create at least the appearance of support from a few domains other than Satsuma, Chōshū, and Tosa whose contributions to the Restoration deserved equal recognition by the Imperial government. Following the *Haihan*, all domains briefly became ken, only to be merged within a short period of time. By the end of 1871, only the largest of the domains retained any semblance of their former boundaries, and the remainder had only token domain identities (see Table 3.9).

The following chapter will offer a more complete picture of the dislocation of the feudal domains by examining the two possible sources of resistance to the *Haihan chiken*. One is the Imperial government, which had protected and depended upon the continuation of the feudal domains. The other is the feudal domains, which were, as William Griffis, a Westerner in Fukui, summarized the sentiment of the Fukui samurai, "victimized"[58] by this sudden shift in the thinking of the central leaders just when their preservation appeared firmly assured. As the foregoing analysis suggests, the developments in the new government and the feudal domains did not lead inexorably to the dissolution of the feudal domains. The following chapter will suggest that underlying the dramatic change of the *Haihan chiken* were other developments that made the decision, though unexpected, far less disruptive than it might have been both to the Restoration government and the feudal domains.

This analysis of the developments leading the *Haihan chiken* by no means lessens the significance of the event, often described as the "second Restoration."[59] The thrust of the analysis, however, differs from a simple characterization of the developments preceding the *Haihan chiken* as a "a test of [the samurai leaders'] nationalist resolution."[60]

# 3

# The Demise of Feudal Politics

THE ABSENCE OF violent reaction to the decision to terminate the feudal domains marked the most important turning point in early Meiji politics. This "bloodless" revolution, as Itō Hirobumi characterized the *Haihan chiken* afterward,[1] does tempt us to assume that the decision was a perfectly logical choice for the Imperial government, that it was consistent with the past course of political development, and that a national consensus may have existed that blocked efforts by the domains to resist the decision. In fact, many historians have made similar assumptions. However, these inferences do not take into account the Restoration leaders' efforts to secure a coalition basis for the Imperial government well into 1871. Further, the absence of strong resistance suggests another possibility—that the political life of the Imperial government and of the feudal domains had been subtly transformed by the summer of 1871 in such a manner that the *Haihan chiken* no longer either adversely affected it or inspired resistance.

The Imperial government, of course, authorized the decision to terminate the feudal domains. However, it was this same Imperial government that had previously reconciled itself to the continued existence of the feudal domains and had founded its survival upon the support of a few southwestern domains. For the feudal do-

mains, the *Haihan chiken* brought an end to the long tradition
dispersed political control. In addition, it meant a sudden shift in
the central government's moves to secure places for the domains
in the new Court-centered political order. Nonetheless, both the
Imperial government and the feudal domains complacently accepted the decision. The earlier efforts by the Restoration leaders
to reconcile the Court with the feudal domains no longer seemed
to matter much to either the central government or the feudal
domains. What changes in the political lives of both parties, prior
to the summer of 1871, were chiefly responsible for this
complacency?

The greatest irony of the *Haihan chiken*'s success may be that
it hinged upon the earlier reconciliation of the Imperial government to the existence of the feudal domains. Consequently, the
scope of its governing authority was limited mostly to the Imperial territories inherited from the Tokugawa family and a few
pro-Tokugawa daimyo houses. This limited authority was clearly
reflected in the makeup of the "central" offices, none of which
was designed to promote the central government's interference
in the affairs of the feudal domains. But this domestic disengagement also prevented the growth of any institutionalized interdependence between the Imperial and the domain governments.
Therefore there were no central officials with vested interests in
protecting the feudal domains, nor did the decision to terminate
the domains mean for the central government to discontinue a
substantial part of its operation and organization.

An equally important consequence of the Imperial government's domestic isolation was the protection of its samurai officials. As seen in the previous chapter, these samurai officials
occupied positions that enjoyed little support from their fellow
retainers at home. They were exposed to merciless criticism for
being the "subjects" of two "lords," their daimyo and the emperor.
However, their assignments in the "central" offices nothwith-
standing, it was obvious that the Imperial government as a whole
was not actively seeking to dictate domain affairs, and thus its
officials were spared far more direct criticism or resistance by the
feudal domains and their members. Instead, the central government provided a protected sphere of action for its officials where

they could work in relative isolation from the usual feudal obligations. The domestic disengagement of the Imperial government, in other words, helped to create a situation in which its officials began to favor the relinquishing of the coalition basis of the Restoration.

On the other side of the new government's domestic disengagement were the feudal domain governments. The Imperial restoration and the ensuing war had renewed the domain officials' sense of feudalistic obligation toward the daimyo houses. The Imperial government's hands-off policy was their reward for surviving the emperor's political ascendancy and the Boshin War. Thus when participation in the war proved to be a threat to the daimyo houses by hastening the depletion of the domain treasuries, the domain officials could find no place for the Imperial government in their efforts to help the daimyo houses survive the financial crisis. Instead, they reduced domain management to simply the maintenance of the daimyo houses. By the eve of the *Haihan chiken*, most of the domain administrations had been cut back to a minimum, making them almost identical with the house administrations of the daimyo houses and rendering them insignificant to the domains at large.

### The Old Problems and the New Order: Political Conditions for Change

One of the pressures for change that had made the old system of rule obsolete remained despite the restoration of the Imperial rule. In fact, the Court's reconciliation with the continued existence of the feudal domains essentially prevented the new system of rule from addressing this old source of several problems.

The original cause of these long-standing problems, the developing market economy, had been particularly detrimental to the feudal domains and the bakufu, who had relied on the continuation of the archaic exchange economy for generating income for their treasuries. The bakufu's elaborate system of political control, the *sankin kōtai* in particular, had only made the deterioration of the financial basis of the domain treasuries more

pervasive throughout Japan. The maintenance of extravagant res-
idences in Edo and the financing of the equally expensive daimyo
trips between the domains and Edo had made it the custom of
the domain officials to turn to rich merchants in Edo, Osaka,
and elsewhere for large loans. To cite one example, the indebted-
ness of the Satsuma had reached such a level that, before
one of its daimyo undertook rigorous fiscal reforms in the mid-
nineteenth century, the domain's annual revenue could repay
only 0.3 percent of the loan.[2]

The domain governments devised various ways to arrest the
corrosive effects or even to take advantage of the development of
a commercial economy. The bakufu's own attempts to mitigate
the effects of commercialization proved largely ineffectual, as
they included the forced appropriation of some of the fiefs of the
loyal daimyo and the *hatamoto*, who not surprisingly became
hostile toward the bakufu's efforts.[3] In contrast, a few domains,
such as Satsuma, Chōshū, Tosa, and Saga, managed to transform
their conservative agrarian economies into commercializing ones.
Admittedly, such a transformation was costly because of the considerable infighting it caused among those who supported it and
those who opposed it. The usual measures taken by these domain
governments included the encouragement of rural hand-
icrafts, for example, the making of lacquer, paper, silk, and por-
celain wares, which were assembled in the domains and sold
through domain-licensed wholesalers. The profits were used for
further investment, which then enabled a few domains, including
Satsuma and Saga, to construct the technological infrastructure
so urgently needed for the Imperial government later on.[4] Beyond
these limited financial improvements, the chief beneficial consequence proved to be an enlarged sphere of action for some retainers of lesser rank who otherwise would have remained outside
the central decision-making process of the domain governments.[5]

At the same time, the unequal treaties concluded with the West
by the bakufu in 1856 and 1866 further weakened the economy.
The unregulated trade sanctioned by these treaties exposed Japan's goods to competition with foreign goods benefiting from
full technological development, economies of scale, and shrewd
management by such tenacious free traders as Harry S. Parkes,

the British consul. As a result, the favorable balance of trade that Japan had momentarily enjoyed was soon reversed. Its specie reserves fell drastically—the government by 1874 had only 15 million yen in specie as opposed to 65 million yen in notes.[6] Even more disturbing, the competition with foreign products also destroyed Japan's handicraft business just as it was beginning to prosper.[7]

The Restoration did not end these bakumatsu financial problems. Financial hardship, deepened by the Boshin War, seemed incidental to the majority of officials in the struggling feudal domains. These men were preoccupied with the ways by which to escape Imperial condemnation for their initial support of, or previous association with, the Tokugawa bakufu. Taking the burden of the war on their treasuries became the price they expediently paid for the survival of their daimyo houses. The need to halt this additional drain was deemed urgent only by those domains confronting the greater economic and military threat of the West. The twin goals of the new government, *fukoku kyōhei*— enrich the nation and strengthen the country—appeared critically linked only to those few who had witnessed firsthand the potential of the Western industrial powers. Satsuma and Chōshū learned this lesson the hard way. Their emotionally charged campaigns to "Expel the Barbarians" had brought only destruction upon them from the tremendous modern firepower of the allied fleets of Britain, France, the United States, and the Netherlands before the Restoration. Thus, they were two of the exceptionally few domains that realized, early on, how much their military strength would depend on advanced technology—which in turn would depend on an enlarged national wealth.

The Court's reconciliation with the feudal domains also failed to bring in potential resources for recovering the financial drain on the nation. No single organization or policy was as yet conceivable for coordinating the mobilization and redistribution of financial, material, and human resources among the 270 feudal domains and the Imperial territories. In addition, each domain's complex form of tax administration remained intact, presenting major difficulties in assessing the potential wealth of each and in coordinating the localities, even if a consensus had existed to do

so. Such was the case even in the Imperial territories under fu and ken, which made it difficult for the government treasury to plan a general mode of management for financial
administration.[8]

The abuse of paper money, stimulated by the need to finance
the domains' participation in the War, also illustrates the problem
caused by the constitutional protection of the feudal domains in
the new Court-centered order. According to one estimate, 244
domains, 14 Tokugawa territories, and 9 *hatamoto* territories had
issued various notes amounting to 38 million yen; as a result,
there were 1,700 varieties of note in circulation as of September
1871.[9] The most immediate damage was done to the circulation
of the new central government paper notes (the *Dajōkansatsu*) in
the majority of the domains. The widespread domain notes dis-
credited the value of the *Dajōkansatsu*, thus nullifying the government's original intention to promote commercial enterprise
through the new money supply.[10] Worse yet, domain notes were
issued and circulated even within Tosa, Okayama, and Toku-
shima, whose daimyo and key retainers were occupying important
offices in the new central government, thus badly damaging the
credibility of the Imperial government as a central authority.[11]
The foreign diplomatic corps was quick to spot this incongruity
and to demand the rectification of these commercially unacceptable practices. To allay these suspicions as to the legitimacy of
the new government, a joint conference of foreign and government
representatives was held on August 29, 1869. However, the meeting only revealed the government's ignorance of the scope of the
widespread financial mismanagement.[12]

Last but not least, because the Restoration did not alter the
status of the samurai, it perpetuated their presence in the new
order as at once a political and a financial problem. The relative
domestic peace of the past two centuries had already rendered the
military function of this dominant class largely obsolete, turning
samurai as a whole into a peculiar, and unwilling, "leisure" class
living off the rice stipends appropriated by the domain treasuries.
Yet at the same time, the cash value of their rice stipends declined
during the Tokugawa period and continued to fall after the Restoration, while the price of commodities went up (Table 3.1). A

TABLE 3.1. Aggregate Samurai Income after the Restoration

| Year | Source | Income (in yen) |
|---|---|---|
| 1868 | Estimated value of rice stipends at the end of Tokugawa rule | 34,612,583 |
| 1871 | Value of rice stipends at current market price | 22,657,948 |
| 1876 | Annual interest payment on pension bonds issued in lieu of rice stipends | 11,568,000 |

SOURCE: *Saishutsunyū kessan hōkokusho*, in *MZZKSS*, vol. 4, pp. 43–44.

revealing description by a mid-Tokugawa Confucian scholar likens the samurai's economic life under the strain of the commercializing economy to one of a traveler who purchases daily commodities as the need arises. Samurai did so, too, except that they exchanged their rice stipends for cash at ever-decreasing rates. In addition, the financial hardships of the domains had forced their samurai retainers to accept greatly reduced rice stipends or, worse, to "contribute" much of their income to the domains' depleted treasuries. Thus, the samurai were deprived of the real financial security to match their privileged social status. Any fiscal reforms could only worsen the samurai's financial condition: efforts to stop the depletion of the domain treasury would mean further reductions of samurai stipends. Such efforts would inevitably widen the gap between the already reduced financial conditions of the dominant class and their seemingly privileged status—a consequence particularly to be avoided when their loyalty to the daimyo had so recently been demonstrated in the War of the Restoration.

## The Central Government and Its Domestic Insulation

Though confronted by the same long-standing problems, the new central government and the feudal domain governments nonetheless differed from each other in one important way: the Imperial government did not have its own "vassals." This unique feature of the new government in a predominantly feudalistic order meant the absence of a rigid, status-bound community, which in the domains had been the basis of political identity and the unit of political action. More importantly, from a feudal domain's perspective, the absence of "vassals" of its own made the new government appear shaky. As Reinhard Bendix points out, this in turn actually made the new government seem much less threatening to the status quo of each domain and its leading stratum than a central government founded on "one territory and its leading strata."[13] One could thus argue that this unique "shortcoming" of the Imperial government helped strengthen, by default, the conviction that the continuation of the feudal domains was constitutionally guaranteed.

Another effect of the absence of "vassals" in the new central government was structurally significant. The presence of samurai retainers in the domains and in the bakufu had long been an asset of the Tokugawa polity, particularly as it was insulated from external contingencies and its domestic stability rested on the maintenance of routinized administrative functions. The samurai retainers provided an ample pool of highly literate administrators, with skills unusual in a society at this stage of socioeconomic development.[14] Drawing upon this pool, the domains and the bakufu collectively had developed a network of meticulously routinized administrative infrastructures throughout the society. To assure orderly transitions over time within each feudal house, a system of rotation for the pivotal positions, those of *karō*, in the administration had been established among the house's ranking retainers. Thus, even when the administration was mismanaged, the *karō* on whom the blame fell could be replaced by another high-ranking retainer before the temporary mismanagement turned into a serious administrative paralysis.

This continuity in political organization was becoming a liability, however. While the peaceful Tokugawa order minimized domestic disruptions, it also removed the occasions for testing the actual administrative skills of likely high-ranking retainers. Furthermore, recruiting for pivotal positions exclusively from within limited the candidates to men from a few privileged houses of the daimyo's vassals, and the position of *karō* inevitably ceased to be a reward for merit. Consequently, the political actions of such pivotal administrators in the domains were often overly conservative. This self-perpetuation of the few privileged vassals now paralyzed the feudal domains in the face of the alarming depletion of their treasuries.

In contrast, the Imperial government at its birth did not have a readily available pool of its own men with administrative skills. With a few exceptions, the numerous but politically unseasoned Court nobles who were mobilized to staff the new organization could only acquiesce to political changes that made the Court "visible" without making it politically responsible. Moreover, the chief concern of the majority of these Court nobles was their own economic well-being, which, many of them believed, had been denied them for some centuries in favor of the dominant samurai class. In fact, Iwakura Tomomi, himself a Court noble, admonished the rest for their inflated expectations of material rewards for their nominal resurrection to political prominence.[15] Therefore, it was just as impossible for the Court nobles to form a viable pool of political and administrative personnel as it would have been for them to become a source of protest and division in the government when their representation in the important offices dropped sharply soon thereafter.

However, the lack of "vassals" of its own for the infant government proved a blessing in disguise. The creation of the new government organization relying heavily on the Restoration leaders proceeded with far less resistance from within and without. The recruitment to the new offices from the ranks of the activist samurai, instead of from the inexperienced nobles, might have invited contempt from those noblemen as well as other samurai back in their domains. Yet, by the same token, it was not subject to a paralyzing resistance from the group of privileged samurai who still ran the feudal governments.

Before the battle of Toba and Fushimi, the Restoration leaders had already begun creating their own organization. On January 3, 1868, they removed the old offices, including that of shogun, that had long kept the emperor cloistered in political obscurity. In their place they created three offices, those of President *(Sōsai)*, Senior Councilors *(Gijō)*, and Junior Councilors *(Sanyo)*, to constitute what is collectively known as the *Sanshoku*.[16] Itself devoid

of clear organizational boundaries, the *Sanshoku* was largely a
selectorate of men from the ranks of both the nobility and the
samurai (daimyo and retainers) active in bakumatsu politics.

These men soon began to staff the somewhat more structurally
distinct organizations of, first, the Seven-Department System
(*Shichi-ka*, created on February 20, 1868) and then the Eight-
Department System *(Hachi-kyoku)*, which replaced the *Shichi-
ka* on February 25, 1868. Instituted in these systems were the
departments of Shinto Affairs, Home Affairs, Foreign Affairs, Finance, Military Affairs (soon divided into the Army and Navy),
and Justice. In addition, and eighth, independent judicial inves-
tigations office enjoyed a brief tenure, existing exclusively to examine the statutory questions of the new regime's incipient
constitution. Replacing the Eight-Department System in turn, the
Oath (April 16, 1868) gave the broad and intellectual, if not practical, inspiration for a short-lived experiment with division of
power in what is known as the *Seitaisho* constitution, instituted
on June 11, 1868. Here the division of power was expressed only
between the legislative and the administrative branches: between
the *Gijōkan* for the Senior and Junior Councilors as well as for
the *kōshi*, and the *Gyōseikan* for the administrative officials.
Furthermore, the boundaries between these branches were un-
derstandably vague, as it was really only a handful of able activist-
turned-officials who interchangeably performed the governmental
functions. Having had so little time to mature, this first division
of power in the *Seitaisho* proved abortive within a few months.

The euphoria of the renewed unity between the Court and the
military houses following the *Hanseki hōkan* (Return of the Fiefs
to the Court) prompted another wave of organizational reform
replacing most of what had gone before. The resurrection of a
more ancient Imperial government was symbolically achieved on
August 15, 1869, by elevating the Department of Shinto Affairs
to the status equal to that of the supreme executive office (the
*Dajōkan*), which oversaw the workings of the administrative departments. The Ministers of the Left Chamber *(Sa-daijin)* and the
Right Chamber *(U-daijin)*, the Senior Councilors *(Dainagon)*, and
the Junior Councilors *(Sangi)* constituted concentric circles at the
core of the *Dajōkan* with differing degrees of responsibility in

assisting the throne in the conduct of national affairs. In addition, there were only six administrative departments instead of eight: Home Affairs, Foreign Affairs, Finance, Justice, Military, and Imperial Household Affairs. One important point to note is that this reorganization of the central government involved a large reduction in the number of Councilors, allowing their positions to become more selective and powerful than ever before.

Another round of reorganization came after the *Haihan chiken*. On September 13, 1871, the Three-Chamber System *(San'in-sei)* was instituted: the Central Chamber *(Sei-in)* for the prime minister *(Dajōdaijin)* and the Councilors *(Nagon* and *Sangi)* performed deliberative functions; the Right Chamber *(U-in)* housed the ministers and their deputies of the administrative departments for policy consultations; and the Left Chamber *(Sa-in)* performed, though largely nominally, legislative functions. Together, these three chambers formed the highest governmental authority until December 22, 1885, when a more modern cabinet system replaced this inner circle of the government.

These constant realignments of the central offices, particularly the earlier shifts, reflected the Court-military unity and the numerical dominance of the feudal elite (the daimyo and their loyal retainers from a few domains). They were responding to the stresses on the primacy of the Court and its necessary reliance upon the forces of the pro-Restoration domains. At its inception, the *Sanshoku* (President and Councilors) was composed almost entirely of the forces most directly linked to the removal of the Tokugawa family (Tables 3.2, 3.3, and 3.4). For example, Owari and Fukui had been known for their moderate stance toward the Tokugawa mainhouse throughout the final stages of the Restoration, and also at the Kogosho Conference. Mainly because of their opportune presence at that critical juncture, men from these moderate domains were rewarded with appointments to the *Sanshoku* offices. In contrast, such appointments eluded the Chōshū members at first, due to their absence from Kyoto at that time. More Court nobles, daimyo, and retainers of the other domains that had been active in, or at least sympathetic to, the cause of the Imperial restoration were added to the new central government. As a result of such additions, the men who were appointed

TABLE 3.2. The *Sanshoku* Appointment
1/3/1868

| Office | Princes of Blood | Court Nobles | Daimyo | Samurai Retainers |
|--------|------------------|--------------|--------|-------------------|
| Sōsai | 1 | | | |
| Gijō | 2 | 3 | 5[a] | |
| Sanyo | | 5 | | 15[b] |

SOURCES: Tōyama Shigeki and Adachi Shizuko, eds., *Kindai Nihon seijishi hikkei*, and Wilson, "Genesis of the Meiji Government in Japan," Appendix.
[a]One daimyo each from Owari, Fukui, Aki (Hiroshima), Satsuma, and Tosa.
[b]Three samurai retainers each from Owari, Fukui, Aki, Satsuma, and Tosa.

Senior and Junior Councilors amounted to 126 by June of 1868. Though the time of appointment and spans of tenure differed, the breakdown of these men by ascriptive attributes was as follows: Princes of Blood, 6; Court nobles, 54; feudal daimyo (including current and former lords, heirs and brothers of lords), 17; Shinto priest, 1; and samurai retainers, 48. The *Seitaisho* constitution, instituted on June 11, 1868, greatly reduced the number of Senior and Junior Councilors, allowing for a total of 42 openings for the new government organization: 13 Court nobles, 14 feudal daimyo, and 15 samurai retainers. However, only one Court noble and one

TABLE 3.3. The *Sanshoku* Appointment
1/3/1868–6/11/68

| Office | Princes of Blood | Court Nobles | Daimyo | Samurai Retainers | Shinto Priests |
|--------|------------------|--------------|--------|-------------------|----------------|
| Sōsai | 1 | | | | |
| Gijō | 5 | 11 | 14 | | 1 |
| Sanyo | | 46 | 5 | 48 | 1 |
| Total | 6 | 54[a] | 17[b] | 48 | 1[c] |

SOURCES: Tōyama and Adachi, eds., *Kindai Nihon seijishi hikkei*, and Wilson, "Genesis of the Meiji Government in Japan," Appendix.
[a]Three were promoted to Gijō from Sanyo.
[b]Two were promoted to Gijō from Sanyo.
[c]Promoted to Gijō from Sanyo.

TABLE 3.4. *Sanshoku* Samurai Officials, by Domain

| Domain | No. of Officials | Domain | No. of Officials |
|--------|------------------|--------|------------------|
| Satsuma | 10 | Akita | 1 |
| Kumamoto | 7 | Inuyama | 1 |
| Chōshū | 7 | Ōgaki | 1 |
| Fukui | 6 | Oka | 1 |
| Owari | 6 | Takanabe | 1 |
| Saga | 5 | Takatori | 1 |
| Tosa | 4 | Tokushima | 1 |
| Hiroohima | 3 | Tsuwano | 1 |
| Uwajima | 3 | Yanagawa | 1 |
| Okayama | 3 | | |
| Tottori | 2 | | |

SOURCES: Tōyama and Adachi, eds., *Kindai Nihon seijishi hikkei*, and Wilson, "Genesis of the Meiji Government in Japan," Appendix.

daimyo entered the central organization at this point, leaving the officials of samurai retainer's ranks to increase their influence.

This picture of the central government as a Court-military co-alition remained very much the same for the first decade after the Restoration, as further confirmed by the *Hyakkan rireki* (*Career Records of The Government Officials*, 2 volumes). Of the 450 (8 Princes of Blood excluded) listed therein,[17] the contingent of Court nobles provided a total of 69, and the four principal southwestern domains together furnished 167 (Satsuma 63, Chōshū 51, Tosa 25, and Saga 28). Twenty-two came from Tokyo, 19 from Shizuoka, 15 from Kumamoto, 11 from Tottori, 8 from Okayama, and 7 from Fukui. In addition, each of some 50 other feudal domains provided a few men.

At the same time, however, the organizational realignments reflected subtler changes that would quickly render the Court-military unity as well as the salience of the feudal elite inconsequential, particularly for the central government's relationship with the feudal domains. The beginning of functional differentiations within the central government, tailored to its limited scope of governing authority, undermined the basis on which the samurai officials (daimyo and their loyal retainers) holding the three highest offices (President, Senior and Junior Councilors)

TABLE 3.5. The *Seitaisho* Appointment
6/11/1868

| Office | Court Nobles | Daimyo | Samurai Retainers |
|--------|--------------|--------|-------------------|
| Gijō | 9 | 12 | |
| Sanyo | 3 | 3 | 15 |
| Total | 12 | 13ᵃ | 15 |

SOURCE: Tōyama and Adachi, eds., *Kindai Nihon seijishi hikkei,* and Wilson, "Genesis of the Meiji Government in Japan," Appendix.
ᵃTwo were promoted to Gijō from Sanyo.

could have exercised their influence upon the general relationship between the Imperial government and the feudal domains.

The first instance of functional differentiation, in the Seven-Department System of February 20, 1868, appeared in the form of a deliberative-administrative division. The Presidential *(Sōsai)* office, occupied by one of the Princes of Blood, was defined in highly abstract terms as responsible for "deliberating on general affairs and deciding all matters" of government and thus remained somewhat above the division. The Senior *(Gijō)* and Junior *(Sanyo)* Councilors were placed in charge of assisting that supreme office in the same function. But the crucial consequence of the functional differentiation is that the group of Councilors became a pool of personnel from which ministers, their deputies, and officials were selected for the administrative departments. Furthermore, when the administrative appointments were made, there remained a surplus of men in the ranks of Senior and Junior Councilors with no administrative assignments. The Court nobles made up most of the surplus, followed by the daimyo. Those who accounted for the fewest in the surplus were the samurai retainers. A similar pattern of surplus Councilors emerged also in the *Seitaisho* constitution, even though the constitution reduced their total number of positions (Tables 3.5, 3.6, and 3.7).

Concurrent with the emerging functional differentiation initiated by this Seven-Department System were even more direct indications of the nature of the central-domain relationship. First,

TABLE 3.6. The *Seitaisho* Samurai Officials, by Domain

| Domain | No. of Officials |
|---|---|
| Satsuma | 5 |
| Saga | 5 |
| Tosa | 4 |
| Chōshū | 3 |
| Kumamoto | 3 |
| Fukui | 2 |
| Owari | 1 |
| Hiroohima | 1 |
| Uwajima | 1 |
| Tokushima | 1 |
| Okayama | 1 |
| Tottori | 1 |

SOURCE: Tōyama and Adachi, eds., *Kindai Nihon seijishi hikkei*, and Wilson, "Genesis of the Meiji Government in Japan," Appendix.

the highest offices for the deliberative functions remained defined only in general terms. The ministers of the Left and the Right Chambers were, as described in 1869, to "preside over the conduct of administration to assist the emperor's rule." Their functions signaled the locus of the highest authority of the nation vis-à-vis foreign powers, such as the proclamation of war or the conclusion of treaties. Likewise, the Prime Minister in the post-*Haihan chiken* government received no more specific definition than before. Senior and Junior Councilors were given, in this regard, roles supplementary to these supreme offices and with the same generalized responsibility.[18] But significantly, there were still not positive specifications linking these offices and the domains. Even though the feudal domains in the *Seitaisho* constitution were designated, together with the fu and ken, as one of the three legs of a tripod on which the "domestic" administration was founded, broad guidelines stated only that the domain administrations, like the fu and ken in the former Tokugawa territories, should function in accordance with the intention of the Oath. But unlike the fu and ken governors, the feudal lords received no further specific directives. The result was that this "benign neglect" of the feudal domains, even in the formal language of the *Seitaisho* constitution, actually undermined the constitutional claim that the high-

TABLE 3.7.  Administrative Appointments
for the *Shichi-ka*, *Hachi-kyoku*, and *Seitaisho* Governments

| Government | Princes of Blood | Court Nobles | Daimyo | Samurai Retainers | Others |
|---|---|---|---|---|---|
| No. of the *Sanshoku* Appointments:1/3–6/10/1868 | | | | | |
|  | 6 | 54 | 17 | 48 | 1 |
| *Shichi-ka* (2/20/1868) | | | | | |
| Heads and Deputies | 5 | 13 | 6 | 0 | 1 |
| Officials | 0 | 2 | 1 | 27 | 0 |
| *Hachi-kyoku* (2/25/1868) | | | | | |
| Heads and Deputies | 3 | 12 | 9 | 0 | 1 |
| Officials | 0 | 4 | 2 | 34[c] | 0 |
| No. of the *Sanshoku* Appointments: 6/11/1868 | | | | | |
|  | 0 | 12 | 13 | 15 | 0 |
| *Seitaisho* (6/11/1868) | | | | | |
| Heads | 1 | 7[a] | 3 | 0 | 0 |
| Deputies and Officials | 0 | 4 | 4[b] | 24[d] | 0 |

SOURCE: Tōyama and Adachi, eds., *Kindai Nihon seijishi hikkei*, and Wilson, "Genesis of the Meiji Government in Japan," Appendix.
[a]Includes one from outside the *Sanshoku*.
[b]Includes one from outside the *Sanshoku*.
[c]Includes two from outside the *Sanshoku*.
[d]Includes eleven from outside the *Sanshoku*.

est offices made to extend their authority, even symbolically, throughout the society.

Second, the creation of the Department of Home Affairs likewise did not clarify the ambiguous relationship between the new central government and the feudal domains. The increasing recognition of the Imperial government by the *individual* domains as the legitimate successor to the Tokugawa bakufu, through the advance of the War of the Restoration, might have justified its label of "central" government, but it also confirmed that, in practice, its "domestic" sphere of action was essentially limited to those territories inherited from the Tokugawa family. Although the term "domestic" for the deliberative offices lacked any specific reference, the Home Affairs Department confined its formal jurisdiction to the areas adjacent to the Kyoto-Osaka region and later to those former Tokugawa lands now under fu and ken.[19] Therefore, the claim of the highest offices to be responsible for overseeing domestic affairs, or any vaguely national affairs, was weakened by the administrative arm of Home Affairs that did not reach the domains. This discrepancy between claims and practices bore testimony to a more fundamental incongruity in an Imperial government that externally claimed to be the sole legitimate governing authority of the nation, yet internally resembled a provincial government with limited scope for uncontested governing authority.

Finally, the emerging functional differentiation encouraged the development of only one of the two roles of the three highest offices to the detriment of the other. The existence of these offices as both the supreme organ in the central organization and the pool of officials for its administrative arms quickly became precarious. The creation of the administrative departments had already produced a surplus of Councilors without administrative assignments. Under the *Seitaisho* constitution, the number of samurai officials who entered the Imperial government by bypassing the Councilors' posts almost equaled the number of those who did enter through the post of Councilors. Thus, the ideal form of government as an organic entity, in which the higher offices would decide and the lower departments implement, began to mean little in practice. The issue was not so much a question of polarization between samurai officials with and without Councilor status, for such distinctions did not mean much in practice for those who had a record of participation in the Restoration movement longer than the life of the Restoration government itself. Rather, the issue was the damaged credibility of a central organization now incapable of sustaining even the facade of organic unity.[20] In regard to the central government-domain government relationship, the effect was the same. The increasing autonomy of the administrative arms rendered even more fictitious the claim of the highest offices to preside over matters of national concern, thus removing them further from the domains.

The most profound impact of these consequences of the increasing functional differentiation within the central government was on the role of the daimyo who usually occupied the Senior Councilors' positions. Confined to supreme yet largely symbolic acts of state, the daimyo's functions in the central government quickly ceased to have any practical bearing upon the political life of the feudal domains either individually (that is, upon their own domains) or collectively. At the very beginning, the daimyo took action to assert what was then considered unequivocal feudal justice. They exhibited a surprising unity and tenacity in attempting to protect the Tokugawa mainhouse as a daimyo house and secure a corresponding position in the new government for its head, Tokugawa Yoshinobu, during the Kogosho Conference and the ensuing month of heated debate with the militant samurai activists. When this action proved largely ineffective, however, the daimyo (Yamanouchi Yōdō of Tosa, Asano Nagakoto of Hiroshima, Tokugawa Yoshikatsu of Owari, Date Munenari of Uwajima, and others) and their loyal retainers in the government (most notably, Nakane Yukie of Fukui) ceased even to try to act in the feudal interest through the new government apparatus.

The institution of the *kōshi* suffered from a similar estrangement, though it had been designed explicitly to represent feudal opinion and interest in the new central government. First instituted with the Seven-Department System, the *kōshi* had been conceived of as a possible institutional link between the central and the domain governments. Each feudal domain was ordered to send retainers (first, 3, 2, or 1 depending upon the sizes of the fiefs of the domains; later uniformly 1) to the central government. Appointment and tenure remained at the disposal of their own daimyo; thus their status remained unmistakably that of domain retainers. But whereas the status of the feudal domains collectively was being decided by the success of the Imperial side of the Boshin War, the decisions on the political life of the individual domains continued to be made and implemented by the domain bureaucracies at home. Furthermore, the *kōshi's* proximity to the deliberative branch in the deliberative-administrative division, most explicitly expressed in the *Seitaisho* constitution, led them to share, with the deliberative offices in general, the political estrangement of the central government from the domain affairs.

As in the action to protect the Tokugawa mainhouse by the daimyo in the central government, the *kōshi*'s active participation was most salient regarding a similar question of feudal justice— the preservation of the military houses in general. Even there, however, the *kōshi* served as a sounding board, at best, from which the central government could obtain feudal reactions to its do- main-related policies.[21] The lack of an institutional mechanism for deliberations by the *kōshi* meant that their discussions or decisions could have little actual impact upon the new govern- ment. Thus, for example, when in the debate on the 1869 *gunken- hōken* alternatives, discussed in Chapter 1, their deliberations were almost completely dismissed by the new government's of- ficials, no recourse existed for the *kōshi* to realize their decisions or preferences.

This neglect was not reversed even when the *kōshi* (later *kō- ginin*) were given the more explicit role of representing their do- mains. The decree of April 21, 1868, for example, ruled that the domains whose daimyo were occupying the central offices did not need to furnish *kōshi*.[22] Nor did their status improve when more specific qualifications for the *kōshi* were added, as ruled by another decree of January 22, 1869, that they be selected from the *sansei* or *shissei*, the equivalent of the *karō*, who were directly engaged in their domain governments at the highest levels.[23] In other words, while gaining on paper as a more distinct group of domain representatives in the center, the *kōshi* remained isolated in practice from actual administration both at home and in the Imperial government.

Such apparent alienation of feudal forces in the new govern- ment, however, did not mean the corresponding increase in the strength of anti-feudal forces. From the very beginning, some of the Restoration leaders showed an acute awareness of the im- minent danger in overreliance on either Court nobles or the priv- ileged military class, the daimyo. Those leaders who had survived the intrigues and violence of bakumatsu politics saw most of these privileged men, whether nobles or daimyo, as emerging from pro- tected places and lacking in the qualifications needed for creating and surviving a new organization. Ōkubo Toshimichi, who rep- resented the militant position against the Tokugawa sympathizers at the Kogosho Conference, viewed the privileged nobles and daimyo as something other than mere political moderates. Having earlier been disturbed by their utter indecisiveness and inactivity, he now voiced concern over their inability to conceive any sound plan for the future. "Virtually none among the men of *Gijō* and *Sanyo* [mostly Court nobles and daimyo at this point] possessed any sense of projection for the future,"[24] wrote Ōkubo to Iwakura Tomomi, a rare exception among the nobles, just before the outbreak of the battle of Toba and Fushimi. Ōkubo's low opinion of these men of the privileged classes led him to entertain the potentially dangerous idea of increasing the infant government's already heavy reliance on Satsuma and Chōshū, and to disregard the inevitable criticisms from within and without that the government was neglecting the Court-military harmony.[25] His condescending views were repeated time and again toward the daimyo and Court nobles who, as Ōkubo characterized them, were as politically naive as "ladies in a harem."[26]

On the positive side, the new government did have access to political talent, particularly from the ranks of samurai retainers. The question was how to use it in the interests of the infant central government, regardless of the retainers' domain affiliations and their resurrected feudalistic loyalism toward the military houses. Here the designation of *chōshi*, which did receive recognition by the writers of the Oath at one point, played a significant role. This institution gave samurai activists more access to the central government by creating positions in addition to those of Councilor.

Under the *Seitaisho* constitution, as the *Gijō* and *Sanyo* positions were greatly reduced in number, the *chōshi*, or Court appointees from among the samurai activists, provided an important alternative access to the new government. Of the 11 who joined the central government then at the department level, all but one were *chōshi*. From a listing in the *Hyakkan rireki*, the significance of this new category of men is evident. Of the 366 samurai listed in the *rireki*, 122, or exactly one-third, were *chōshi*. (Of the 122 *chōshi*, 39 also held Councilors' positions as well.) Considering that the *chōshi* category ceased to exist a year and half later (it was abolished on August 4, 1869), the preponderance of men who joined the central government through these entries is indeed impressive. In fact, 109 of the 122 *chōshi* came in before the end of 1868. Moreover, the *chōshi* placed under the aegis of the central government those who also performed important administrative functions in the isolated fu and ken. In the *rireki*, 182 held the highest offices in fu and ken before the *Haihan chiken;* of them 158 were samurai, more than half of whom were *chōshi*.

The samurai from Satsuma, Chōshū, Tosa, and Saga were dominant among the *chōshi* men, and thus the creation of this institution was still consistent with the reliance of the new government on a few southwestern domains. However, the *chōshi* were not typical of the Tokugawa-era samurai serving one lord methodically and unerringly. The peculiar visibility of the *chōshi*, even when it meant little to the majority of the provincial samurai, was particularly disturbing to their fellow retainers at home, especially in those domains most instrumental in bringing about the Restoration. "The unpopularity of the *chōshi* is by and large attributed to their extravagance and arrogant attitude,"[27] wrote a Satsuma retainer, Takasaki Seifū, to another who was himself a *chōshi*, Godai Tomoatsu. This unpopularity was in effect a recognition that these men appeared to be above the familiar strictures of feudalism and also that the new government actually legitimized the existence of such uncharacteristic samurai.

Another factor helping to produce a potential selectorate among the samurai retainers was the distribution of court ranks and pension-bearing rewards for the participation in the Restoration movement and the Boshin War. As the war ended, the court ranks were given to individuals and the pensions to both individuals and daimyo houses.[28] These rewards were actually an addition to, not a displacement of, the same instituted privileges that the members of the feudal political order had always respected. Furthermore, the rewards affected the members of the old order, the samurai, *only* when in the service of the Court; inside the domains they might have generated new and potentially destabilizing relationships among its members. The net effect was obvious: in the eyes of the Imperial government, the vast and previously unbridgeable differences between the daimyo and their retainers could be reduced merely to distinctions, as expressed in court ranks, in their commitment to the Restoration cause. This effect was most meaningful where it needed to be, in the Court and the new government. In other words, in a similar but perhaps less direct manner like the *chōshi* system, these new privileges of rank and reward served as an entry for samurai activists to the new government, by virtue of their proven talent during the Restoration movement and the Boshin War. Unlike the *chōshi* system, these practices, seemingly less selective and more consistent with the feudalistic practice of honoring military virtue and status, could protect the vulnerable recruits against any hostility from their fellow retainers at home.

The political estrangement of the traditional feudal elite (especially the daimyo members and the *kōshi*) in the center was therefore a complex process. They were not actually removed from the central government. Rather, their central *offices* were made irrelevant to the affairs of the domains largely because of the dual character of the central government—national in symbolic status only, while preserving the domain autonomy. At the same time, these privileged individuals did play one significant role: by virtue of their presence, they made the central government look less foreign and hence less threatening to the continued existence of the feudal domain governments outside its boundary.

On the other hand, the new recruits in the central government did not provide any tangible solutions to problems such as the precarious financial and military foundations of the new government. Their internal struggle, as will be discussed in the following chapter, was no less inhibitive to them than the jealousy and hostility of their fellow retainers at home. The positive result of isolating the new samurai recruits lay, rather, in their recognition that, beyond the boundary of the new government and its territories, the feudal distinctions among men had not been erased. That recognition was also the basis for the directing of their allegiance more exclusively to the new central government, the maturation of their talent beyond feudalistic obligations, and their corresponding awakening to the inhibitive influence of the coalition basis of the new government on them. In short, the domestic disengagement of the central government both inhibited its institutionalized dependence upon the feudal domains and promoted the notion among some of its members of forgoing the constitutional protection of the feudal domains.

## The Demise of the Feudal Domains

For the domains, the familiar problem of financial difficulty had a paradoxical dimension to it: their efforts to protect the daimyo houses in the Boshin War accelerated their fiscal demise, thereby eroding the very foundation of the daimyo houses.[29] In fact, before the *Haihan chiken*, a score of impoverished feudal domains voluntarily liquidated themselves due to bankruptcy (Table 3.8). Included in this group were the pro-Restoration Tsuwano han, the pro-Tokugawa Morioka han, and the Nagaoka han, which, even before Aizu, staged something of a one-domain war against the superior Imperial forces. Likewise, this group also included the Takasu han, the size of whose samurai population suggests an unusually heavy burden on its treasury (369 per 1,000 *koku*), and Yoshii han, with only 51 per 1,000 *koku* at the opposite pole. In terms of financial stability and of attitude toward the Restoration, these domains had little in common. They liquidated themselves in a variety of ways, from simply renouncing their existence as self-sufficient political units to becoming absorbed into larger domains. In this case, the lord-governor of domains such as Mariyama, Takasu, and Tokuyama stepped down to become deputies of the larger domains. It is important to note that these domains positively chose a course of action that the rest of the feudal domains would have had to follow sooner or later even without the *Haihan chiken*. Our concern is the process by which this situation arose in most of the remaining domains.

As we have seen, the end of the Tokugawa bakufu did not introduce any significant change into the relationship among the domains or between the domains and the new central government. The formal recognition of the feudal domains as part of the triumvirate of "domestic" administration in the *Seitaisho* confirmed them as autonomous governments and testified to the

TABLE 3.8. Voluntary Liquidation of Domains, 1870–1871

| Domain | Agricultural Productivity in koku | Domain Revenue in koku | Samurai population per 1,000 koku of domain revenue |
|---|---|---|---|
| Fukumoto (1/13/1871)[a] | 10,573 | 3,204 | 166 |
| Morioka (8/6/1870) | 130,000 | 68,580 | — |
| Mariyama (10/11/1870) | 10,000 | 4,950 | 64 |
| Marugame (5/16/1871) | 51,512 | 33,120 | 218 |
| Nagaoka (11/15/1870) | 24,000 | 10,500 | 783 |
| Ōmizo (July or August 1871) | 20,000 | 6,730 | 132 |
| Sayama (1/27/1870) | 10,000 | 5,470 | — |
| Takasu (2/11/1871) | 30,000 | 6,630 | 369 |
| Tadotsu (5/11/1871) | 10,000 | 7,400 | 170 |
| Tatsuoka (7/2/1871) | 16,000 | 5,140 | 127 |
| Tsuwano (7/9/1871) | 43,000 | 30,753 | 138 |
| Tokuyama (7/2/1871) | 40,000 | 21,410 | 193 |
| Yoshii (1/27/1870) | 10,000 | 2,160 | 51 |

SOURCE: Michio Umegaki, "From Domain to Prefecture," in Jansen and Rozman, eds., *Japan in Transition: From Tokugawa to Meiji*, p. 101.
[a]The dates refer to when the Imperial government received the request for self-liquidation. For Mariyama and Tadotsu, however, the dates refer to when these domains submitted their requests for self-liquidation.

resilience of what was earlier referred to as a "calculated indifference." Thus, the domains showed no intention of seeking access to resources outside their boundaries. The extra income of the new central government from the former Tokugawa territories and from some of the pro-Tokugawa domains was partly consumed by military expenses and partly reserved for the rewards to participants in the Restoration movement and the war. Little was left for the majority of the domains in desperate need of financial relief. Moreover, it is, in fact, doubtful that the domains themselves would have demanded the redistribution of such war spoils. After all, most of the domain officials had willingly contributed their own human and material resources to the war in exchange for their places in the new Court-centered order.

At the same time, the initiatives by the Imperial government to engage the domains in reforms necessitated by the changes in the center of the political order made little headway because they bypassed the source of political sanction within the domains— the daimyo or the domain officials acting in their names.[30] As seen in Chapter 1, the proposed reforms of the domains' internal organization, encouraged by the Imperial government, had only indirect and limited consequences. For example, orders to promote new men, in defiance of hereditary practices, to high administrative positions in the domains were heeded only by receptive domain officials, as in the case of Wakayama han.

Thus, the need to address the problem of the diminishing domain treasury, too, would have to presume this basic distance, or the absence of cooperation, between the new central government and the domain governments. Entrenched in this legacy of the old system of rule, the domains could only repeat an old method of financial relief: internal redistribution of the ever-decreasing resources. Participation in the war did not help the domains but only narrowed their options, for the reward for participation was the confirmation of this noncooperation and the cost for the reward was the hastening of the depletion of the domain purses.

In the wake of the Restoration, then, domain autonomy was rapidly becoming a fiction. Most of the domain governments were no longer able to perform what was expected of politically autonomous communities—public services for their population such as police protection, taxation, and rural administration. Thus, the domain officials faced the necessity of disengaging themselves from the political life of the domains as a whole in order to commit themselves, instead, to their essential feudalistic obligation: the house administration of the daimyo. For their own relief, they began to seek a more positive role for the central government, whose noninterference had been the mark of the domain autonomy.

The domains' acceptance of their financial demise and of the new-found role for the central government began almost concurrently. The central government made a few attempts to show the domains that the Restoration was not an affair "only of the Court." The new government encouraged all the domains to follow broad guidelines for the internal management of domain affairs, instead of enforcing a uniform mode of domain administration with threats of punishment. The domains gradually acquiesced to these modest efforts as their officials began to recognize that the new role of the central government could help avert the final collapse of the daimyo houses.

The *Hanseki hōkan* (the Return of the Fiefs to the Court) of 1869 was one attempt that both observed the domain autonomy and initiated some necessary reforms for the domains. The *Hanseki hōkan* was intended to set things right between the old feudal governments of the daimyo and the new central government by officially making the daimyo the imperial governors of their own territories. The symbolic unity thus achieved between the Imperial government and the daimyo was strengthened further by its extension to all members of the domains' governments. The Imperial government uniformly designated the daimyo, along with the court nobles, as members of the new privileged class, the *kazoku* (literally, "Flower Families"), while their retainers were categorized into two classes, the *shizoku* for the upper and middle ranks and the *sotsuzoku* for the lower rank. Not surprisingly, the *Hanseki hōkan* did little to redistribute the domain resources for appropriation by the Imperial government; the central treasury was still 1,000,000 *koku* in debt as of 1870.[31] Neither did it produce any beneficial consequences for the domains. However, this symbolic unity on the one hand strengthened the guarded acceptance of the Imperial government by the domain officials; on the other hand, it also induced the domain governments to accept the central rulings on domain affairs that followed.

The first of these, the eleven-point guideline, issued to each of the domain lord-governors by the new government on August 2, 1869, dictated that one-tenth of the domain revenue be separated from "public" expenditures and allocated to the daimyo's household as income.[32] This guideline, implemented by the domain bureaucracies themselves had three immediate results. First, it had been customary to claim that the domain's resources, theoretically, were the property of the bakufu or the emperor and that the shogun and the daimyo were empowered to administer them, often as they saw fit. The eleven-point guideline was the first formal recognition by the domains that the fiction of "trusteeship" over their lands no longer held, and that there could be a practical distinction between what belonged publicly to the domain at large and what belonged privately to the household of the daimyo. Second, this separation of public and private expenses allowed the earlier, virtually unheeded, decree differentiating public and private affairs in the conduct of the domain administration (issued on December 11, 1868),[33] to gain effective institutional and material bases. And finally, the stated limit of one-tenth of domain revenue for daimyo income prompted a spontaneous reduction of the retainers' incomes, even though the guideline lacked any actual stipulation to that effect and domain officials retained the power to determine the reduction of the samurai stipend throughout the vassalage. As a paradoxical result, the samurai of high income brackets often received only 10 percent of their previous stipends, whereas those in lower brackets, already suffering from impoverishment, escaped such drastic reduction.[34]

Using the momentum of the *Hanseki hōkan*, the new government experimented in another way with limited interference in the domains' internal affairs. The government's efforts to streamline the taxation systems had always been hindered by the domains' retention of, as part of their fiefs, villages in geographically remote areas. As the daimyo were made, in effect, Imperial appointees, thereby legally incorporated into the central nexus, the new central government attempted to exchange these less accessible villages for ones closer to the domains concerned. The substitution was put into effect slowly at first. When it incurred little resistance from the domains, even with an unequal rate of exchange of the nearer villages, the government pushed its plan more audaciously. In some cases, the new government even confiscated some portions of the land or its products in the process of exchange.[35] In terms of practical or material gains, the resources redistributed to the central treasury were still negligible. Nonetheless, in terms of symbolic effect, this practice drove an important wedge into the domain bureaucracy's unfettered control over domain resources and into the closed community of the daimyo. As a result, the government was even able to decree on April 3, 1871, that the vassals in those detached territories confiscated in the process of exchange no longer need to return to their home domains.[36]

On October 4, 1870, another, thirteen-point, guideline replaced the eleven-point guideline. Although the *Hanseki hōkan* still observed the unequivocal autonomy of the daimyo and the domain bureaucracy, the new orders addressed the redistribution of the domain resources in a still more specific manner. The 10 percent of the revenue set aside for the income of the daimyo's household remained the same. However, interfering directly with the domain bureaucracy for the first time, one of the directives touched upon the distribution of the remaining revenue for public expenditure. The new guideline ordered 9 percent of the revenue to be allocated to military expenditures and 81 percent to administrative expenditures, including stipends for the house retainers.[37] Compounding such interference, the new guideline also called for the incorporation of the higher officials of the domain governments into a national system of ranking, matching the court ranking system of the central government officials.

By now one thing was clear, however: the depletion of the domain treasuries had gone unchecked to the extent that any marginal changes were of little use. In response, the domains began to devise ways in which their financial difficulties could be halted, or at least slowed, more directly, and these efforts inevitably presumed some role(s) for the Imperial government. A curious sort of evidence for such domain efforts was the increasing frequency with which they asked the Imperial government for permission not to repair their own deteriorating castles toward the close of 1870.[38] In addition to providing telling evidence of the depleted purses of the domains, these requests for austerity measures demonstrated that the domains no longer ignored the presence of the new central government.

The domains' new recognition of the central government's existence was also shown in their direct requests for relief, such as those made by the Tsuruta han (formerly the Hamada han) and a few other domains. These requests for aid confirmed a larger picture of the domains' financial plight and its consequences across Japan, to which the new government was increasingly exposed. For example, a central government official, sent to northern Japan, an area far more destitute than most because of its longer war experience, described the region as "lying in complete devastation" and its domains "unable to maintain their vassals and govern the local populace" because of the impoverishment due to the war, the bad harvest, and the partial confiscation of their fiefs.[39]

These requests for relief were followed by yet another pattern of recognizing the central government exhibited by some of the domains toward the close of 1870. Following the lead of the Kumamoto han, a few domains began to send appeals to the Imperial government that it allow the domains to use some portion of the daimyo's income (the 10 percent of the domain revenue) for the purpose of relief. Then more domains began to send similar appeals for the reallocation of the daimyo's incomes for the use of wider purposes such as maintaining the operation the domain administration and defraying the domain debts. All together, the *Dajōkan nisshi* recorded twenty-eight such cases.[40]

These appeals provided clear evidence that even the daimyo houses, the centers of the domain communities, were no longer unaffected by deteriorating domain finances. It was only logical, then, for the domain administration to respond with rather drastic measures such as the reduction of the number of retainers. Thus, a score of domains began encouraging their retainers to return agriculture, which would help trim the cost of maintaining samurai, who were now even condemned as "living off the stipends for nothing,"[41] and help reclaim the lands within the domain. In a few exceptional cases, the impoverished domains repeated voluntarily what the Imperial government had advised the Tsuruta han to pursue—turn to other, related daimyo for aid.[42] The Obama han (100,000 *koku*, ruled by the Sakai) absorbed another of the Sakai house, the Mariyama han (10,000 *koku*) on September 19, 1870. Likewise, the Owari han absorbed the Takasu han on February 11, 1871, and later Chōshū and Tokuyama (both the Mōri houses) followed suit on July 2, 1871. In all cases, the participating parties stressed the need for trimming the administrative costs of having two separate domains, and proposed amalgamation by making the daimyo of the inferior houses the deputies to those of superior ones.[43]

These developments prefaced a drastic and abrupt change in the domains' preservation of their own autonomy: the decision by some of them to liquidate themselves voluntarily. Yet in real terms this decision was far less disruptive than it may appear. The situation at hand simply denied any saving alternative. As summarized by the lord-governor of small Yoshii han, "the public costs have only grown larger; there are no conceivable measures to meet the costs; and the people's cry for relief has come to fill the air around us." With this memorandum to the Imperial government, Yoshii han became the first to fold: "We humbly request the Imperial government to extend its rule to us." Requesting that the domain be annexed to the nearby Iwahana ken, this memorandum stressed two points: first, that the daimyo was financially unable to perform his expected role as governor, and second, that the annexation would impose no additional burden upon the ken authority since the domain's populace was very well disciplined and the retainers could readily perform the necessary police duties.[44] The other domains that voluntarily terminated themselves explained the need to do so in similar financial terms, as necessitated by inability of the lord-governors to govern when overwhelmed by growing public costs in proportion to the domain productivity, to the "excess of samurai," to natural disasters, to poor harvests, and the like.

In feudal terms, this voluntary termination was the only conceivable recourse for protecting the very core of the domain community, the daimyo's house, from being engulfed by the consequences of his treasury's depletion. This was because the Imperial government still guaranteed the daimyo and their households one-tenth of their former domain revenues when the domains were annexed by the nearby fu and ken. The samurai stipends for the retainers were likewise assured of continuation. The majority of the remaining domains, which kept on repeating the redistribution of their worn-out resources, only delayed, but did not prevent, their own financial death. Hence, by the time of *Haihan chiken* in 1871, none of the feudal domains was in a position to stage or even to contemplate any resistance to the decision by the Imperial government to terminate them altogether. In fact, the lord-governors of the remaining domains were thus spared the embarrassment of admitting formally the "inability to govern" that had often prefaced the daimyo's requests for relief or self-liquidation.

To some of the Restoration leaders in the central government, the collapse of the feudal domains presented a clear picture of a feudal political order that had exhausted all resources for resistance, and would now accept further interference by the central government. Ōkubo's and Kido's fears of disruptive reactions to the *Haihan chiken* proved unwarranted. Once it became obvious in the aftermath of the *Haihan chiken* that the domains would remain passive, the central government had little hesitation about erasing many of the remaining feudal distinctions.

The Imperial government now could rearrange the feudal distinctions left in the residual administrative structures. After a brief period following the *Haihan chiken*, the Imperial government began to reduce the domains-turned-ken to fewer local administrative units. After the first phase of this amalgamation was completed, very few of the individual feudal domains' old territorial boundaries remained (Table 3.9). Within each of the new local units, too, few traces of the old community of the domain survived. Table 3.10 shows the composition of the upper echelons of the local administrative structure of a few ken selected for purposes of comparison. The period during which the local officials were appointed at different ranks covers slightly differing time spans but in general extends throughout the period between 1871 and 1875. (Changes in the order of offices and their corresponding grades, *tō*, brought about by the reform of offices in 1873, have been adjusted so that the systems before and after the

TABLE 3.9. Amalgamation of Domains into Ken
Jurisdiction, 1871

FU AND KEN

| No. of Former Domains Incorporated | No. | Names |
|---|---|---|
| 0–1 | 25 | Hamada, Hamamatsu, Hiroshima, Iruma, Kagoshima (Satsuma), Kanagawa, Kanazawa, Kōchi (Tosa), Kumamoto, Mizusawa, Morioka, Myōdō, Nanao, Nihonmatsu, Obi, Oitama, Okayama, Sendai, Shinagawa, Shizuoka, Tokyo, Tottori, Wakamatsu, Yamanashi, Yatsushiro |
| 2–4 | 25 | Ashigara, Asuba, Chikuma, Fukuoka, Hōjō, Hyōgo, Kagawa, Matsuyama, Mimizu, Mitsuma, Nagahama, Nagasaki, Nagoya, Osaka, Ōtsu, Saitama, Sakai, Sakata, Tochigi, Tsuruga, Uwajima, Wakayama, Watarae, Yamagata, Yamaguchi (Chōshū) |
| 5–7 | 14 | Akita, Anotsu, Hirosaki, Ibaraki, Imari (Saga), Imba, Iwasaki, Kashiwazaki, Kokura, Kyoto, Nagano, Niigata, Ōita, Utsunomiya |
| 8–10 | 8 | Fukatsu, Gifu, Gumma, Nara, Niiharu, Nukada, Shikama, Toyo'oka |
| 11 or more | 1 | Kisarazu |

SOURCE: Michio Umegaki, "From Domain to Prefecture," in Jansen and Rozman, eds., *Japan in Transition: From Tokugawa to Meiji*, p. 92.

reform are comparable.) The most noticeable feature is that the offices at levels where interaction with the central government was expected to be most active, those of the seventh grade and above (which required Imperial approval for appointment), were held mostly by samurai from elsewhere. The proportion of local samurai increases as the grades of office descend along the hierarcy of the ken administrative structure, and one can safely assume that the offices below the thirteenth grade were monopolized by the local samurai. In other words, these local samurai, who once constituted concentric circles according to their ranks around the center of the domain community, the daimyo, were now almost entirely removed from positions that could influence the political life of the new local government.

TABLE 3.10. Local Appointment at the Prefectural Level, 1871–1876

| Prefectural Office | Grade | Social Origins | NO. OF OFFICIALS / NO. OF POSITIONS | | | |
|---|---|---|---|---|---|---|
| | | | Yamaguchi | Shizuoka[a] | Gifu | Aomori |
| Governor (or deputy) | 4 | Nonlocal Samurai | 2/2 100% | 1/1 100% | 2/2 100% | 3/3 100% |
| | 5 | Local Samurai | | | | |
| | | Nonlocal Commoners (heimin) | | | | |
| | | Local Commoners | | | | |
| Sanji | 6 | Nonlocal Samurai | 1/3 33% | 5/7 71% | 2/2 100% | 4/5 80% |
| | | Local Samurai | 2/3 67% | 2/7 29% | | 1/5 20% |
| | 7 | Nonlocal Commoners | | | | |
| | | Local Commoners | | | | |
| Tenji/Taizoku[b] | 8 | Nonlocal Samurai | 2/20 20% | 6/9 67% | 3/4 75% | 8/15 53% |
| | | Local Samurai | 8/10 80% | 3/9 33% | 1/4 25% | 4/15 27% |
| | 9 | Nonlocal Commoners | | | | 3/15 2% |
| | | Local Commoners | | | | |
| Taizoku/Chūzoku[b] | 10 | Nonlocal Samurai | 10/32 31% | 4/22 18% | 13/29 45% | 20/37 54% |
| | | Local Samurai | 22/32 69% | 15/22 68% | 15/29 52% | 14/37 38% |
| | 11 | Nonlocal Commoners | | 2/22 9% | 1.29 3% | 3/37 8% |
| | | Local Commoners | | 1/22 5% | | |
| Shōzoku | 12 | Nonlocal Samurai | 11/71[c] 16% | 10/38 26% | 7/24[d] 29% | 18/39 46% |
| | | Local Samurai | 51/71 72% | 22/38 58% | 15/24 63% | 14/39 36% |
| | 13 | Nonlocal Commoners | 1/71 2% | 6/38 16% | 1/24 4% | 7/39 18% |
| | | Local Commoners | | | 1/24 4% | |

SOURCES: *Fuken shiryō*: Aomori, book 13; Gifu, books 33, 34, 35, and 35; Shizuoka, books 18, 19, 20, 21, 22, 23, 24, 25, and 26; Yamaguchi, books 46 and 47.
[a]Suruga region only.
[b]After 1873.
[c]Eight officials, unclassifiable by the four categories, are excluded.
[d]This total does not include officials below the twelfth grade.

The shrinking of the collective life of the domain to the innermost circle of the daimyo house preceding the *Haihan chiken* was paradigmatic: the han having its own territory and populace as an integrated whole had become a fiction. The feudal order had worn itself out. The Restoration leaders exhibited more than simple relief at having witnessed no resistance to the *Haihan chiken*. To Kido Kōin, once torn between the need for a stronger central government and the need to protect the daimyo houses, a han separated from its daimyo house had expediently become a mere area and a cluster of populace that were easily subjected to mergers and partitions: "... divide the large domains like Satsuma into three, Chōshū into two, or Kanazawa into three ken; combine two or three small domains to make one ken."[45]

What is identifiable in the developments leading to the *Haihan chiken* may be no more than a convergence of the decision of the Restoration leaders to end the feudal domains, the growth of the Imperial government into an organization of men increasingly distant from the political life of the domains, and the shrinkage of the domain bureaucracy into a household administration. Or one may posit at least an indirect causal chain connecting these three developments. Yet, one should also detect an important void, or an attenuated sense of the real instrumentality of the Imperial government itself in sustaining and linking these developments. As this close analysis shows, it was largely a specific combination of financial and political impulsions that enabled the fledgling central government to continue. Itō Hirobumi's reference to the *Haihan chiken* as a bloodless revolution betrays underlining relief—relief over the opportune convergence of these developments—rather than shrewd management of a rational change designed by men, himself included.

# 4

# The Emperor's Government:
# The Community of Strangers

THE *HAIHAN CHIKEN* freed the new central government from the self-induced domestic isolation it had maintained since 1868. The leaders in the Imperial government now found themselves liberated, rather abruptly, from the often inhibiting constitutional equality among the feudal domains before the Court. With conditions now favorable to the expansion and consolidation of its rule, however, the Imperial government also had to face two problems: the lack of cohesion among the central leaders and the low level of acceptance of the Imperial government by the populace. Both problems had previously remained concealed precisely because the Imperial government had been far less than a central government in domestic affairs.

The first of these two problems was internal to the Imperial government. As examined earlier in Chapters 1 and 2, many of the emperor's proxies, the former Restoration activists, continued their mutual and often debilitating suspicion and jealousy in addition to competing among themselves on policy issues. Their earlier engagement in the common cause of creating the emperor's government had not made them a community of the equally committed. Their subsequent affiliation with the emperor's government did little to foster a shared identity either; although they all had various posts in the same governmental organization, the interactions necessitated by these posts did not generate a stable relationship among them.

In the past, the continued importance of the feudal domains had kept these emperor's proxies constantly aware of the precarious foundation of *their* government, thereby reducing the competition and suspicion among them. Now liquidation of the feudal domains removed that source of self-restraint. However, the Imperial officials did not seem to perceive this potential internal conflict as a particularly serious problem. Thus, within six months after the *Haihan chiken*, the Imperial government decided to send what is known as the Iwakura mission to the United States and Europe. The most important goal of the mission was to improve Japan's unequal treaty status via-à-vis the Western powers based on treaties the bakufu had concluded in 1858 and 1866.[1] But the mission's most serious impact at home was the fact that it deprived the Imperial government of those key figures who had been particularly crucial in maintaining the minimal cohesion among its members. The central government was left without the services of Ōkubo Toshimichi, Kido Kōin, and Iwakura Tomomi for nearly two years. In addition, Itō Hirobumi, Sasaki Takayuki, and others of lesser visibility but of no less importance to the central cadre accompanied these three pivotal men on the mission. Leadership in the central government during the Iwakura mission was left to Saigō Takamori and Itagaki Taisuke, whose realms of action had been confined primarily to their own domains. It will be shown below in Chapter 6 that the absence of the key figures from the central government during this crucial period played a significant role in destabilizing the internal relationships among the central leaders.

The purpose of this chapter, however, first, is to trace the instability in the years 1871 through 1877 to the problems of the community of powerful proxies of the emperor. These problems were already evident even before the *Haihan chiken* and the formation of the Iwakura mission.

Second, this chapter will examine another problem that did not surface until the liquidation of the feudal domains: the reception of the Imperial government by the local populace, most of whom had been under the jurisdiction of the domain governments. The removal of the feudal domains alone could not promote the acceptance of the central government, as the long history of feudalistic divisions had prevented a sense of "national" government from growing among the people. In addition, before the *Haihan chiken*, the new government, which was something less than central, did not make systematic efforts to woo the local population, and it lacked the means to encourage the people to accustom themselves to it. The manner in which the Imperial government was initially viewed by the populace, therefore, is a crucial question. The clarification of these two problems furnishes the basis for the analysis of the post-*Haihan chiken* politics in the second half of the book.

## Government Within a Government?

In the turbulent wake of the Restoration and the ensuing war, one particular administrative arm of the new central government, the Finance Department, became essential to the operation of the entire system of rule. Yet its rise to a position of paramount importance had also engaged the members of the Imperial government in a dynamic and often unpredictable internal struggle for power among themselves, a divisiveness so intense that their common loyalty to the Imperial government as a whole had little effect in moderating it. The preeminence of the Finance Department and its impact upon the Restoration leaders points to this far more serious problem of the Imperial government, namely, its inability to generate cohesion among its own members through their common affiliation.

Like other departments, the Finance Department (called the *Kaikei-jimuka* first, then the *Kaikei-jimukyoku*, and finally the *Ōkurashō*) had a rather undistinguished presence in its first few months. Iwakura Tomomi and Yuri Kimimasa, at its head, were the only well-known Restoration activists in the department. In addition, the task that should have been the department's specific concern—ensuring financial resources for the War of the Restoration—had to be undertaken by all the leading figures in the government, who naturally were more concerned about the survival of the new government as a whole than about the performance of any of its parts.

A critical turning point for the performance of the department came early in 1869 with the ousting of Yuri Kimimasa, the key figure responsible for its operation. Yuri's fall from grace resulted from his rather simplistic approach to stabilizing the central finances. Replicating the monetary policy enforced earlier in his own Fukui han, Yuri had attempted to circulate irredeemable paper notes *(Dajōkansatsu)* as the monetary stimulus to local manufacturing and as a supplement to the growing central expenditures. The value of the paper notes, however, soon amounted to 38 million yen, fifteen times the value of the reserves. In addition, the new central government could not even replace the notes widely issued by the feudal domains, as pointed out in Chapter 3. These problems quickly eroded confidence in the paper notes to the point where the monetary stimulus was completely ineffective. Yuri was apparently oblivious to the fact that the new central government had neither the power nor the credibility to back the value of the *Dajōkansatsu*.[2] Consequently, by the beginning of 1869, Yuri's inflationary policy had proved itself a miserable failure even within the Imperial territories. Yuri's economic mismanagement impeded the new government's efforts to gain the confidence of the all-too-suspicious Western powers, forcing the Restoration leaders to take steps to protect it from the Westerners' relentless criticisms.[3]

One major step was to bring into the Finance Department some officials who had dealt with the foreign powers in earlier assignments in the Department of Foreign Affairs. Thus, early in 1869, Ōkuma Shigenobu, then at the Foreign Affairs Department, was also attached to Finance. Itō Hirobumi, Godai Tomoatsu, and Inoue Kaoru were called back to Tokyo from their posts in cities with open ports, such as Nagasaki, Hyōgo, and Osaka. By the summer of 1869, these three had been transferred to the Department of Finance or given double assignments in both Foreign Affairs and Finance.[4] On September 16, 1869, the revamped Finance Department and the Department of Home Affairs were made practically into one department, under a single minister, to improve the efficiency of both departments whose jurisdictions and functions were too closely parallel to justify a division.[5] With Matsudaira Yoshinaga serving as the minister of both Finance and Home Affairs, Ōkuma, Itō, and Inoue again all received double assignments within the two departments.

With these changes in personnel and organization, the Imperial government began to correct some of Yuri's mistakes and to tighten the reins over those economic matters important to Japan's position vis-à-vis the foreign powers. For example, the government declared the *Dajōkansatsu* redeemable, printed new notes, and sought tighter control over the widespread varieties of domain currencies. Additional corrective and preventive measures included the transfer of the Bureau for Trade and Commerce from the Department of Foreign Affairs into the expanding Department of Finance in order to establish better management of foreign trade.

The changes in personnel and organization had unexpected results in consolidating the Finance Department but, at the same time, isolated its operations. First of all, the core members of the combined Departments of Finance and Home Affairs were men whose actions were inspired by the need to protect the fragile Imperial government as a whole, particularly against any doubt of its legitimacy by the foreign powers. Because of their earlier assignments in the port cities, they already had seen signs of the foreign powers' grudging acceptance of the Imperial government as the central authority of a new Japan. Consequently, they were more inclined then others to overlook the dominant coalition basis inhibiting the action of the Imperial government. They were willing, when possible, to disregard the underlying rule of the territorial autonomy of the feudal domains in favor of policies promoting the "central" authority. Accordingly, they devised policies that could collectively enhance the status of the central authority even to the detriment of that of the domain authorities, enabling the Imperial government to interfere with the autonomy of the domains. Examples included the prohibition of the sale of bonds by the domain governments to the foreign powers without the permission of the new central government (February, 1869), restrictions upon the use of foreign-registered vessels by the do-

mains (June 1869), promotion of government paper notes in the
domains (January, February, and April, 1869), and prohibition of
coinage by the domains and other feudal authorities.[6] These
policies inevitably made their designers and the Department
of Finance a unique presence among the central officials,
whose concern still lay in managing the coalition basis of the
government.

Second, the vigorous administration now reinforced by the
transfer of such men as Ōkuma Shigenobu, Itō Hirobumi, and
Inoue Kaoru to the Finance Department also resulted in the department's greater importance to the Imperial government as a
whole. This increased importance, in turn, provided greater leverage to its key members in the intricate politics of the emperor's
proxies. For Itō and Inoue, this new status countered the presence
of Kido Kōin, who had become something of a dean of the members of the new government from Chōshū. For Ōkuma, it com-
pensated for the lesser weight that his own domain, the Saga han,
could carry in the Imperial government vis-à-vis Satsuma, Chōshū, or Tosa. Thus the realization by these men that their services
were badly needed by the rest of the central leaders placed them
on a stronger footing in the Imperial government than they would
otherwise have had.

By the fall of 1869, then, the Finance Department, together with
the Department of Home Affairs, was well on its way to becoming
the pivot of the entire Imperial government. This sudden rise of
the Finance Department and the increased importance of the officials who managed it nearly turned the department into a government within the government. But the real significance of the
rise of this administrative arm lay in the number of hostile reactions it provoked among the rest of the key members of the
Imperial government. These reactions revealed that the Imperial
government was far from the ideal community of the equally
committed.

One reaction was resistance. Despite the combined departments' wish and claim to monopolize domestic affairs, at least
for the Imperial territories under fu and ken, their ability to enforce their preferred policies was often impeded by the noncompliance of some of the central officials assigned to these territories.

These officials based their contention on the departments' ignorance of local conditions. Moreover, viewing themselves as the emperor's proxies, some of these officials were supported by credible power sources of their own. For example, Matsukata Masayoshi, the governor of Hida ken on the island of Kyūshū, was from the powerful Satsuma; Maebara Issei, the governor of Echigo fu facing the Sea of Japan, was from the equally powerful Chōshū. The ultimate leverage these officials had in contradicting and criticizing the departments was the fact that they were from two of the most influential domains in the coalition.' Actually, even the combined departments and their members had little real power to overrule such noncompliance. This resistance to the combined departments reveals several problematic aspects of the complex dynamics of the competitive relationship among the government officials. First, the increased importance of the combined departments did not necessarily provide *more* powerful leverage than that more conventionally based on domain backgrounds in the competition among the emperor's proxies. Second, the competition between the government officials on different power bases also suggests that they sought every possible source of influence both inside and outside of the Imperial government. And finally, as such an almost undisciplined competition among the emperor's proxies implies, their shared membership in the Imperial government had not facilitated communication and coordination among them.

A far more significant reaction was the attempt by the key Restoration leaders to adjust to the overall operational impact on the Imperial government of the emergence of the combined departments. The issue, at first, involved the disquieting effect on the leaders' hopes of maintaining the appearance of unity within the new government on the basis of a balanced division between the deliberative and administrative functions. The reorganization of the central government in the summer of 1869, following the *Hanseki hōkan*, seemed to have attained such a balance by sharply reducing the number of Councilors, thereby making them far more selective positions responsible exclusively for deliberative functions. However, the simultaneous rise of the combined departments quickly undermined such an effect. The ensuing at-

tempts at readjustment proved even more divisive for the central
government as a whole, for they inevitably engaged these leaders
in unstable and shifting alignments among themselves and with
the key officials in the combined departments.

By the summer of 1870, the Imperial government had settled
into two groups in a division that even their shared domain backgrounds could not help moderate. Ōkubo Toshimichi emerged as
the major critic of the accumulation of power in one administrative arm, as had happened in the combined departments. He represented a group of Councilors that included Sasaki Takayuki of
Tosa, Soejima Taneomi of Saga (the domain of Ōkuma Shigenobu,
the *de facto* head of the combined departments), and Hirosawa
Saneomi from Chōshū, the domain from which Itō Hirobumi and
Inoue Kaoru, flanking Ōkuma in the departments, had come. This
group defended the status of Councilors, with whom the deliberative responsibility formally rested but which the vigorous administrative initiatives of the combined departments appeared to
have made useless.[8] Their proposed "adjustment," accordingly,
was the clear separation of Finance and Home Affairs, which
would certainly dissipate the power of the officials in the combined departments. In the meantime, Kido Kōin of Chōshū
emerged as the guardian of the strong Finance-Home Affairs Department, whose management was in the hands of lieutenants
from Chōshū—Itō Hirobumi and Inoue Kaoru—as well as Ōkuma
of Saga. Kido's suggested "adjustment," in opposition to that of
Ōkubo's group, was to reinstate the parity between the deliberative and administrative branches at a higher level by promoting
one of the officials, Ōkuma Shigenobu of the combined departments, to the status of Councilor.[9] The division between the two
conflicting groups thus clearly suggests that shared domain backgrounds were hardly the basis of a stable alignment among the
members of the Imperial government.

Furthermore, the bickering and wrangling that ensued quickly
obscured the initial issue of how to maintain balance between
the deliberative and administrative branches of the new central
government. Compromises were sought and made not on the basis
of the two proposed adjustments, but on the basis of the intricate
power politics among most of the participants, which uncovered

other issues that some deemed more pressing. Being from Satsuma and acutely aware of the precarious coalition basis of the Imperial government, Ōkubo Toshimichi did not press his preference too far in contradiction to Kido Kōin's because he was aware of the even more crucial need not to displease the leader from Chōshū at this critical juncture. Conversely, Kido's defense of the strong Finance Department and its able administrators was also influenced, more than he himself might have been willing to admit, by his nagging feeling at this time that the "Court seems to listen only to Satsuma lately...."[10]

In the end, neither camp won. Political bickering and compromising led to the constant reshuffling of personnel at a furious pace once the two Departments of Finance and Home Affairs were separated on August 6, 1870. First, Date Munenari, the daimyo of Uwajima han who had been openly accused of incompetence in the Department of Foreign Affairs earlier, became the minister of Finance. The Kido-backed trio of Ōkuma, Itō, and Inoue were placed in the next three highest positions in Finance. Ōkuma Shigenobu then also became Councilor the following month, on September 26, 1870. At the same time, Ōkubo Toshimichi, as Councilor, became the head of the Department of Home Affairs. A few months later, however, a newly created Department of Construction took several of the key divisions (Mines, Railroads, and Steel Mills) away from the Home Affairs Department. It also took Itō Hirobumi away from the Finance Department and made him its first de facto head. Two weeks before the Haihan chiken, Finance and Home Affairs were combined again, only this time the former completely absorbed the latter. The minister was Ōkubo Toshimichi and the first vice-minister, Ōkuma Shigenobu. The central government remained without a Department of Home Affairs until December of 1873.

What thus became clear from the reactions to the rise of the Finance Department was the apparent discrepancy between what appeared to be the formation of a powerful administrative arm and the extreme susceptibility of that arm to realignments. The inconsistencies following the fate of the department suggested larger problems characterizing the entire Imperial government, both as an organization with a clear boundary of its own and as a community of men supposedly joined by a shared commitment. To begin with, the Imperial government suffered from several organizational deficiencies. Before the *Haihan chiken*, it had no firmly established procedures to examine and screen policy proposals or to review their development and outcome once implemented.[11] Furthermore, appointments to central offices were often at the disposal of, or actually made by, backstage negotiations among a handful of the members of the government.[12] And finally, there was still no established system of control or coordination among the administrative departments by way of central budgeting.[13] These deficiencies made the Imperial government unable to enforce a unified system of procedures on its members, thereby causing each to draw upon individual sources of leverage to strengthen his own position and press his preferred policies. They could derive such support from many sources: from their domains, from other powerful figures within the government, and even from powerful figures within the foreign diplomatic corps, as in the support by the British consul Harry Parkes of Ōkuma Shigenobu.[14] During these machinations, however, the source of support they still ignored was any sense of their shared identity with the new government. The powerful Finance Department owed both its quick rise and its susceptibility to realignments to the organizational deficiencies of the Imperial government, which allowed its leaders the freedom to tamper with their own organizations as they saw fit.

What aggravated the organizational problems of the Imperial government was in fact its dual character: it was domestically far less than a central government, while it was *the* government of the new Japan vis-à-vis the foreign powers. Given this duality, the members of the Imperial government had two pressing needs: a need to maintain and improve the legitimacy of the Imperial government externally, and to protect the coalition basis of the Imperial government internally. Both these objectives had led the key members of the new government to allow fairly extensive autonomy to the officials in the departments but at the same time to keep a tighter rein over the administrative departments through appointments to the important positions. Because a greater autonomy improved the performance of the officials, it was worth-

while to grant it in order to improve also the credibility of the
Imperial government to the foreign powers. Yet undisciplined
actions by the administrative departments could easily lead the
Imperial government to violate the domains' autonomy, thereby
provoking resistance and protest from the feudal domains—hence
the necessity to keep strict control over the departments. Maintaining a dialectical equilibrium between autonomy and control
was the prerequisite for a stable central government that had not
yet overcome this duality. But since these two needs allowed two
groups of leaders to emerge, each more concerned with one need
than the other, the attempt to maintain the equilibrium led to
debilitating conflicts.

Against this background, the emergence of a powerful (and, for
some, all-too-autonomous) Department of Finance, given its key
members' inclination to sidestep the coalition basis, was particularly destabilizing to the Imperial government at first and served
as a catalyst for divisive disputes. However, the problem that the
Finance Department had initially posed for the rest of the members of the Imperial government in the summer of 1870 soon
changed its nature. Some central officials involved in the disputes
began to see that an alignment with the officials in the Finance
Department, whose administrative skills had proven crucial to
the operation of the new government, was a possible source of
greater influence. In other words, as Ōkuma, Itō, and Inoue of
Finance recognized their worth to the government, some of the
rest of the members of the Imperial government recognized the
worth of these Finance officials to their own bases of power.

Thus, this unpredictable dynamic of alignment among the
key members of the new government, which the rise of Finance revealed, caused even some of the more powerful and
seemingly more secure leaders to be drawn into the disputes.
For example, Ōkubo Toshimichi had initially tried to weaken
the Finance Department for fear that the necessary balance between the deliberative and executive functions might have
otherwise been permanently upset. To him, Kido Kōin's idea
of promoting Ōkuma, head of Finance, to Councilor would
have only facilitated this breakdown. Yet Ōkubo's initial resistance to Kido's idea was not a categorical denunciation of

the autonomy which the Finance Department and its key officials seemed to have acquired. In fact, Ōkubo was not averse to making compromises, particularly once it became clear that the conflict over the promotion in and of itself could become even more divisive than the "excessive" autonomy of the Finance Department. Moreover, on the eve of the *Haihan chiken*, which promised to end the duality of the central government, Ōkubo was even more willing to yield autonomy to the administrative departments, although their activities would now be expanded in the absence of domain resistance.

An important factor allowed Ōkubo Toshimichi, rather than Kido Kōin, to maintain a particularly flexible response within these shifting political alignments. These two leaders were equally committed to the Imperial government and aware of their importance as stemming from their own domains' military strength. Also, both, from time to time, were accused of serving two "overlords." However, with Saigō Takamori instead of Ōkubo himself firmly in command of the Satsuma troops and with Shimazu Hisamitsu being one of the most consistent critics of the new regime, Ōkubo's position in the new central government *as* a Satsuma retainer was considerably more vulnerable than Kido Kōin's, whose domain of Chōshū was firmly behind him. According to Japanese historian Haraguchi Kiyoshi, of these two leading samurai, Ōkubo Toshimichi was much more reluctant to tamper with the coalition basis of the Imperial government because of his stronger "attachment" to vestiges of the old order.[15] I would argue, instead, that Ōkubo's relatively weaker position vis-à-vis his own domain left him with a much more limited ability to exploit the power of Satsuma. It seems very likely that his awareness of his weakness compelled him to exercise more flexibility and seek a source of power primarily within the new central government.[16] One reward for Ōkubo's flexibility was that, as it soon turned out, he earned the allegiance of Ōkuma and Itō Hirobumi, who had established their worth to the new central government as administrators less concerned with its coalition basis.[17]

In contrast, Kido Kōin had a firmer control of his fellow Chōshū retainers in the new government and at home; the Chōshū men appeared to be united under Kido's leadership. By the same token, however, Kido also had a tendency to rely more on the Chōshū members as a power bloc in the central government, a practice that deprived him of the flexibility necessary to steer through the unpredictable currents of power among the arrogant and often insecure proxies of the emperor in the new central government. An interesting evidence of Kido's misplaced confidence in the Chōshū men's ability to remain united was his angry reaction to Hirosawa Sanemi, a Councilor of Chōshū origin, who betrayed Kido's confidence by siding with the other Councilors on the issue of the combined departments.[18]

In the final analysis, the members of the Imperial government were, by and large, victims of their own creation. The common memory of the Restoration movement had deceptively raised their hopes that the Imperial government could be a community of the committed. But the dispute over the Finance Department drew them into unpredictable and shifting power relationships in which all sought different sources of support, ultimately proving to themselves that they were strangers who happened to be working within the same government. Precisely because of this, some were quicker than others to begin seeking a power base within the Imperial government itself.

One other significant group of Restoration leaders had remained aloof from the internal struggle of the new central government. These were the leaders whose source of power rested almost exclusively in the local forces of the major domains. In particular, Itagaki Taisuke of Tosa and Saigō Takamori of Satsuma distinguished themselves primarily by their capacity to command the allegiance of their respective domain troops. The prevailing constitutional language legitimizing the coalition basis of the Imperial government assured them of a power base founded on their control of domain troops. Because they therefore might have not fully questioned the continuation of the domains, they were prevented from recognizing, first, that the coalition basis of the Imperial government was indispensable to their power and, second, that the control of key officials and some of the administrative departments in the central government could also be exploited as a source of influence once the coalition basis ceased to exist.

For these two Restoration leaders, the control of their domain troops provided one significant moment before the *Haihan chiken* to demonstrate their substantial influence upon the Imperial government. Ironically, that moment was also the last. They had mobilized the troops of Satsuma and Tosa earlier in 1871 as a contribution through the *sampan kempei*, only to see them used as a convincing, if untested, show of force to back the government's decision to terminate all the domains later in the same year. When the *Haihan chiken* was successfully enforced, both men were in fact destroying their own power basis. Thus, following the *Haihan chiken*, their appointments as Councilors, along with Kido Kōin and Ōkuma Shigenobu, were merely symbolic rewards of little political consequence now that their control of the Satsuma and Tosa troops hinged precariously upon the personal allegiance of only some of their troops.

When the Iwakura mission took Ōkubo Toshimichi and Kido Kōin abroad, the actual management of government was left to men such as Ōkuma Shigenobu and Inoue Kaoru, both in the Finance Department. These two men might have felt vulnerable to Saigō's and Itagaki's prominent, if originally symbolic, presence in the central government. Indeed, Inoue did feel as if he were a "skinny horse with a loaded back struggling to get over high mountains."[19] At the same time, however, Ōkuma and Inoue no longer really needed protectors. Once the *Haihan chiken* was complete, Saigō and Itagaki were without the source of power that could have rendered their presence in the government more substantial than symbolic. Inoue's initial apprehension in fact betrayed his deeper conviction that only men of Inoue's and Ōkuma's caliber could or should steer the government. Thus, recalling this period later, both Inoue and Ōkuma remained proud that they alone in the Finance Department did "70 to 80 percent of the business of the administration."[20] As will be seen in Chapter 6, this left Saigō and Itagaki feeling "disenfranchised" from the politics of the Restoration, even as they themselves helped achieve the most radical change in the new political order. They were to seek power again outside the Imperial government, this time among the displaced samaurai.

## The Arrival of the Restoration: The Local Populace

The contacts with the local populace established by the new central government since the Restoration were at best ad hoc, due largely to the government's limited governing authority. Measures designed by men such as Ōkubo Toshimichi were meant to free the emperor from his long-standing political obscurity and protection by conservative nobles and to impress the Japanese with his presence as the symbol of the new regime. One such measure was the emperor's long journey to Tokyo, formerly Edo, which had been renamed on September 3, 1868. The Imperial procession left Kyoto on November 4 and reached Tokyo three weeks later. The long procession, which was accompanied by some 2,300 Court nobles, daimyo, and samurai officials, made a great show of the "benevolent rule" to be expected under the emperor as it left thousands of barrels of sake, measures of poor relief, and the like in its wake.[21] At considerable cost to the central treasury, the procession left a strong impression of the emperor's presence and even contributed to his deification in the minds of the people. Yet for that same reason, such a show could not be exploited too regularly as a means of familiarizing the populace with the new central government that had replaced the bakufu. As a result, the local population in general was left without any clear perception of the new central government. In addition, their governance remained largely in the hands of the feudal domain authorities. Even within the Imperial territories, the attempts by the central governing authority to establish new relations with the local populace lacked any coherent pattern.

From the very beginning, the need to maintain an idealized image of benevolent Imperial rule, while carrying out the practical requirements of keeping the floundering new government afloat, led the Restoration activists now in the government to follow often contradictory courses of action toward the local population even in the Imperial territories. On the one hand, the activists often devised benevolent policies such as the reduction of taxes; but on the other hand, they also implemented more cautious monetary policies to fill the fiscal needs of the newborn Imperial government. The resulting inconsistency was often aggravated by the new government's dismissal (or sometimes even prosecution) of those who exercised this type of "benevolent" rule, as demonstrated in the incessant appointments and replacements of local officials in the Imperial territories who had been sent by the new government itself. A stark example of this type of contradiction can be found in the Kasamatsu area, previously under bakufu control and now an Imperial territory, northeast of Kyoto in the months following the battle of Toba and Fushimi. Sagara Sōzō and his pro-Restoration vanguard originally spread promises of reduced taxes in the area under new Imperial rule; Sagara was then replaced by Takezawa Kunimitsu from Awa, who was in turn replaced by Umemura Hayami of Mito. In each case, the Imperial government condemned the ruling official for his "arbitrary" exercise of its authority: " . . . ignorant of the very art of governing society, you simply offered petty charity in order to please the local people. . . . "[22] Each dismissed ruling official was followed by someone who was, seemingly, better informed of the will of the new government; in each case, however, the succeeding official found that his predecessor had left the populace with ever-higher expectations for improved rural life and more lenient taxation. Umemura, the last of the three, was not only dismissed but arrested by the new government at the end of a three-week rural uprising in the area.[23]

This type of inconsistency, which only confused the local population, was also related to the fact that the Imperial government was less than an autonomous organization. Each former activist sent to the Imperial territories was highly motivated to popularize the new Imperial regime; and to that extent, each, in his own way, embodied and projected the new central governing authority in the eyes of the people. At the same time, however, those in the Department of Home Affairs or the Department of Finance authorized to oversee the administration of these Imperial territories were acutely aware that the survival of the new government depended not so much upon the popularization of the Restoration as upon careful fiscal management. These administrators had their own expectations of the roles to be performed by the officials sent to the Imperial territories. The approaches of the administrative departments and of the new territorial officials were thus rarely congruent: each party criticized the other for neglecting the fundamental task of presenting and promoting the strength of the Imperial government.[24] In addition, the attempts of the central officials to impose their wills on the local officials sometimes met with another difficulty. Precisely because they were the central officials, they were not always powerful enough to overrule the resistance of some of the local officials. A resulting inconsistency was evident when officials such as Takezawa Kunimitsu, Umemura Hayami, Ogō Kazutoshi (the governor of Sakai ken from a small Oka han), and Bōjō Toshiakira (the governor of Yamagata ken from the ranks of the nobility) were summarily dismissed for "abusing" the authority of the Imperial government in measures for poor relief,[25] whereas the powerful Matsukata Masayoshi of Satsuma and Maebara Issei of Chōshū were free to pursue such policies.

The need for sound fiscal management also kept the Imperial government from much contact with the populace under the domain governments. Beginning in late 1869, the Imperial government began to seek ways to remove the excessive diversity and complexity of local administrations, the chief source of wastefulness in local expenditures. One measure, noted in Chapter 3, was the removal of remote villages from the feudal fiefs and their consolidation with geographically adjacent domain authorities or, in some cases, to nearby fu and ken governments. However, for the villagers, the result of such reassignment was separation from their familiar feudal authorities and placement under the jurisdiction of new rulers who might or might not have the same policies of taxation and rural administration as before. Even before the effects of the new policy on the revenues of the central treasury became apparent, the new government began to realize the adverse consequences of this measure. Thus the combined Departments of Finance and Home Affairs reported: " ... the people, who had been accustomed to the regulations and practices of the old authorities, refused to accept new rules with any comfort; so much so that their protests, their voices of anger and sorrow are everywhere, and have reached to our department directly."[26]

The *Haihan chiken* of 1871 imposed this apparently unsympathetic government on the local population by bringing it under the governorship of the new regime, whose presence had either been remote from the non-samurai populace or was by now associated with inconsistent policies. Furthermore, this imposition affected every locality. Not surprisingly, when this alien Imperial government was presented to the local populace after the familiar governments of the daimyo disappeared, it evoked only unpleasant images and led to an outcry for a return to the old order. "The *Dajōkan* government is where the foreigners reign," or "[they] sell girls of fifteen to twenty years of age as well as cattle to foreigners" were among the desperate rumors that outraged the peasants in Hiroshima. The people of Hiroshima were quick to demand lenient policies on taxation and the return of their old daimyo, the Asano, following the *Haihan chiken*.[27] In Niigata ken in 1872, the uncertainties brought about by the discontinuity in local administration drove the populace to demand an outright restoration of Tokugawa rule.[28]

After the *Haihan chiken*, the expansion of the central governing authority was viewed suspiciously by a local population to whom the Restoration and the emergence of the new regime had been remote at best. Within the Imperial government, which had survived the duality of being less than a central government at home while representing the nation abroad, the fear of a breakdown of its coalition basis could no longer exert even a minimal restraint against the competitive politics of its members. Thus, the *Haihan chiken* ended the coalition basis of the new central government, thereby removing at least one factor that had kept it from achieving a degree of autonomy. Both internally and externally, however, new sources of polarization emerged soon after.

# 5

# Politics of Integration and Local Order

BEFORE THE *Haihan chiken*, the stability of the local order was intimately related to feudal revenues. The domain authorities assigned differing tax rates in each domain, determined by combining an estimate of annual harvest with several other factors, such as the financial needs of the daimyo household and the number of his vassals whose stipends were appropriated from the same feudal revenue of the domain. Surtaxes varied, too, again depending on what the feudal authorities deemed taxable, primarily crops, other than rice. Social relationships within villages, within each domain, and between the villages and the domain's castle town, were determined by the manner in which the limited variety of resources was produced, allocated, and consumed; social norms and customs served to preserve and refine the existing class distinctions based upon the division of labor.[1]

Local variations in the predominantly agrarian order were determined mainly by two factors: the geophysical characteristics of the land, largely untouched by technological innovations, and the sociopolitical devices designed by the feudal authorities to maximize the use of such land. In the absence of *systematic* interlocal and interclass mobility and diffusion, instability in the social, political, and economic relations of each locality tended to be contained, providing the key to the security of most of the Tokugawa era.

But the rural unrest that had intensified since the closing decades of the eighteenth century did begin to shake the Tokugawa order. In addition, increasing upward mobility among rich merchants and farmers out of their prescribed social strata was signaling the erosion of social order before the Restoration. But it was the *Haihan chiken* that directly challenged the foundation of the old order by allowing communication between localities and social strata. For example, many villages, previously insulated from one another, were now incorporated into the same fu or ken jurisdiction, increasing the likelihood that a village with a tax burden as high as 80 percent of its agricultural produce would be placed next to another with a tax rate only half as high.[2] Furthermore, rural administration was complicated by the incorporation into one local governorship of many villages previously under different feudal authorities.[3] Indifference to each other at best and hostility at worst now prevailed among the newly incorporated villagers.

The *Haihan chiken* gave rise to another factor contributing to local political instability: the impoverished samurai in the new localities under fu and ken. The issue was no longer simply the excess of samurai officials—"the greatest curse for ages"[4]—that had formerly been contained within each feudal domain. As shrewdly perceived by Kido Kōin, the samurai impoverishment was part of a chain of problems. With the abolition of the domains, samurai first faced unemployment because the former daimyo households had far fewer employment opportunities to offer their former vassals. These newly unemployed samurai also faced decreasing employment opportunities in the society at large. In commerce, many of the castle towns were reduced in significance, following the mergers of the 270 domains-turned-ken; in agriculture, only a limited amount of land was left to be further developed by these "newcomers." And even if the capacities of the job markets could have met some of these extra demands, the proud samurai themselves had difficulty adapting to their new vocations,[5] and many of them simply relied on the samurai pensions that the central government decided to provide at the time of the *Haihan chiken* in lieu of feudal stipends. Finally, these samurai pensions made the issue of rehabilitating the displaced samurai a national one, as the pension program now claimed more than 30 percent of the central revenue and forced the new government to devise ways in which its sources of income could be multiplied and stabilized.

The displacement of the old institutions and structures of rule thus gave rise to feelings of insecurity among the local populace with regard to the new system of local government. The *Haihan chiken* also brought on jealousy caused by the perception of others being better off, which only deepened the hostility of previously distant communities. The displacement also meant the loss of a mechanism for containing conflict locally. At the core of post–*Haikan chiken* politics, then, was the question of how the fu and ken came to be valued by both governors and the governed as legitimate political institutions expressing the authority of the central government and commanding local public support for its policies.

At the same time, the question of public support suggests the uniqueness of post–*Haihan chiken* politics: the fu and ken institutions did not merely replace the old governments of the daimyo; they also exposed the local populace to the previously unfamiliar Imperial government and, more broadly, to the central arena of politics, which had been even less familiar. The degree of acceptance of, and reliance on, the fu-ken institutions by the local populace would thus indicate how well the Restoration government might integrate the people into the expansion of its rule. The acceptance was progressive, considering the suddenness with which the fu-ken institutions came into contact with the local populace. Moreover, this acceptance awoke the people to the fact that the central arena of politics was no longer closed to them, whether in the fu-ken or in national politics.

The important catalyst for the progressive acceptance of the fu-ken institutions by the local populace was the creation of the *ku* system of districts delineated for census-taking purposes by a decree on May 22, 1871, and abolished on July 22, 1878. The positive contributions of these short-lived, intermediate districts to the expansion and consolidation of the new system of rule have never been critically evaluated. Nearly all of the scholarship treats the *ku* system as the manifestation of an authoritarian bent in the Imperial government: it is viewed exclusively as a means of strengthening central control, or as a device to exploit the ruling stratum within the local populace in order to enforce the policies of the central government.[6] As a result, many scholars stress that the local order was disturbed by the intrusion of this system, but none attempts to establish the relationship between the *ku* system and the existing fu and ken institutions, which were equally alien to the local populace. Our purpose in this chapter is to cast the *ku* system in a new light and to examine its broad range of functions at this critical point in post-Restoration politics.

## Problems in Norms and Organizations of the New Local Institutions

The *Haihan chiken* itself did not allow for any consistent local checks and balances on the expansion of the central governing authority. As reported in a government document, the mergers of the 270 domains-turned-ken into 41 fu and ken by the summer of 1876[7] were determined by "short-sighted considerations, and not provisions for particular local conditions, for the people, or for improvements in local administration."[8] Nonetheless, the mergers produced significant long-range effects. The abrupt reductions from the 270 ken to 73 fu and ken by the end of 1871[9] increased the efficiency with which the new governing authority maintained contact with the local populace. Within each new locality, too, the reduced number of local officials, averaging no more than sixty in most cases, allowed the fu-ken authorities to achieve a similar kind of efficiency.[10]

A close analysis suggests that several notions must have been underlying the promotion of this efficiency either directly or indirectly. For example, a need had been felt to overcome the inefficiency of the old feudal governments, as indicated in the Imperial announcement justifying the *Haihan chiken*. The announcement strongly denounced the excess of samurai officials and, no less strongly, the unnecessarily diverse administrative styles perpetuated by the feudal domains.[11] These legacies of the old structure were deemed detrimental to the manner in which the Imperial government hoped to gain both quick acceptance of its existence and conformity to its policies among the local populace. In line with such denunciations of the old structure of rule, there was another concern that the *Haihan chiken* allowed to surface among the central officials—how best to express, symbolically if not actually, the emperor's direct rule of the nation as a whole. What underlay this concern was the desire to make the new central-local relationship universalistic in nature: the central authority would not sanction decisions nor exercise its governing power on the basis of any particular relationship that it held with individual localities. The central authority would not descend, as it were, to the local level simply to resume the kind of particularistic authority relationship that previously had existed between the feudal authorities and their local populations. Indeed, the primary difference between the Imperial governors and the feudal daimyo was that the governors were merely conveyers of laws and regulations originating in the inviolable will of the Imperial government.

The Department of Finance in particular, the central office for the fu and ken, often expressed these overriding considerations. As seen in Chapter 4, the department, through close cooperation with or absorption of the Department of Home Affairs, had expanded its sphere of action for domestic administration. Following the removal of the feudal domains, one obvious change that some of the Finance members entertained was the removal of the intermediate fu-ken institutions as well. In fact, the idea of abolishing the intermediate institutions had been proposed before the *Haihan chiken* by the governor of Wakamatsu ken and by a Finance official reporting on the ken in Kyūshū. Expressing irritation to the Imperial government over the slowness with which the local offices in the Imperial territories received the proper central instructions, the Wakamatsu governor offered as a solution a reduction of local autonomy:

We might as well confine the function of the local office solely to tax administration, like the old bakufu's *daikan* office, and let the

rest of the local administration be handled by men from the center
who would regularly move from one locality to another.[12]

Similar conclusions about the redundant role of the local offices
were reported near the end of 1872 by a Finance Department
official who was sent to the island of Kyūshū in order to examine
the performance of the ken institutions:

> Many ken officials [below the level of Imperial appointees] are local
> natives, badly informed of the current situation, and incapable of
> comprehending central instructions and orders.
>
> Time is being wasted on useless efforts and concerns because of the
> lack of understanding among these officials . . . ; the gist [of the new
> regime] is never understood by these officials; and every adminis-
> trative process is falling apart here.
>
> How shall one, how shall people in coming generations try to explain
> it to themselves when the system does not work and no prospect is
> yet insight for the protection and enlightenment of the local popu-
> lace, in spite of the ken institutions that were established at unlim-
> ited cost as the measures for governing the nation?
>
> It is now imperative to abolish the ken, and divide the country into
> five or six districts wherein the branch offices of the central de-
> partment [of Finance] are to be established, each headed by the cen-
> tral officials [of medium-high ranks, *daijō* or *shōjō*], so that the
> foundation for improving the local government system and reducing
> its cost can be laid.[13]

This growing opinion by those in the localities in favor of direct
rule prompted some of the central officials to entertain the extreme idea of uprooting the new intermediate institutions of fu
and ken. Yet there still remained methods, much less disruptive
than a total uprooting, by which the new center and the new
localities could be well integrated. One of them was simply to
change the names of the fu and ken, a method deemed particularly
effective in fostering the sense of discontinuity. This method also
had an ulterior motive of inflicting a sort of punishment on regions formerly sympathetic to the Tokugawa bakufu, thereby im-
pressing them with the presence of the new central government.

Accordingly, Sendai ken (the former Sendai han) was changed to Miyagi ken, and Morioka (the former Morioka han) to Iwate, so as to encourage the "populace to rise above the old provincial orientations."[14] But the most systematic and concrete method was to expand the boundary of the central governing authority by integrating the fu and ken offices into the overall governmental organization. The result of this expansion of central power was the creation of a concentric system whose center was the emperor. The distance of all government officials from that center indicated both their degree of integration into the government hierarchy and their administrative level within it.

The first of the means of defining these concentric circles was the System of Ranks for the Fu-Ken Officials (*Fu-Ken kansei*, December 10, 1871).[15] The system placed the local officials on a scale of grades, called the *tō*, encompassing all officials in the government. The governors' posts were the third and fourth grades in the fu and the fourth and fifth grades in the ken, roughly corresponding to the position of section chief in the central organization. Another means was the institution of Court ranking, which enjoyed renewed prestige in the wake of Restoration euphoria. The governors were usually awarded lower-fourth (*juno-shi'i*), which made them the equivalents of "colonel or lieutenant colonel in the Army ranking order."[16] In addition to these rankings, the types of appointment helped to define the place of the government officials in the concentric circles while offering still another linkage between the emperor's government and the prefectures. These were the *chokunin* (appointees chosen by the emperor), the *sōnin* (appointees confirmed by the emperor), and the *han'nin* (appointees chosen locally). The governors of a few exceptional localities with major ports were *chokunin* appointees, while all other governors were invariably *sōnin* appointees.

The most peripheral men in this system of expansion were officials of *han'nin*, or entirely local, appointment, mostly samurai recruited locally for clerical functions. However, notwithstanding their remoteness from the source of power, these petty officials still operated within the system and in fact constituted the boundary between those "inside" and those "outside." Be-

tween them and the local people in general lay the distinction
that the dominant euphemism of that era expressed, that of the
*kan* and the *min*—the governors and the governed. Or, to put it
another way, the more directly tied to local origins an official
position was, the less prestige and power it carried, despite the
oft-voiced desire to link the new central government as closely
as possible with the localities.

In conjunction with the incorporation of fu-ken offices at the
middle level (*sōnin*) into the government hierarchy was the division of governmental responsibility by which the fu-ken offices
were clearly placed under the central departments. The Ken Government Ordinance (*Kenji jōrei*, January 7, 1872)[17] defined the
extensive scope of practical supervision to be undertaken by the
governors and the fu-ken offices, extending from the "protection
and enlightenment of the populace within their jurisdiction" and
the "observance and enforcement of ordinances, decrees, and regulations" to the "collection of taxes." However, when it came to
initiating and devising policies that were likely to touch upon the
local financial resources or public order, the fu-ken offices were
required to consult with the relevant departments of the central
government. The fu-ken offices were thus administrative arms of
the central government extended into the localities.

Thus the integration of the prefectural offices into the overall
government organization was thorough, satisfying the need to
project the emperor's direct rule to a limited degree. One result of
this integration was the emergence of a clear boundary between
the governors and the governed. On the inside of this boundary,
among those fu-ken officials who found themselves benefiting
from their positions, there was even a tendency to emphasize the
boundary itself. These officials were usually from places outside
the localities in which they served and were continually transferred from one locality to another, or in and out of the central offices. Accordingly, they looked to the hierarchy of the overall
government organization not so much for confirmation of their
current status as for opportunities for upward mobility. As a result,
they tended to deemphasize the lower end of their center-local role
to facilitate their own advancement; the more strongly they felt
about being on the inside of the boundary, the more unapproacha-

ble they made the crossing of the boundary to those on the outside. This orientation was reflected in their perception of the local populace, whom they saw as only the products of the old order and old customs, the "illiterate," "stubborn," and "uncivilized" who refused to accept the benevolent rule of the new regime.[18]

At the same time, however, there was constant pressure to make the overall government organization open and responsive to those outside the boundary. These pressures in fact served to counter the tendency toward a more direct rule. First, there were those officials who hovered near and yet did not quite cross the boundary. For example, Kōno Hironaka, a major figure in movements for popular political participation in the 1880s, developed a deep-rooted aversion to that *kan-min* distinction dramatizing the boundary. Half-samurai and half-farmer in social origin, with a fairly distinguished record of Restoration activities in his own Miharu han, Kōno was appointed by Fukushima ken authorities following the *Haihan chiken* to a position of rural administrator that did not quite fit the category of *kan*, or one of the "governors." Instead, he found himself at best in the circle farthest from the center, which promoted his belief that the expansion of the central governing authority had not fulfilled the Restoration's promise of responsiveness to the people. Consequently, he became involved in the constitutional movement for popular representation, which challenged the rigid boundary separating the governors and the governed.[19]

There were also those within the boundary who tended to see their prefectures as their own territories to govern in accordance with both the traditional belief in a benevolent ruler and the newer constitutional experiment in local autonomy.[20] If they increased their insistence upon autonomy, it was not to contest the authority of the central government but rather to assert their conviction that they were the embodiment of the emperor's government. As will soon be seen, these governors themselves instituted a framework for a limited popular political participation in their own jurisdictions, and it, too, challenged the boundary between the government hierarchy and the populace.

In addition, there was a more general problem affecting the assimilation of the emperor's rule by the populace: the relationship between the traditional communities of cooperative life at village and township levels on the one hand and the fu and ken institutions on the other. Any immediate and further governmental integration would have imposed tremendous readjustments on all involved, as the *Haihan chiken* had simply dislocated the lower levels without any provision for linking them to the fu-ken. Some of these traditional communities such as those in Kyoto, Osaka, and Tokyo, had already felt the effects of the earlier change in the central government. After the Restoration, these cities were reorganized into compounds of various sizes, the smallest of which was often a group of a few households. The purposes of such reorganization varied from streamlining neighborhood control and administration to removing the traditional community elders in the hope of quickly introducing the new central governing authority among the people. However, the reorganization served more to impress upon the community members the passing of the bakufu, with its long-established administrative control, than to prepare them for the coming of the new central-local relationship. Thus further integration of the governmental process could risk alienating these traditional but displaced community leaders, which would certainly have been detrimental to the need to project the emperor's direct rule.

In other words, the integration of the prefectural offices into the overall governmental hierarchy did not proceed unchecked. First, there was the positive and passive resistance of men within the hierarchy and at its boundary to be considered, a resistance that collectively countered the orientation of some in the central government toward more direct rule. Furthermore, the absence of any provision for a systematic link between the governmental hierarchy and the traditional communities made the former appear even more alien in the eyes of the latter. The more integrated the overall governmental organization became, the more likely it was to be distant from the populace, and the fu-ken institutions, as part of that organization, were less likely to be assimilated by the local populace.

## Ku: *The Agent of Assimilation*

In contrast to the structure of the fu-ken institutions in which the roles were rigidly defined, the system of community administration at village and township levels before the *Haihan chiken* had been no more than a cluster of loosely defined functions customarily performed by community leaders. The distinctions among these functions had remained ambiguous even though their performance had ritual precision. Village heads and town elders now continued to oversee a wide range of community affairs such as fulfillment of the collective responsibility of tax payment, supervision of community rituals such as seasonal festivals, maintenance of public order, and enforcement of directives and regulations handed down from the fu-ken authorities. It was at this village and township level that the positive link between the local populace and the new institutions of fu and ken was to emerge. By mobilizing and employing the community leaders in their traditional roles, the fu-ken authorities were able to promote the acceptance of the new politics by the local populace.

A few months before the *Haihan chiken*, a decree by the Imperial government announced the establishment of the Household Residence Registry (the *koseki*, issued to the fu, ken, and han governments on May 22, 1871, with a provision that the survey for the registry commence a year later). The underlying motivation for this decree was a belief that accurate information about every household in the country could improve the "foundation for promoting the people's welfare and enlightenment." The decree began with a preface addressing the problems created by the lack of communication among too individualized localities:

> Since ancient times, the governing of our people has differed from one locality to another. Even the slightest distance between them had rendered the customs therein peculiar to each.... None have shared any common orientations. Accordingly, the various practices of residence registration have fallen victim to bewildering confusion....[21]

In order to do away with these local peculiarities and enrich the government's knowledge of the population by way of a national census,[22] the decree proposed new districts, called *ku*, that were in effect compounds of several villages and townships brought together for administrative efficiency and convenience in completing the census. Much leeway was given to the individual local authorities as to how to draw a boundary for a *ku*.

In this, the central government did not provide any exact guidelines. It even granted that the already existing village or township could be used for preparation of the registry under certain circumstances.

Likewise, there was flexibility in defining the *ku* officials who assisted the fu-ken authorities in performing the census-taking responsibilities. The *ku* officials, variously called *kuchō, fuku-kuchō, kochō,* and *fuku-kochō* (the first two meaning "heads" and "deputies" of "districts," and the second two meaning "heads" and "deputies" of groups of "households"), were to be appointed by the fu-ken governors, sometimes from the villages and townships within the designated *ku,* sometimes from elsewhere in the same fu or ken, or in some cases even from outside. But the decree was ambiguous in its ruling that the number of *ku* officials in one *ku* could vary and that community elders such as *shōya, myōshu* and *furegashira* could perform the responsibility of the *ku* officials as well.[23] It was, in fact, the old community leaders who quickly provided the pool for the *ku* officials.[24]

The census originally proposed by the decree was completed without adding too much extra responsibility in community administration for the traditional leaders. Yet, the *ku* and *ku* officials quickly underwent significant changes that kept them from remaining merely a well-defined and restricted, though purposeful, administrative unit. More functions began to be added to the *ku,* more responsibilities were demanded of the *ku* officials on an irregular basis by both the governors and the governed, and the *ku* and *ku* officials became something of an ad hoc action unit. More often than not, they ended by fulfilling the functions of the old community leaders. The post-*Haihan chiken* influx of reforms accelerated this expansion of the functions of the *ku* officials and the transformation in the traditional mode of community administration. The interaction between the fu-ken authorities and the traditional community leaders, set in motion by the new district system, served as the catalyst for the emergence of a new authority relationship between the governors and the governed.

This mobilization of the traditional community leaders was never written into any coherent, integrated government process.

Originally, their new role was invented to implement one particular policy—the census-taking, explained below—and was not meant to exist beyond the fulfillment of that goal. Neither was the new role intended to induce a major change in community life or in the life of the new localities under fu and ken. Nonetheless, once introduced, the new role of the community leaders generated consequences of major significance. It now brought about an interdependence between the fu-ken authorities and the traditional community leaders, exposed the local populace to new varieties of political and social life, and began to undermine the rigid *kan-min* distinction.

## Policies of Innovation and Local Order

To understand the growth and function of the *ku*, it is helpful to examine the larger framework of the major post-*Haihan chiken* reforms and their effect on the relationship of the populace to the fu-ken officials. In the period following the *Haihan chiken*, numerous reforms introduced innovations in political, social, and economic life. Some of these were intended to facilitate the larger social changes that the *Haihan chiken* produced, such as the decline of samurai as a privileged class. Such change increased mobility between classes, necessitating decrees that permitted marriages across class boundaries (October 7, 1871) and the free selection of vocations (January 27, 1872).[25] These policies, which explicitly overturned institutionalized class distinctions, extended the campaign against the privileged strata including the majority of former samurai and some groups of traditional village notables.[26]

These and other reforms were meant to be adjustive. Yet the populace did not always see themselves as benefiting from these and other new social schemes. Often the reforms were introduced too abruptly, leaving the people little time to assimilate them. Frequently they were greeted with rioting and protests, as exemplified by the violent resistance to the legalization of Christianity, the establishment of a conscript army, the land survey, obligatory vaccination, the introduction of the new Western calendar, and the opening of nationwide government schools. However, in all of this seemingly reactionary resistance, the local populace was always somewhat justified in its suspicion, because reform policies meant something more specific than a broad and abrupt break with the past. Focusing on three of these reforms, E. H. Norman points out the valid reasons behind this mistrust:

> When the new calendar was introduced, consequent indignation could easily arise from the not unjustifiable fear that money-lenders would take advantage of the reform to juggle accounts to their advantage. The feeling against the school system arose possibly because government schools might necessitate an increase in the local tax. Conscription meant less hands to help on the farm.... [27]

Many of the post–*Haihan chiken* reforms combined ideals and concerns touching upon the very foundation of agrarian order. The central reformers had been entertaining these ideals for some time since the Restoration. First, there was the idea of equity of land in tax assessments and payments, a notion that received strong approval among the central reformers who were inspired by the notion of just government under the emperor. Even before the *Haihan chiken*, the Finance Department had attempted to realize the idea by devising a few policies to tax the land owned by shrines, temples, samurai, and townspeople.[28] Second, there was an equally pervasive belief in the commercialization of agriculture to meet the challenge of international trade. Both of these ideas were strengthened by the urgent concern of the central leaders that the central revenue would soon have to overcome two particular problems caused by the *Haihan chiken*: the burden of samurai stipends and pensions transferred from the feudal domains to the central treasury, and the disruption caused by the fluctuation of wholesale rice prices.

If these ideas were to be implemented successfully, they would have to touch upon the heart of the feudalistic order—the land. And, because the economic and social customs and the values of the local populace had been rigidly tied to the agrarian order, the announcement of the new policies needed to be balanced by reinforcement of the local benefits of the changes as well. Thus, one proposal that suggested the lifting of the ban on the export of rice and grains was quick to point out a chain of beneficial results: the commercialization of agriculture, diversification of farm produce as trade commodities, and the overall increase in agricultural productivity and profit.[29] A similar strategy was employed by another proposal intended to remove the feudalistic restrictions on free farming that had prevented "the farm land from being developed to its fullest potential. . . . " These restrictions, originally enforced by the feudal authorities to secure rice income and provisions for military purposes,[30] were deemed the major "hindrance to enriching our nation's wealth" now that "domestic and foreign trade has been progressing day by day, and land as well as maritime transportation facilities are being improved at an unprecedented pace." Therefore, the proposal concluded, "it is imperative to lead the people in the promotion of various enterprises. . . . "[31]

Some of the policies concerning farmland proved to be no more than the legal recognition of existing practices. An example was the removal of the ban on the permanent alienation of land. Kanda Kōhei, one of the central government architects of the Land Tax Reform, had already seen the incongruity between the regulation banning sale and actual practice:

> Since the time of the civil war [in the fifteenth and sixteenth centuries], it has been common practice for the people to purchase and sell land at their own discretion. Farmland is not something that the governing authority [by the emperor's proxy] has given to the people, but something that was acquired by the people through transactions among themselves. . . . Even though the ban on the permanent alienation of land has been upheld since the mid-Tokugawa period, the ban has never been quite effective, for it was never relevant.[32]

The removal of the ban, instead, provided confirmation of the shift from a view of land as valuable in and of itself to one in which its worth was measured increasingly by the "profits" it could return. Post hoc recognition or not, the results were still profound. More attention was now given to the productivity of the land and to measures that could help maximize crop production. Land became a market commodity whose value was deter-

mined by supply and demand; and, even more profitable for the
central government, a tax could be more easily assessed on the
values of land thus appraised.

The drive to modernize the feudalistic system of taxation remained the major reform goal for the central leaders. To this end,
ideas for a land tax and the commercialization of agriculture were
integrated into a set of proposals prepared by the Finance Department for nationwide reform of the taxation system.[33] The
equity principle in tax-payment responsibility was promoted
partly to lessen the burden of the peasants, who had been the sole
taxpayers, and partly to undo local variations in tax rates. Included
was the determination of land values by the market mechanism,
which the central reformers found expedient for three reasons.
First, the tax estimation could take into account the real productivity of different pieces of land, which was likely to vary with
qualities of soil. Second, it could identify landowners from among
the usual collective owners of land through certificates of ownership (the *chiken*) issued upon transactions of land. These certificates were first issued at the time of a transaction and later to
all landowners generally, regardless of whether or not there were
actual transactions at the time.[34] The third reason reflected a
particular fear on the part of the central reformers. The government needed ways to avoid the troublesome land surveys used
for tax estimation that had been the signal, to many peasants, of
the feudal authorities' maneuvering for tax increases and were
therefore likely to be greeted by the peasants' "bamboo spears."[35]

On the basis of these preliminary developments, the Land Tax
Reform (the *Chiso kaisei*, 1873–1881) was announced. The Reform was intended to advance each of its underlying ideas further,
stating them in more concrete terms. These included: (1) the
application of a standardized and fixed tax rate of 3 percent of the
land value to extend the equity principle across the localities; (2)
the change in tax estimates from those based upon annual crop
yield to those based upon land value, which would enable the
central revenue to count on a steady income regardless of good
or bad harvest years; (3) tax payment in cash, instead of the traditional payment in kind, which would make the central revenue
less susceptible to natural disasters or to fluctuations in the price

of rice and at the same time would provide the farmers with an incentive for the commercialization of agriculture;[36] and (4) the transfer of the responsibility for tax payment from villages to individuals, which would add important momentum to the rise of private landownership.[37] As discussed elsewhere in great detail,[38] the consequences of the Reform were numerous and far-reaching. Among the positive ones were the stabilization of revenue to the central treasury and higher agricultural productivity. Negative consequences also resulted from the systematic commercialization of agriculture promoted by the Reform: such commercialization generated a simultaneous increase in large landowners and tenant farmers, and the transformation of rice into a market commodity allowed rich farmers and large landowners to become even richer.

The implementation of this Reform also created diverse kinds of difficulties for the central government, the local populace, and many fu-ken officials who carried out this time-consuming task in the prefectures. There were practical problems of how to identify owners in places where different kinds of collective landownership had been widespread, where there were only unreliable, old records of transactions involving land, and where tenant farmers had been engaged in production for generations.[39] Furthermore, central reformers needed to maintain a delicate balance between two conflicting requirements: retaining effective control of the fu-ken officials so as to minimize misinterpretation of the intent of the Reform; and allowing a degree of autonomy for the fu-ken offices in order for them to cope with the local conditions upon which successful implementation of the Reform might hinge.[40] Finally, for the local populace, the Reform was doubly draining. It was they who bore nearly 80 percent of the cost of implementing the Reform,[41] a measure that also epitomized to them the disruptions of all the post–*Haihan chiken* reforms. The Land Tax Reform was thus often seen by them as a systematic intrusion into local affairs by the central governing authority; this only deepened their animosity to its administrative arms, the fu-ken offices.

In light of these consequences of reform, the evolution of the *ku* system and its resulting political significance comes into

sharper focus. The *ku* and its officials did not escape the post–
*Haihan chiken* reforms, including the Land Tax Reform, either.
First conceived as convenient tools for completing the Household
Residence Registry, the *ku* officials had begun to absorb more
responsibilities over a short period of time. In so doing, they
transformed themselves into administrators capable of fulfilling
the wider responsibilities of the fu-ken authorities. At the same
time, they also became channels through which the local populace
could express its demands and protests to those very fu-ken
authorities.

From the outset the individual fu-ken authorities had had an
almost completely free hand in designing and creating the *ku*
system, tailored to individual local conditions. When and in what
manner the *ku* were actually instituted varied from one locality
to another. In some cases, the *ku* were created around the time
of the *Haihan chiken*. For example, Kanazawa ken created seven
*ku* in the Kanazawa township following the *Haihan chiken* in
the summer of 1871 but left the rural areas without any until the
spring of 1872.[42] In other cases, it was not until or even after the
first wave of mergers of the 270 domains-turned-ken in late 1871
that any record of the *ku* and their officials appeared in local
government archives.[43] Mergers and separations of the *ku* were
also common practices that the fu-ken authorities repeated during
the short period between 1871 and 1878, the year that the *ku*
system was abolished altogether.

It should also be noted that in the creation of *ku* in various
localities, the roles of the traditional communities at village and
township levels remained untouched; any attempts by the fu-ken
authorities to distinguish the *ku* officials legally and institutionally from the traditional community leaders were largely abortive.
It was thus inevitable that the *de jure* boundary between what
was demanded of the *ku* officials and what the old community
leaders were expected to perform became merely a token. With
the disappearance of the distinction between the *ku* officials and
the traditional community leaders, the latter were able to seize
the momentum for participating in the politics of prefectural
government.

Once the interchangeability of the *ku* officials and the community leaders was established, the fu-ken authorities and the local populace expected the *ku* officials to take on more of the former responsibilities of the traditional leaders in the wider scope of community affairs. A telling example was the case of the School District Ordinance of 1872, issued by the central government. The Ordinance instituted yet another type of district to serve the purpose of administering public schools and seeing that the district directors (*gakku torishimari*) were appointed from village heads and other notables in the area. However, the *ku* quickly took over the financial responsibility for running the schools, and *ku* officials frequently became the district directors. Consequently, the local populace began to expect the *ku* officials to perform what used to be the traditional leaders' responsibilities vis-à-vis the governing authority, even to the extent of channeling appeals and complaints to the fu-ken offices.[44]

This transformation of the well-defined administrative unit of the *ku* and the *ku* officials into an ad hoc action unit depended upon the extensive autonomy that the fu-ken authorities possessed in designing their own modes of internal administration. It also depended upon ambiguity in the central directives as to how to institute the new district system. It is reasonable to assume that the transformation began after the confusions had cleared about the mergers of the 270 domains-turned-ken late in 1871, which reduced substantially the total number of fu-ken. The central government, for its part, did not remain unaware of this subtle transformation. Thus, on April 22, 1872, Inoue Kaoru, then the Vice-Minister of the Finance Department, sought to clarify where the *ku* officials stood in relation to the community leaders by abolishing the traditional titles of village heads and leaders, variously called *shōya*, *myōshu*, or *toshiyori*. But Inoue's attempt left untouched the more important but blurred distinction between the administrative responsibilities of the *ku* officials and those which the community leaders had previously performed.[45]

Many fu-ken officials were puzzled by the meaning of this attempt by the Finance Department: whether the "abolition" of the traditional titles literally meant their replacement by the *ku* officials (i.e., that the *ku* officials were to take over the business of village and township administration), or whether it simply meant that the old titles were no longer to be used but that the traditional leaders' responsibilities remained intact and distinct from the *ku* officials' formal responsibility.[46] In the end, the exigencies of time and convenience dictated the former interpretation. The *ku* officials, originally instituted through a legal decree, thus became identical, in effect, with the traditional community officials—not by formally changing their original legal status, but by default. The abolition of the old titles for the community officials left those called *ku* officials as the only institutional, recognized channel between the local communities and the fu-ken authorities.

The *ku* officials were now performing more than the one specified function of household registration, and they became more than instruments to be employed for administrative convenience by the governing authorities. Well established among the community members and well informed of community affairs, their systematic participation in the implementation of large-scale reforms such as the Land Tax Reform became indispensable to the fu and ken authorities. And, as their importance increased, these community leaders ceased to be merely the obedient recipients of the reforms. Instead, the *ku* officials became active participants in remaking the local order as their collective voices began to grow into a political force that the fu-ken authorities found increasingly difficult to ignore.[47]

One example of the *ku* officials' increasing importance involved the distribution of the landownership certificates (the *chiken*), a task requiring the active engagement of the *ku* officials—the *ku-chō, fuku-kuchō, kochō,* and *fuku-kochō*— in the necessary survey.[48] For the higher fu-ken officials, always apprehensive that the "naive" and "ignorant" farmers would easily be subjected to "irresponsible demagogues," the new political positions of the former community leaders were important tools for gaining the acquiescence of the local populace to new policies such as the distribution of the certificates. It quickly became a common practice for the fu-ken governors to circulate among the local populace variously worded announcements that there were no hidden intentions behind these reform policies on the part of the central government, such as purchasing the land for itself if the estimated land values were low or raising taxes if the values turned out to be high.[49] These public announcements, along with others, were usually addressed to the *ku* officials. In other words, even though none of the articles in the Land Tax Reform referred to the role of the *ku* officials, the governing authorities took it for granted that the *ku* officials (and, by extension, their stratum in the community) would play substantial roles in the implementation of the Reform.[50]

The fu-ken authorities' growing dependence upon the *ku* officials, in turn, furnished important political leverage for these community leaders. Some of the *ku* officials, to be sure, used this newfound power to their own advantage. Sometimes they manipulated the land registration to add to their own land ownership or attempted to increase the estimates of the public expenditures of the communities, which they then appropriated for their own benefit.[51] In both instances, they exploited their legitimization by the fu and ken authorities. However, just as often, the interests of the *ku* officials and of the communities were identical in their efforts to oppose the fu-ken authorities, as occurred in their pressure to lower the 3 percent tax rate, which they eventually reduced to 2.5 percent. Therefore, instead of resigning themselves to mere compliance with the higher fu-ken authorities, the *ku* officials joined and often even organized protests opposing the ways in which the land values were estimated and determined, or the manner in which the costs for the implementation of the Reform were imposed upon the communities.

Thus, as valuable as the *ku* officials could be for the fu-ken authorities in solidifying the relationship with the populace, they also could be a serious hindrance to the pace at which the fu-ken officials wished, for their own sakes, to advance the reform. At times, the inability of the fu-ken officials to foresee and preempt the communities' resistance or to halt their protests effectively resulted in the replacement of the fu-ken governors by the central government.[52] To avoid such a fate, the higher fu-ken authorities often took measures against the *ku* officials in order to protect themselves. In 1876 the Wakayama ken authority arrested a dozen *ku* officials as "ringleaders of misconduct." The Aichi ken authorities forced a *kuchō* to resign and appointed in his place one of the ken governor's own relatives.[53] These events were responses to but also causes of the mounting rural unrest of 1876 and 1877.[54]

By that time, the newly established *ku* officials had taken on a dual role in local politics. When their actions were deemed unjust and when they were held to be conspiring with the fu-ken authorities against the communities' interests, they became the targets of the peasants and farmers. At the same time, when they were viewed as manipulating the community members into protests, they were denounced by the fu-ken authorities. The emergence of this group of individuals, then, meant something quite profound. Their role as both victims and beneficiaries, implementers and recipients, of the new policies was quickly obliterating the line between the governors (*kan*) and the governed (*min*).

## The Changing Authority Relationship

The growth in importance and scope of the *ku* officials' activities inevitably caused subtle changes in their political recognition and status. Despite having witnessed substantial increases in their importance, the *ku* officials were still categorized in 1873 as *ippan jin'min*, or "ordinary commoners," as opposed to those in the government. Such a designation was not really surprising, since the *ku* officials' only distinction was the status given to them initially to carry out the Household Residence Registry Act and by the abolition of the traditional titles for the community leaders. But the visibility of the *ku* officials in government was growing. A *Dajōkan* notification toward the close of 1873 gave the *ku* officials higher places in the order of recognition on public occasions than both commoners and former samurai.[55] Later, still another *Dajōkan* notification, acknowledging the fu-ken officials' own awareness of the *ku* officials' importance, enlisted them on the side of *kan*: the *ku* officials were called "semi-government officials" (*kan ni junzuru*).[56]

Furthermore, significant recognition of the *ku* officials was expressed through a change in the character of the *ku* itself. The *Kaku-ku-chō-son kinkoku kōshaku kyōyūbutsu toriatsukai do-*

*boku kisoku* (Regulations on Borrowing Money and Grains for Public Purposes, Usages, and Appropriation of Public Properties and Public Construction by *Ku*, Townships and Villages) of October 17, 1876,[57] no longer treated the *ku* simply as an instrument for a particular purpose. Recognizing the emerging cases in which the *ku* officials also managed the public properties of the traditional communities in villages and townships, the Regulations gave the *ku* the attributes of corporate communities. According to the Regulations: "When a *ku* borrows money or grain, and sells or purchases lands and buildings for its public purposes, it is required that the seals of the *ku* officials and of 60 percent or more of the total of each pair of representatives from each township and village within the said *ku* be obtained." In other words, the *ku* were no longer mere compounds of villages and townships without their own identity. A *ku* now had its own constituent members (even though some overlapped with those of existing villages and townships), its own properties, and its own right to manage them.

These signs of the changing recognition of the *ku* and its officials by the new government reflected an even more fundamental change in the boundary between those in the government and those outside of it. For the first time, the commoners realized that the Restoration government could be made accountable to them through the actions of men in the same category as themselves. For their part, the fu-ken officials recognized that the boundary between the rulers and the ruled could best be maintained by having the responsibilities of rule shared, to a degree, with those formerly outside the political arena. This change in attitude was most clearly manifested in the measures the fu-ken officials began to provide for the *collective* participation of the *ku* officials in the fu-ken governance.

In some localities, these measures amounted to no more than the creation of offices to which the *ku* officials were summoned by the fu-ken officials to receive the latter's instructions, though the *ku* officials hoped that the fu-ken authorities would thus make themselves receptive to demands by the community members.[58] In others, however, the measures actually instituted assemblies of *ku* officials elected by or selected from among the local populace. The initiative in these cases rested with the individual fu-ken governors, who found in their measures something consonant with the symbolic reference to an open society expressed in the Oath of 1868. Thus, Kanda Kōhei, the governor of Hyōgo ken, prefaced the establishment of elected assemblies in his villages, townships, *ku*, and ken with a reference to the first clause of the Oath which called for public discussion through the deliberative assemblies in making decisions.[59]

A more interesting development was the trend toward popular representation in the Oda ken (which was later amalgamated into the Okayama ken). Here, in 1874, the collective pressure of the *ku* officials prompted the governor to pledge to open assemblies of *ku* officials by popular election both at the *ku* and fu-ken levels. The conditions preceding this pledge were typical of the people's rising political awareness and their search for meaningful methods of expressing this awareness. Beginning in 1872 Oda ken first saw a brief period of occasional experimentation with a form of popular representation in the assemblies of the *ku* and the fu-ken officials. This experimentation was still dictated by convenience in policy implementation and was thus ad hoc in its nature. Next, the "wisdom" of the elected assemblies established by Kanda Kōhei inspired the local Oda populace to seek popular representation on a more regular basis. Finally, the coming of the Prefectural Governors' Conference (1875), in which the Oda ken governor was to participate as the "representative" of the Oda ken residents, offered an opening for their collective pressure.[60]

The Prefectural Governors' Conference (the *Chihōkan kaigi*) of June 20 through July 17, 1875, itself spotlighted the differing views on popular representation, while acknowledging the trend through its very debate on the subject. To be sure, the responses to popular pressure for political participation and popular representation varied from one locality to another, since it had been primarily the political predispositions of the fu-ken governors that made possible a greater or lesser acquiescence in popular participation. However, by the time of the Prefectural Governors' Conference, the trend toward positive responses to elected assemblies had already become irreversible. Seven ken had already instituted assemblies of elected members, and twenty-three more had opened assemblies with mixed memberships, that is, a combination of members appointed by the fu-ken governors and members returned by popular election.[61] In addition, important momentum was added to the trend by the Conference itself. Even though it ended by leaving the matter of establishing local assemblies by popular election, the *minkai*, up to the judgment of the individual governors, it had at least identified this possibility as one of the key issues for the conferees. In so doing, it both highlighted the already existing trend and rescued it from remaining purely a matter for individual governors.

At the center of the debate during the Conference was the question of who should and could govern. The majority of the governors predictably questioned the level of "enlightenment" and the political immaturity of the populace at large, which had led some of them to believe that the participation of the people in politics would only be harmful. As one Conference participant put it:

> The opening of elected assemblies to the populace, if it could be assured of proper members, might prove beneficial. If not, the assemblies are simply an imitation of civilization and only do harm to government. To be sure, now is the time to undo the evils and wrongs of the past three hundred years at one stroke, and it is only natural that any attempts at improvement are likely to bring about some mistakes. Yet, it must be remembered that a blind insistence on logical reasoning alone produces vice, not the virtues promised by reason....After all, the majority of the Japanese are still old Japanese.[62]

If still naive, this "majority of the Japanese" might only prove susceptible to incitement by "frivolous men" enticing them with the idea of opening the *minkai* throughout Japan. As another participant pointed out:

> If we openly allow popular assemblies now, the people will overstep the limits [set for the assemblies] and engage in discussion that would touch even upon the conduct of the great [Imperial] government. Supposing, then, a measure is taken to restrain them, the people will

call this oppressive and despotic. Before long, ... the assemblies will turn into an arena for useless political debate.[63]

One governor likened popular elections and participation to a rudimentary "schooling" for infants not yet capable of true learning. Still another flatly declared that, as far as he could see, "not even one percent of our 30,000,000 people are capable of reasonable thinking."[64]

The issue that polarized the governors at the Conference, however, was not popular participation itself. The disagreement among them came, rather, from their perception of who among the local populace were more or less capable of representation and of sharing the responsibility of local governance. In other words, they all foresaw the eventuality of gradually increasing popular participation. Furthermore, they had all already realized that those gradual steps began in the stratum that produced the *ku* officials. To be sure, some viewed this stratum among the "governed" in negative terms: only the *kuchō* and *kochō* might be literate and able to represent the people. Others saw the *ku* officials more in terms of potentials: "It is for the sake of enlightening the populace that the assemblies should start with the *ku* officials."[65] Finally, some saw no point of making any distinction among the local populace. Thus, one governor who supported assemblies by popular election first emphasized the "educational" effect of the assemblies and then went on to conclude: "Would you insist that the *kuchō* and *kochō* are necessarily better prepared simply because they are appointed by you?"[66]

In short, the new political climate among the fu-ken officials was tolerant of certain measures of popular political participation as a matter of principle. Informing their tolerance of such measures was their belief in the capacity of a limited portion of the populace to engage in the decision-making of a central or local government, rather than a firm belief in the political right of every citizen to help make the decisions that would affect his welfare. Limited as it was, this political recognition of the *ku* officials was indeed a paradigmatic change in a constitutional sense. Politics was no longer the exclusive preserve of a specific category of men—*kan*, the governors—or a particular kind of phenomenon attendant only upon government action.

The responses to this debate varied. First of all, some of the immediate observers from a dozen localities at the Conference were concerned primarily with the increased influence of the *ku* officials in the ongoing Land Tax Reform.[67] Included in this group were those who were aware not only of the elevated status of the *ku* officials among the local populace, but also of the preliminary constitutional steps that should logically follow such an elevation. Thus, upon returning home after the Conference, Kōno Hironaka drew up a personal draft of ken constitutional guidelines to regulate popular political participation in his Fukushima ken politics.[68]

Second, there was a wider, if less directly involved, audience that had begun its own political movement toward popular participation a year and a half earlier in the national debate over the establishment of a popularly elected national assembly. The political arena for that debate had been unmistakably national, since it had originated in the controversy over the military expedition to Korea late in 1873, an issue that divided the central government leaders. Yet the debate at this later Conference of the governors was still meaningful for that audience. On the one hand, the Conference raised much the same issue of popular participation within the specific context of fu-ken politics, an indication that the earlier national debate was not solely limited to the power struggle within the central government and that the issue had wider and more diverse support. In fact, the Conference discussion itself was dictated by the political semantics that the national debate a year and half earlier had developed. Thus, the notion of the people's rights activists—the *minkenka*, which the earlier national debate had helped popularize, or the "frivolous men" of "useless political debate" as some participants of the Governors' Conference called them—became a collective term encompassing all activists seeking a responsive government. It was applied to activists within the prefectural context, to those from a selected social stratum among the commoners, and even to former Restoration leaders with prominent careers in the Imperial government.

Finally, some in the central government itself, such as Kido Kōin and Ōkubo Toshimichi, were equally sensitive to the emerging trend of popular participation. Having chaired the Governors'

Conference, Kido was able to fashion his own way of joining the rising tide of popular political participation. Although he had earlier encouraged the appointment of outsiders to local positions, he now changed his opinion:

> Recently, the central government has extracted money and stores of grain from all over Japan, . . . yet allowed each prefecture no access to them. . . . If the central government is to avoid [adverse consequences], then, nothing is as desirable as the separation of the central and prefectural budgets, the division of the governing power among them, and the local recruitment and promotion of men for the prefectural offices.

Now was the time to correct the problems of the earlier measures, Kido argued, such as the lack of communication between the governors and the governed; now was the time for local affairs to be returned to the hands of the local populace.[69] However, Kido's sympathy for popular participation differed in a very subtle way from that of the others; what appeared to be his defense of popular political participation on the basis of local expertise actually had another constitutional theme behind it: the decentralization of government. This notion did not necessarily accord with the predominant campaign for political participation led by many *min-ken* activists, which was not incompatible with the stronger authority of the Imperial government itself, as will be seen below.

In contrast to Kido, Ōkubo Toshimichi was as sensitive to the elements that had formed this dominant political climate as he was perceptive to how they had gathered momentum. In a proposal dated March 11, 1878, which shortly became the framework for a new local government abolishing the *ku* altogether,[70] Ōkubo wrote:

> From time to time there have been difficulties in local government. Currently, in some of the fu-ken, the local orders are in turmoil due to violent unrest. In point of fact, this is due not necessarily to mismanagement by the fu-ken authorities . . . , but [more to the tendency on the part of the local populace] to attribute every misconduct that the petty officials, that is, the *ku* officials, have committed, to

the central authority.... If we provide a measure for opening local popular assemblies, then all the responsibility for the mismanagement, wrongdoing, and mistakes as well as merits and benefits [of the prefectural administration] shall inevitably rest with the assemblies and the local populace; and even the slightest discontent with the central government will be minimized.... Thus, the useless and harmful event which they call the *minken*, I believe, will cease to exist.[71]

Ōkubo saw in the constitutional measures for political participation the chance both to put the abstract notion of the Oath into practice and to moderate the otherwise destabilizing pressure of the unrepresented upon the governing authority. His hostility toward the *minken* notwithstanding, Ōkubo thus did not stray too far from the constitutional practitioners of the day. In not resisting what seemed the irreversible trend toward more political participation, Ōkubo again exhibited his usual shrewd calculation of political risks.

Limited political recognition of the local populace would grow beyond the interdependence between the fu-ken authorities and the local community leaders in the proscribed field of prefectural administration. Such a recognition now entailed the "enfranchisement" of the stratum that had been at best peripheral to Restoration politics. This being an irreversible development, many of those who had been central to Restoration politics would have to allow for it in their actions. The development would affect even the central arena of national politics that they had monopolized, and inevitably would draw them into unfamiliar political terrain where actions were no longer informed solely by the actors' conviction of their being the emperor's proxies.

The catalyst for this acceptance of wider political participation, however, did not come from a uniform response among the central leaders to the government's liberation from its coalition basis of the feudal domains. It came from the different reactions to the painful fact that the central authority had turned out to be barely capable of commanding its own members, the self-styled proxies of the emperor, when it was freed from its dual status. The following chapter examines the evolution of post–*Haihan chiken* politics within the central government that contributed to the divisive competition among its key members, finally "disenfranchising" some of the very Restoration leaders who had been central to Restoration politics.

# 6

# The End of the
# Restoration Coalition

THE post–*Haihan chiken* reform policies required difficult adjustments on the part of many groups in Japanese society. The adjustments were in part to the fundamental transformation of the political order and in part to their own unfulfilled expectations. In the case of the samurai, their impoverishment became more than a simple economic issue, as they were further threatened with social displacement by the establishment of a conscript army in 1872, which ended their monopoly of arms. For the farmers, their hopes for the relaxation of taxes, for relief from feudalistic social restrictions, and for the betterment of rural life were dashed by the continued confusion in rural administration and the time-consuming Land Tax Reform. The Court nobles, too, in some cases, resented their reduction to utter political insignificance just when they had seemed to gain power by being adjacent to the throne.

Consequently, the difficult tasks of adjustment gave rise to the conviction that something else was also fundamentally wrong, and that just as unacceptable as the policies of westernizing and defeudalizing Japan was the ruthlessness of a small group of men in the Imperial government acting in the name of the emperor. Even before the *Haihan chiken*, the disgruntled had detected the

coming of these dissatisfactions and had resorted to armed revolts
to check them. One of these attempts, initiated by Otagi Michiakira in the spring of 1871, had enlisted men from among
Otagi's fellow Court nobles, as well as among samurai from Kyūshū, Shikoku, and the regions facing the Sea of Japan. Their manifesto exemplifies the language and ideas of the continuing post–
*Haihan chiken* protests and resistance:

> After the accomplishment of the Restoration, while the Imperial
> person should have grasped political power, instead, *officials who
> were not true officials ruled separate from the palace;* the new gov-
> ernment was tyrannous; peasant revolts sprang up here and there.
> Again, after the capital had been moved to Tokyo, although some
> officials remained in Kyoto, both the upper and lower classes, priests
> and laity, fell into impoverishment. The masses of people are in
> acute distress from the rise in the price of commodities which comes
> from foreign trade. Before the present time it was the policy to expel
> the barbarians, but since the Restoration, relations with the barbar-
> ians have become closer and *the Imperial mind is disquieted.* It is
> a fact that by *neglecting true administration* we are forfeiting the
> prestige of our country.[1] (Emphasis mine)

Despite its apparently traditionalist overtones, this manifesto
expressed a political message that soon became the dominant
theme of protests against the government, a theme that was also
to be shared by some of the more progressive voices within society. Its message was clear: "officials" had abused Imperial power
and unjustly intruded into the Imperial government. While it
separated and upheld the sanctity of Imperial rule, the manifesto
accused the intermediate actors of violating the tenet of direct
rule and attributed to them all the evils consequent upon their
rapid reform policies. And although the government successfully
quelled Otagi, and other rebels and rioters, their acute sense of
injustice was not silenced. Moreover, this manifesto was not
merely the distant cry of those who were permanently alienated
from the central arena of politics. Soon after the *Haihan chiken,*
in fact, the Restoration leaders themselves began to voice the
same message in their attacks upon each other, although their

protests were less noticeable because they occurred between actors within the same central arena of politics.

## Polarization in the Making

Within two years of the *Haihan chiken* reforms, the Restoration
leaders were deeply divided and involved in an exchange of harsh
criticism and denunciations of each other. At the close of 1873,
nearly half of the top Restoration leaders, who were from some
of the key domains, defected from the central government. The
sudden breakup marked the beginning of the period during which
the central government came under the strain of protests and
criticisms raised by some of its founders themselves.

All the leaders initially expressed their relief at the success of
the *Haihan chiken* and at what appeared to be the first genuine
sign of concord among themselves that it had produced. Kido Kōin
noted in September 1871, following the termination of the feudal
domains: "Unlike before, we are able to embark upon reforms
without much trouble and resistance. Around the time of the
Restoration, everyone was everyone else's adversary.... Now
[that the *Haihan chiken* has been successfully enforced], many
of the past adversaries have become our allies."[2] A few months
later, Saigō Takamori also showed his sense of relief in a letter
to Ōkubo Toshimichi, then abroad on the Iwakura mission:
"Everything seems in order here.... I feel rather lost not having
much to do."[3] This success, however, concealed the seeds of
conflict.

Following the *Haihan chiken*, the central leaders began to op-
erate under a false sense of relief that they were, like the Imperial
government itself, free of the constraints previously imposed by
the existence of the feudal domains. On the one hand, this sense
of relief led them to concentrate on measures to improve Japan.
The formation of the Iwakura mission was one such action, aimed
at improving Japan's unequal status vis-à-vis the West. On the
other hand, this sense of relief also led the leaders to believe that
any disharmony among them could be contained simply by representing the four major Restoration domains in the pivotal po-

sitions within the Imperial government. However, as discussed in Chapter 4, the termination of the domains had already removed a deterrent against divisive competition among the central leaders. With the feudal domains gone and conditions favorable to strengthening and expanding the central government, there was little to deter each of the central leaders from reinforcing his own sense of proximity to the emperor, in whom the governing authority was embodied. Each leader's insistence on being just as close as anyone else to the emperor—and allowing no one to be closer than himself—only weakened the very authority entrusted to the Imperial government *as a whole.*

By the beginning of 1874, Kido Kōin was becoming increasingly frustrated by the sharp criticism of the Imperial government voiced by some of the men who themselves had helped create it. These critics, who had defected from the central government at the close of 1873, began to promote the notion of popular political participation as a means to check the threat of "oligarchical" rule by a few in the government. Kido, however, was not at all convinced of the legitimacy of their criticism:

> The radicals of yesterday have become the advocates of gradual change today as their private concerns dominate; and the advocates of slow progress this morning will be entertaining radical changes tomorrow morning as their personal frustrations prompt them to. ... As it should be assured that our actions will follow upon public decisions, I cannot help condemning the fact that everyone lets his private considerations dictate his position, and justifies his support of it on the basis of personal dissatisfactions. ... [4]

In the critics' allegation of "oligarchical rule," Kido detected the partisan interests of the individuals who themselves had abandoned the government. It was these "private" interests and ambitions, to Kido the antithesis of politics, that were now at the root of protest and opposition to the government.

Kido's condemnation had a specific political context. In a letter of introduction to an associate on behalf of Komuro Shinobu, a young popular rights supporter who had recently returned from England, he wrote: "He himself is a very sincere person. However, having joined with a band of malcontents who had recently defected from the government and having little familiarized himself with the current situation in Japan, his writings have inadvertently contributed to causing the disturbances in society. . . . "[5] Komuro and Furusawa Shigeru, who had also recently visited England, had drafted a petition in English to the Imperial government early in 1874 that was to become the first significant document advocating a national assembly by popular election.[6] The "malcontents" at whose request the draft petition was prepared included Itagaki Taisuke (Tosa), Gotō Shōjiro (Tosa), Soejima Taneomi (Saga), and Etō Shimpei (Saga), all formerly Councilors in the central government. Along with Saigō Takamori, they had defected from the central government in the fall of 1873, when their resolution on a military expedition to Korea was defeated by another group of Councilors, led by Ōkubo Toshimichi and Iwakura Tomomi. The "disturbance" Kido Kōin spoke of was the merging of these powerful "malcontents" with the wider movement for popular political participation, which claimed it would check the government from outside.

Kido's condemnation, however, did not address the major cause of the division itself. In fact, despite the distance that Kido presumed between himself and the critics of the government, there was a fundamental commonality in their political outlooks. Itagaki Taisuke, the chief spokesman for the popular political movement, quickly contradicted Kido's characterization of their venture as motivated by partisan intention or private interest. Instead, he argued that his *Aikoku kōtō* (the "public party of the patriots," established in 1874) took its name from its aim to represent and serve the interests of the "public" and not any partisan group (*shitō*).[7] Thus Kido and Itagaki used the same rhetorical attack in their attempts to discredit each other's claim, that is, by emphasizing the other's failure to be responsive to the "public." What made reconciliation between the two difficult was their underlying disapproval of politics as incessant competition and compromise among conflicting partisan interests. This attitude, perfectly consonant with the ideals of the Restoration that unified Japan under the emperor, ran particularly deep among the Restoration leaders, for it was they who held the strongest belief that their displacement of the bakufu had been motivated and sustained by their commitment to the nation as a whole. But this common intolerance of political conflict now served to intensify the divisive competition among them.

However, the key source of division, which became directly responsible for the first serious breakup of the community of the Restoration leaders, lay elsewhere. The basic agreement on the need for domestic reform and for the improvement of Japan's status in relation to the West still allowed disagreement on questions of the method and timing of these reforms. Yet complex political competition became intensified as these post–*Haihan chiken* debates tested the ability of the central leaders to transcend their differences. The competition was also a serious threat to each leader's belief that he was fully entrusted with the authority of the government, as each instance of conflict was taken as proof that his position and authority were contested by the others. It was in this climate of increasingly unstable interaction that the final disagreement erupted, as will be examined below, over the issue of the military expedition to Korea in 1873. The central government initially made a decision at the insistence of some of its members to launch a military campaign against Korea. Yet in four months, under pressure from the others, it reversed the decision and consequently nearly half of the top leaders resigned.

It should be noted, however, that this dramatic end was not a result of irreconcilable differences about the need for a military expedition to Korea. In fact, the central leaders generally agreed on this method of defusing domestic tension, that is, the exploitation of a real or fictitious external threat. As early as 1868, for example, Kido Kōin had urged the government to launch a similar expedition.[8] Yet in 1873, when Saigō Takamori, the key proponent of the expedition, insisted on the urgent need to rechannel "internal turmoil towards problems outside Japan,"[9] Kido Kōin was his staunchest opponent. Saigō and the other advocates resigned from the government on the heels of the reversal of the government's decision; yet within six months, Ōkubo Toshimichi, another opponent of the expedition, himself authorized a different military campaign. In May 1874, the government, under Ōkubo's leadership, sent a few thousand troops to Formosa on a punitive expedition against the islanders, who had massacred Ryūkyū fishermen.[10]

The major issue of the dispute over the Korean expedition was thus the credibility of the central governing authority among the central leaders themselves. During the post–*Haihan chiken* reforms, the leaders had conceived and sanctioned many policies as they saw fit, as if each one individually embodied the governing authority. The net effect was a central governing authority increasingly paralyzed by disputes and differences among the central leaders themselves. The Korean expedition was the last of a series of cases in which each leader asserted his right to prevail over the others in the name of the emperor. The dispute brought into sharper focus the absence of a governing authority transcending the individual leaders and revealed the government's inability to command the conformity of its own members to the policies they authorized.

The problem of the credibility of the governing authority underlay the basic character of the political competition that quickly dissolved the community of the Restoration leaders. The present argument differs from Tōyama Shigeki's influential proposition that the political conflict in the ensuing years was based on the incompatibility between the "absolutist" government and its critics, who ranged from the defected Councilors to the people's rights activists.[11] The following analysis of political conflict also differs from the commonly held view that the partisan conflict arose from a basic disagreement between two groups of leaders—those who were concerned with the domestic problems of rural unrest, by which category is usually meant the leaders remaining in the government, and those who were concerned with the displaced samurai, by which is usually meant the defected Councilors who supported military action abroad.[12] In contrast, my emphasis on the problematic status of the governing authority calls attention to two developments that reached their climax in the Korean expedition dispute of 1873. These were the continuing divisive politics of the central leaders in the years after the Restoration, and the particular impact of the *Haihan chiken* upon their unstable relationships.

## The Failure of Concord:
### Saigō's Caretaker Government, 1872–1873

On the day the *Haihan chiken* went into effect in 1871, the leading members of the central government resigned from their positions in a ceremonial gesture to dramatize the historical turn toward national unification. This move was followed on the same day by the reappointment of four of them as Councilors to the *Sei-in*, or pivotal Central Chamber of the government: Saigō Takamori (Satsuma), Kido Kōin (Chōshū), Itagaki Taisuke (Tosa), and Ōkuma Shigenobu (Saga). The reappointment was another significant signal of the concord between the Court and the four key domains which continued to be the "pillars of the nation."[13] The predominance of men from these domains, along with some Court nobles, extended throughout the top cabinet positions. Ōkubo Toshimichi of Satsuma headed the Finance Department, with Inoue Kaoru of Chōshū as deputy. Terajima Munenori (Satsuma) was deputy of the Foreign Affairs Department under the Court noble Iwakura Tomomi. The Department of Education had two Saga men, Ōki Takatō and Etō Shimpei, as head and deputy. The departments of Justice, Military Affairs, and Construction had no ministers but were managed by deputies: Sasaki Takayuki of Tosa, Yamagata Aritomo of Chōshū, and Gotō Shōjirō of Tosa respectively. Finally, Sanjō Sanetomi, a Court noble, became prime minister (*Dajōdaijin*). These men were the major forces behind the reorganized central government after the *Haihan chiken*.[14]

The central leaders wished to project their hope for continued harmony in this allocation of key posts, which was primarily a tacit pledge among them to preserve the long-sought concord between the four major domains and the Court. A far more explicit arrangement for the sake of preserving harmony was required at the close of 1871, when Iwakura Tomomi, Ōkubo Toshimichi, Kido Kōin, and others left Japan on the Iwakura mission to the United States and Europe. This time, a formal pledge was exchanged among the leading members to the effect that a "caretaker" government would freeze new appointments and new reform projects during this absence of nearly half of its key leaders. The fear that prompted such a peculiar arrangement was that the government as a whole might otherwise disintegrate, since half of the government would have little say in deciding major reform policies.[15] Predictably, not all were pleased. Itagaki Taisuke, one of the leaders remaining in Tokyo, soon remarked that the very absence of "the members of the mission practically controls our actions mechanically."[16]

This "mechanical control," however, turned out to be the least of Itagaki's and the others' problems, because concord also proved to be of little concern to the remaining members. The maintenance of the four-domain equilibrium was no longer as meaningful as it had been before the *Haihan chiken* to the practical workings of the Restoration government. Instead, the departure of the Iwakura mission now brought to the fore different divisions that circumvented the central leaders' explicit arrangement to prevent the disintegration of the government.

The cause of these new divisions was the fact that the remaining members differed in their perceptions of their true roles in the central government. The formal definition of the roles provided for their posts never produced the harmony they expected. First, only a few of the remaining leaders derived any practical directions for the joint conduct of government from these formal descriptions of their functions. This was especially true for a government facing the pressing need to transform society. Ōkuma Shigenobu, for one, was quick to perceive the discrepancies between their formal role definitions and what they actually did to manage the administration. In his recollection of the caretaker government soon after the departure of the Iwakura mission, he noted:

Those who constituted the core of the central government were Sanjō, Saigō, Itagaki, and I. Of them, Sanjō stayed in the government simply because of his fame and status; in practice, he was merely another number in the government. Saigō and Itagaki had won their distinction at the time of the Restoration. However, they had secluded themselves in their home domains for most of the years since then and rarely involved themselves in central administration. It was only after the *Haihan chiken* that they began participating in the actual administration, and they had done so at the most for only three or four months. Consequently, they hardly knew their way around the conduct of government affairs at the center, not to mention matters concerning the cabinet and its interdepartmental intricacies.[17]

As further shown in his account of cabinet meetings, Ōkuma's consternation derived both from the others' negligence of practical procedures and from their indifference to government altogether:

Saigō and Itagaki, when the lunch break came, would hurriedly retreat to the anteroom [for cabinet members]. Thereafter, they would pass the time engrossing themselves in nonsensical conversation and never return to the cabinet meeting. Rarely would they show up again even when someone was sent to call them back for the meeting. What they invariably conversed about were stories of battle, which always fascinated both men, or of sumo wrestling, or else of hunting and fishing. . . . They would spend the rest of the day simply indulging themselves unconcernedly in such tête-à-tête chatting.[18]

The actual responsibility for administration, Ōkuma claimed, now rested with the lower but more competent government officials.

Nonetheless, to call the brief period between 1871 and 1873 the "Saigō administration" (Saigō *seifu*), as some do,[19] is not exactly a historical distortion. Unlike Itagaki Taisuke, whose recklessness often prevented him from being an inspiring leader, Saigō was expected to be pivotal in preserving the community of the Restoration leaders. His outstanding military record, his perseverance in times of crisis, and his command of a silence that only added to the dignity of his words when he did speak lent weight to his presence in a central government from which Ōkubo Toshimichi, Kido Kōin, and Iwakura Tomomi would be absent for some time. However, a paradox did emerge from the fact that these attributes were predicated only upon the *person* of Saigō Takamori and did not directly derive from his particular role and office as tacitly prescribed by the formation of the caretaker government. Saigō's views on government in theory and in practice contributed to a peculiar isolation from the other members because their effect was more to moralize than to instill practical principles for collective action. Some fragments of his thoughts were recorded by his admirers and attest to this problem:

> If our nation has been wronged, it should be in the character of the government to restore justice to its cause in a righteous manner, even if this risks the life of the nation. Nonetheless, our men [in the Imperial government], whom you think are of extraordinary caliber when discussing financial matters, often come to a standstill when faced with a decision which might require bloodshed and, instead, they indulge themselves in debate on and concede to considerations for short-term gains. Oblivious to the word "fight," they degrade the character of the government. It no longer is a true government but merely a business office.

> No matter how much you elaborate the institutions and methods [of government], they do not work until there are the right men who know how to make use of them.

> The Way resides in the natural order [*tenchi shizen*] and in men practicing it....[20]

Many could believe in these high-flown teachings and political discourses only because of Saigō's personal integrity and actions, not because of the actual conduct of the administration. In other words, the more Saigō sounded like himself in this personal capacity, the more he embodied the kind of *esprit de corps* that many samurai leaders had treasured and yet the less capable he actually became of commanding the others, who found their commitments to action in the operation of the government as a problem-solving organization. He represented the notion of the concord they wished to preserve but could do nothing tangible to help them realize this notion.

In fact, ironically, Saigō's very aloofness from practical administration allowed others to attempt certain reforms. The lower but more competent echelons of the caretaker government engineered a number of post–*Haihan chiken* reform projects, despite the pledge to the Iwakura mission at the close of 1871. One important reason for the rush of such projects was that the central treasury continued to be depleted: Japan's unequal treaty status in relation to the West drained wealth from the nation, and the abolition of the domains placed a tremendous burden on the central treasury in the form of feudal domain debts and samurai stipends. Furthermore, given the liquidation of the feudal domains, the troops mobilized in the spring of 1871 by the *sampan kempei* were the only legitimate armed forces and became a power of their own. Thus, a measure was deemed necessary to integrate these troops into a more modern system of armed forces by centralizing the control over them. Saigō, far from attempting to moderate or discourage these measures in accordance with the pledge to the Iwakura mission, did little to intervene in these reforms.

This drawing up of reform measures preserved, on the surface, the old four-domain concord among the central officials. The Land Tax Reform and the abolition of samurai stipends had as their chief architects Inoue Kaoru and Yoshida Kiyonari (from Satsuma; the under-deputy [*shōyū*] of Finance). A Chōshū man, Yamagata Aritomo, and two Satsuma men, Kawamura Jungi and Saigō Tsugumichi (Takamori's younger brother), were mainly responsible for the creation of a conscript army.[21] A Saga man, Ōki Takatō, designed and effected the rapid preparation of the government school system, which took less than six months between the time it was conceived and put into effect. Etō Shimpei, also from Saga, who had become the head of the Justice Department in mid–1872, embarked upon an ambitious project that instituted the autonomy of the judicial branches, especially at the fu-ken level, where the governors alone had previously exercised judicial power along with executive power.[22] Most of these reforms, which laid the foundations for more modern political, economic, and social institutions, were conceived and rapidly implemented, if not completed, during the Saigō administration.

Then the political rifts began to emerge. None of these reforms was above criticism, particularly from the members of the Iwakura mission. Informed of the measures while on the mission, Ōkubo Toshimichi was concerned more with their overall effect than with the specific features or desirability of each reform: "Perhaps we are reaching the level of civilized nations in terms of form. I can only wonder, though, about the substance [of each reform]."[23] Objections came from within the government, too, and served to voice a general wariness of precipitous change, if not to frustrate the reform policies themselves. Typically, internal critics advocated a more gradual approach in terms of pace and scope. For example, in the case of military reform, Yamada Aki-yoshi (a high official in the Department of Military Affairs, from Chōshū) suggested an alternative to the sudden creation of a conscript army. His idea was to provide a smooth transition to full-scale conscription by first forming a solid officer corps and providing military training for civilians.[24]

Although most of these reforms inspired only mild criticism, the program of reduction and eventual abolition of samurai stipends began to provoke far more tenacious opposition, even though the program itself won the approval of the *Sei-in* (the Central Chamber) early in 1872. The reform was necessary because of the continued drain on the central treasury of well over 50 percent of its revenue for payment of the feudal stipends and the debts inherited from the abolished feudal domains. The program proposed the drastic measure of immediately cutting the stipends by one-third and terminating them completely within six years.[25] The first resistance to its implementation came from the members of the Iwakura mission, rather than from those within the caretaker government. These measures were "much too severe,"[26] Iwakura Tomomi responded to Yoshida Kiyonari, who came to Washington, D.C., in the spring of 1872 to confer about them with the members of the mission. Kido angrily received Yoshida with the assertion that the former samurai "deserve sympathy," even though Kido was very much aware of the necessity of reducing the hereditary stipends. Kido argued that, though the samurai were admittedly the greatest drain upon the central revenue, "they are not the only ones to be blamed, but all Japanese" who had acquiesced in the historical fact of samurai privilege for several hundred years.[27] Yoshida in his turn reported back to Tokyo: "They hold steadfastly to the old bygone customs; none is willing to support us."[28] This proved to be only the be-

ginning of a sequence of heated exchanges between the members
of the Iwakura mission and the Finance Department that in the
end came close to ruining the stipend-reduction plan.[29]

Yet the caretaker government had done everything possible to
defend itself against likely criticisms by the mission members for
violation of their pledge to freeze major reforms. Even Saigō took
pains to write a letter to Ōkubo Toshimichi, informing him in
advance of the purpose of Yoshida Kiyonari's trip to meet the
mission: "The Finance Department has prepared measures to reduce the samurai stipends.... We must not miss this opportunity
[to implement it]...."[30] The problem unveiled by this incident
thus lay deeper than the obvious violation of the pledge between
the caretaker government and the Iwakura mission. The problem
was the inconsistency of the Saigō administration itself, which
had originally endorsed the program and then quickly retreated
into silence when it incurred unexpectedly fierce resistance from
the mission members. This reversal left only Inoue Kaoru, Yo-
ida Kiyonari, and a few others in the Finance Department to strike
back.

The dispute over the stipend-reduction program was particularly serious because it clearly revealed the caretaker government's inability to override the mission members' objections.
Furthermore, it unearthed two larger problems: the fact that Saigō
Takamori had not solidified his political control by virtue of his
prominence and, more generally, that the Saigō administration
was far from a unified system of decision-making and implementation. Each administrative department with its distinct function
proved to be an isolated unit, ignoring the other departments and
the imperative to coordinate with them. Each fought to push its
own projects through the *Sei-in*. Even the other reform projects,
perhaps less dramatically in the absence of visible resistance,
depended on and contributed to this counterproductive practice.

All of this conflict resulted in discrediting what should have
been the supreme authority formally resting with the *Sei-in* for
the Prime Minister and Councilors. The Saigō administration
was eroding from within. Some came to recognize this problem
when their pet projects saw no advance. The government school
system was a case in point. This project of the Education De-

partment won the approval of the *Sei-in* at first, but the budgetary appropriation for it did not follow for quite a while. During the period of impasse, an irate member of the department, Fukuoka Takachika, threatened to postpone the project altogether and urged the *Sei-in* members to design a "long-range fiscal plan" and hold a "conference of the heads and deputies of the administrative departments at the *U-in* (the Right Chamber)" to define the duties each department could and should undertake, thereby promoting better coordination within the government. Fukuoka also warned that further harm was resulting from other such instances. In the same request to the *Sei-in*, he pointed out that every department had drawn up and insisted on its own administrative districts: Education had the school districts, Military had its six garrison stations, and Justice had its judicial districts for the newly established local courts. These districts "should also be designed in a unified manner so as to enable Finance to manage financial administration, Construction to administer industrial policies, and the Imperial decrees to be enforced by all simultaneously...."[31]

Nonetheless, when further pressed by the Education Department on the budgetary appropriation for the school system, Sanjō Sanetomi of the *Sei-in* had little to offer, simply responding, "... the *Sei-in* does not have any objections to the government school system...." Instead, Sanjō attributed the delay in budgetary appropriation to complications in budgetary planning and estimates, for which he held the Finance Department chiefly responsible. In his request to Ōkuma Shigenobu in Finance to apply pressure upon Inoue Kaoru, the Finance deputy, Sanjō acknowledged the powerlessness of the *Sei-in* and the inability of the administration as a whole to solve its own problems of coordination: "Despite the authority credited to the *Sei-in*, we still cannot override the unwillingness of the Finance Department" to grant budgetary appropriations for approved policies.[32]

With its power of the purse, the Finance Department was an obvious target of criticism from all the other departments and even from the *Sei-in*. From Finance's perspective, however, the crux of the matter was the tendency of each department to arrogate to itself the authority of the administration as a whole, and to devise and justify its own policies to the neglect of the others'. Each department separately sought to win the approval of the highest authority, the *Sei-in*, for its courses of action; therefore, Finance's inevitable reluctance to go along with the already approved policies only rendered meaningless the authority of the *Sei-in* as the pivot of the government. This in turn pitted all the other departments directly against Finance in a stalemate. Inoue Kaoru first wrote of this standoff to Kido Kōin in the summer of 1872, explaining his own ineffectual position as the *de facto* head of the Finance Department:

> It is an absurd practice of the Japanese to plan and begin things without due consideration concerning the material bases of the nation. Yet, if we insisted on this logical argument, we would sacrifice the sense of compassion; and if we simply let the plans through, there would be no prospect for building a fiscal plan and the foundation of the nation would surely be in danger. Consequently, I believe, no matter what means we chose to raise the level of civilization, there would be no way of making use of it.[33]

In another letter to Kido Kōin, on January 22, 1873, Inoue expressed his frustration more directly:

> Even though we [the Finance Department] alone have tried to curb government spending, the other departments, with the intention of gaining an equal footing with the West, are insisting upon positive policies. The *Sei-in*, too, pardon my saying so, has had a hand in this tendency, placing all the blame on the Finance Department and leaving us with no choice but to resist the *Sei-in*. Consequently, we have incurred the displeasure of the *Sei-in* in addition to that of the other departments.[34]

To make matters worse, in the period between these two letters from Inoue, scandals occurred involving misappropriation of government funds by a few merchants who had been taking advantage of patronage by government officials, especially those, like Inoue, of Chōshū origin. The involvement of Inoue himself, Chōshū's most prominent official, in these scandals only aggravated the deterioration of the Saigō administration when Etō Shimpei of the Justice Department tried to take advantage of the situation to press his anti-Chōshū campaign.[35] To him, the actions of Finance as a department, which had included halving the funds the Justice Department requested for instituting the judicial districts, and those of Inoue Kaoru as a corruptible individual were one and the same. In the ensuing scramble for self-preservation, the two sides took similar actions. Both Inoue Kaoru and Etō Shimpei, as well as a few others such as Fukuoka Takachika (who had recently moved to Justice from Education), used threats of resignation in order to strengthen their own causes. Not surprisingly, such moves did nothing to restore stability to the faltering Saigō administration.

By the beginning of 1873, the deterioration had become irreversible. Matters had worsened when Shimazu Hisamitsu, the powerful lord of Satsuma who was known for insisting that his conservative views be reflected in government policy as a whole, forced Saigō Takamori to return temporarily to Satsuma late in 1872. Contrary to his initial idea of pacifying Shimazu's anger with a brief visit, Saigō wound up staying in Satsuma for nearly four months, leaving the central government without his services during this critical time. Saigō's absence only deepened the sense of alienation among the key members of Finance, as the pressure against it from the other central officials was now free even of Saigō's minimal deterrence. Shibusawa Eiichi, another official of Finance, writing on January 15, 1873, to Ōkubo Toshimichi and Itō Hirobumi in defense of Inoue Kaoru's position, lamented: "Even the legislative power as well as the executive power seems to be exercised by the individual administrative departments, leaving the *Sei-in* with only nominal political authority. . . ."[36]

Sanjō Sanetomi, Prime Minister and head of the *Sei-in*, was thus unable to act and could only request the return from abroad of two of the key leaders, Ōkubo Toshimichi and Kido Kōin, early in the spring of 1873. The two did not return to Japan until May and July, respectively. "Each department has come to an immovable standstill with the others,"[37] Sanjō wrote to Iwakura Tomomi in a letter that went on to explain a move he had conceived to strengthen the besieged *Sei-in*. Again in violation of the pledge and its hoped-for concord, this move involved the promotions to

Councilor of Inoue Kaoru's opponents, Etō Shimpei (Saga), Ōki Takatō (Saga), and Gotō Shōjirō (Tosa) on April 19, 1873. Also, on May 2, the *Sei-in*, which was now far less sympathetic to the Finance Department and its key officials, took under its jurisdiction the primary functions of Finance, such as those concerning budgetary appropriation, minting, and foreign and domestic loans. The first visible loss of harmony followed immediately. On May 7, both Inoue Kaoru and Shibusawa Eiichi resigned from their posts in Finance. In consequence, and of serious concern to the others in the central government, Saga men now dominated the *Sei-in* for the first time, as indicated in the composition of its Councilors: Saga (3), Satsuma (1), Tosa (2), and Chōshū (0). This development prompted a meeting between Saigō Takamori and Yamagata Aritomo (Chōshū) to discuss ways of reinstating the equilibrium among the four principal domains.[38] These two consequences of Sanjō's action made it clear that the Prime Minister had failed to fulfill the promise in his letter to Iwakura Tomomi to restrengthen the *Sei-in*.

## The Collapse of the Caretaker Government

The passive reaction of Saigō Takamori to all these developments was hardly indicative of the conflict that was to develop by the fall of 1873 over the Korean expedition. Saigō was even quoted as expressing his desire, earlier in that year, to withdraw from politics altogether: "Mr. Itagaki, my opinion is rarely acted upon. I might as well retreat into Hokkaidō and spend the rest of my life farming. . . ."[39] This reported conversation with Itagaki Taisuke took place during a meeting necessitated by the earlier financial scandals involving several government officials. The disillusionment Saigō expressed came from his awakening to a profound sense of his failure to inspire the government with his own kind of moral commitment.

The first half of 1873, which saw a rapidly disintegrating Saigō government, was followed by Saigō's positive moves to command the *Sei-in*. The issue Saigō decided to exploit was the question of a military expedition to Korea to "chastise" the neighboring nation for its alleged slighting of the emperor's authority. The immediate catalyst for this move was an appeal in June to the *Sei-in* from a Foreign Affairs official which urged the government to take action against Korea's supposed "contempt" for the Japanese governing authority.[40] Soejima Taneomi, Minister of Foreign Affairs, happened to be in China at the time discussing the massacre of Ryūkyū fishermen by the Formosans, a matter that provoked the fear among some of the central leaders of a military confrontation with Ch'ing China. Nevertheless, Saigō's response to the Korean issue, which was just as likely to invite such a confrontation, was simple and straightforward: set up the assassination of a Japanese envoy to Korea at the hands of the Koreans to provide a *casus belli* for Japan's direct incursion into the Korean peninsula. Most importantly, Saigō himself volunteered to be the victim: "Perhaps I may not have the diplomatic skills and caliber of a Soejima, but one thing I can do well is to prepare myself for my own death. . . ."[41]

Saigō's insistence on taking this extraordinary mission into his own hands quickly won the approval of the *Sei-in* on August 16, 1873, with Itagaki Taisuke's strong support in the deliberations.[42] The reasonable fears of a military confrontation with Ch'ing China and of the financial burden of war on the central treasury and society did not moderate the peculiar enthusiasm Saigō's proposal elicited in the *Sei-in*. However, just as unexpectedly, the approval for the mission was then overturned in October. Both the approval of the plan and its reversal only reconfirmed the fact that the *Sei-in*, as the locus of political authority formally making and sanctioning government decisions, was incapable of commanding the members of the Imperial government themselves.

First, the initial approval did not have the support of Ōkubo, Kido, and others who had not participated in the making of the proposal to send the expedition. Ōkubo did return from Europe to Japan in May, but he made himself deliberately scarce during Saigō's efforts to obtain his endorsement.[43] Ōkubo consciously avoided the heady excitement and the unanimity in the *Sei-in* that the Saigō-Itagaki leadership managed to create for the proposal. In fact, the day before the *Sei-in*'s approval, Ōkubo left Tokyo and did not return until late in September, remarking,

" . . . affairs of state cannot be determined by the kind of reckless undertakings that feed on impulse and that lead to more exhilaration. . . . "[44]

The return of Iwakura Tomomi from the West on September 13 did not help Saigō's position either. Iwakura began efforts to reinstate the kind of credibility he believed the central government had had following the *Haihan chiken*. The reappointment of Ōkubo, who opposed the expedition, to Councilor on October 12 was the first result of Iwakura's efforts. As an obvious attempt to mitigate Saigō's influence on the initial approval of the expedition, Iwakura's efforts were more than just a challenge to Saigō's personal commitment to the plan. They were also, and contradictorily, a direct challenge to the political authority of the *Sei-in*. Alarmed by Iwakura's countermoves, Saigō wrote to Sanjō Sanetomi on October 11: "If there is any change in the approval at this stage, it will have the effect of belittling all other imperial orders throughout our society. . . . "[45]

With Ōkubo and a few others on the Iwakura mission fully reinstated, new rounds of cabinet deliberations began on October 14 and included those who had been absent from the government for some time. The participants were Saigō Takamori, Itagaki Taisuke, Ōkubo Toshimichi, Kido Kōin, Iwakura Tomomi, Sanjō Sanetomi, Ōkuma Shigenobu, Gotō Shōjirō, Etō Shimpei, Ōki Takatō, and Soejima Taneomi. The meetings resembled the Kogosho Conference on the eve of the War of the Restoration, in which the final outcome—the denunciation of the Tokugawa—resulted from the maneuverings of the rival parties and from unforeseen events. The polarization among the participants was clearly marked: one group supported the original approval of Saigō's mission to Korea, and the other pushed to reverse it. Ōkubo's and Iwakura's persuasions notwithstanding, reversal appeared almost impossible just when the submission to the throne of the *Sei-in*'s approval of the mission was imminent. At that point, however, Sanjō, who was to carry the approval to the emperor, became ill and lapsed into a coma. Iwakura, whom Saigō next requested to take on Sanjō's responsibility, also made himself unavailable, seemingly because of a sudden illness, for the next few precious days. Because of the delay, Iwakura successfully managed the reversal of the decision to "punish" Korea, which was finalized by Imperial order on October 24.[46] Saigō resigned from the government on the same day, and Itagaki, Gotō, Etō, and Soejima followed suit on the next day. The failure of the Korean expedition was the final blow to an already fragmented government whose formal governing authority was clearly unable to command its members. The Saigō administration thus came to a sudden end.

With it ended the harmony among the principal Restoration leaders from the four key domains that had lasted since the *Hai-han chiken*. Now styling themselves the legitimate critics of the government, Itagaki, Gotō, Etō, and Soejima found they could most forcefully express their dissatisfaction by resigning from the central government and aligning themselves with the popular movement for a more open political system. Their joint action culminated in January 1874 in the signing of the Petition for a National Assembly, which Komuro Shinobu and Furusawa Shigeru had prepared, as noted at the beginning of this chapter. And finally, two of them were dissatisfied enough with the central government to take arms against it. One month after signing the Petition, Etō Shimpei plunged himself into an armed revolt in his former domain, Saga, which never amounted to more than a local skirmish. The Saga revolt coincided with another sequence of disruptions that started with the attempted assassination of Iwakura Tomomi in January 1874 by a band of Tosa samurai and ended in the six-month Satsuma Rebellion of 1877, with Saigō Takamori as its leader.

For those remaining in the government, the task was to regroup themselves and recover the credibility of the *Sei-in* as the locus of the governing authority. Ōkubo Toshimichi became the head of the newly established Interior Department (the *Naimushō*) as well as Councilor, flanked by his new lieutenants, Itō Hirobumi and Ōkuma Shigenobu, who became the heads of Construction and Finance, respectively, as well as Councilors. Kido Kōin, soon to leave the government in protest at its decision to send the military expedition to Formosa in May 1874, had lost his earlier enthusiasm for using intrigue and political manipulation to maintain his kind of "fit" between realities and ideals. He set himself up as a lone critic, sometimes of Saigō and Itagaki, at other times of Ōkubo and Iwakura. Kido's self-seclusion, as well as Saigō's and Itagaki's defection, signaled the end of the period of significant continuity in the efforts of these samurai activists to sustain a faltering Imperial government. Kido's shift, first of all, left Ōkubo's ascendancy in the government uncontested.[47] Moreover, as William Beasley points out, the parallel rise of Itō Hirobumi and Ōkuma Shigenobu marked the training of a "new generation of officialdom in the habits and ideas that were to characterize the next phase in the modern history of Japan."[48]

## The Nature of the Governmental Opposition

The Korean issue irrefutably marked the diverging courses of action that the Restoration leaders had developed, leaving the Imperial government in unfamiliar terrain as its first decade of existence neared its end. First, the petitioners, the defected leaders such as Itagaki, Gotō, Soejima, and Etō, had opened the way for the various movements toward wider political participation to converge. Second, Saigō's failure to command the government during the dispute over the Korean expedition was a sign that the Imperial government had ceased to be readily swayed by the influence of the residual feudalistic forces. And finally, the failure indicates the emergence of a unified front of officials determined to quell the forces that were preventing domestic reforms.

However, it is dangerous to overemphasize the divisiveness of the Korean issue. One false assumption is that the division over the issue reached deeply into society. Some of those whom it directly affected were the few hundred military and government officials of Satsuma and Tosa who followed the defections of Saigō and Itagaki. However, as closely involved observers such as Iwakura and Tani Tateki (Tosa) remarked, these followers acted out of loyalty to their clan leaders, whose position in the government seemed to have been unduly slighted by the others.[49] There were also the "Conquer Korea" parties, the *seikantō*, among the former samurai in a limited number of localities. These organizations or, rather, ad hoc action groups were no more than the historical coincidence of disgruntled and jealous samurai. They found it particularly expedient to glorify their frustration and search for an outlet for it in a party whose name dramatized the reason for the defection of some of the most prominent samurai leaders in the new regime.[50] Overall, however, the outcome of the Korean dispute only indirectly affected those outside the central government.

Of greater significance is the problematic credibility of the governing authority, which had lent itself to divisive competition among the central leaders *before* the Korean dispute. The fact that all the participants in the dispute had retained or reinforced their conviction of being the emperor's proxies did not help stabilize their relations. At this point, it is useful to recapitulate what had sustained this resilient conviction, before assessing the significance of the diverging courses of action the Restoration leaders next took.

The initial causes of this conviction may be traced to the dynamics that lifted the Restoration leaders from relative political obscurity in their own domains. Most of them were of middle or lower samurai origin from a limited number of the feudal domains. During the phase of domain reforms before the Restoration, they seized control of their domain governments in intense power struggles that in the end profoundly altered the feudalistic access to power in the domains. The incorporation of middle- and lower-ranking samurai into the higher domain posts dispersed among them the power that had previously been monopolized by a few privileged vassals. At the same time, the new leaders reconsolidated that power. The movement leading to the overthrow of the Tokugawa bakufu was the exploitation of these two seemingly incompatible dynamics, the dispersion and the consolidation of political power, at a national level. In order to supersede the Tokugawa bakufu, a few feudal daimyo (or, more precisely, samurai activists on their behalf) acquired political influence by gaining access to the national political arena where the bakufu monopoly of administration had long been uncontested. Their consolidation of political power in their domains coincided with the formation of a cross-domain coalition among these new political forces, sustained by the ensuing increase in support from more domains. It was in these parallel processes that samurai activists began to style themselves the emperor's proxies, in order to justify their challenge of the existing governing authorities. Toward the close of the bakufu, the conviction grew stronger in each samurai activist that he alone was the proxy of the emperor, and it provided the mental and ideological foundation for the national exploitation of the two political dynamics of dispersion and consolidation of power.

The Oath of 1868 was a highly political document in this light, too, as it was an attempt to accommodate one dynamic to the other. Its unequivocal stress upon the sanctity of Imperial rule reflected the drive toward consolidation, while the simultaneous defense of "public discussion" expressed the opposite thrust of dispersion. First, the emphasis upon the concentration of political power was more than a passive response to the disintegration of Tokugawa feudalism by the Imperial government in its first few years of uncertainty. In theory, it was intended to promote an exaltation of national prestige in which differences in feudal backgrounds as well as in policy orientations might be surmounted, by designating the locus of the governing authority that they were all to serve on an equal basis. In practice, it was meant to keep the members of the central government from contradicting each other because of their provincial orientations. Finally, the Oath's emphasis on consolidation of power was meant to give the members of the central government the leverage of Imperial authority, however symbolic, vis-à-vis other feudal members in their home domains. In tandem with the drive toward consolidation, the emphasis upon the dispersion of political power through "public discussion" was intended to bring in wider support from the feudal domains and, as its corollary, to diffuse the obvious predominance of the four major southwestern domains.

However, the pressure to move in both directions began to result in peculiar consequences when reinforced within the central community of the Restoration leaders. Hardly a cohesive group from the beginning, each member viewed himself unequivocally but individually and separately in terms of his perceived proximity to the single source of political authority, the Imperial person. And insofar as they did so, they remained equidistant from one another, being equally adjacent to the throne and equally capable of obtaining Imperial approval. Internally applied, the principle of dispersion of power and "public discussion" served to block any one of the members of the Imperial government from becoming more powerful at the expense of the others. At the same time, the principle of the concentration of power served to advance the consolidation of the central leaders' positions both individually, in relation to each other within the government, and collectively, in relation to those outside the government.

Thus the impact of the *Haihan chiken* upon the Restoration leaders was indeed profound. To some, the decision to liquidate the domains in the summer of 1871 was itself evidence of the violation of the rule of "public discussion," or the principle of dispersion of power. As explored in Chapter 2, neither unanimity nor majority rule was employed to arrive at the decision. Itagaki Taisuke, whose control of the Tosa troops was indispensable for the enforcement of the decision, was not even kept informed of the progress toward this decision. Not surprisingly, his reaction to it and its implementation was far from enthusiastic. The execution of the decision critically eroded Itagaki's power base in the Imperial government; his control of the Tosa troops became private in nature, as his battalions were now incorporated into the royal army. Thus, even when Itagaki was made Councilor shortly thereafter, he was without allies in any of the administrative branches that were to play a crucial role in the post–*Haihan chiken* reforms. His bitterness came precisely from the disparity between his belief in his proximity to the locus of the governing authority and his actual, minimized, role in the critical decision. He subsequently characterized the decision as an abuse of "fiat" (*eidan*) by a small group in the government, and he saw it as having preempted what he argued was "dominant public opinion" already in favor of the displacement of the feudal domains, that is, as having neglected the dispersion-of-power principle.[51]

Furthermore, the *Haihan chiken* removed the threats from outside the central government that had prompted the Restoration leaders to seek support from the feudal domains in the first place. Once the government established itself, the leaders lost the momentum to maintain the political dynamics of dispersion and consolidation that had helped preserve their coalition in the preceding years of more acute uncertainty. At least for the time being, these dynamics were suspended when the unification of Japan gained a firmer foothold. That left their effect to be internalized within the Imperial government alone.

The issues therefore became, first, how to maintain the balance between the two dynamics within the community of the Restoration leaders, as had been explicitly attempted in the pledge prior to the departure of the Iwakura mission; and, second, how to reestablish it when it was upset. Itagaki's reaction clearly illustrates the evolution of this issue after the *Haihan chiken*. Frustrated by the incongruity between his imagined and actual roles, he became particularly sensitive to the two dynamics and how they could work to his advantage or disadvantage. After more than a year of merely ceremonial performance as Councilor, Itagaki chose to exploit the Korean expedition issue to consolidate his power. A few months before this issue became divisive, he is said to have told Miyajima Seiichirō, one of the early proponents of a parliamentary movement, that he was interested in consolidating political power by allying with Saigō Takamori.[52] When this attempt proved abortive in the defeat of Saigō's Korean mission proposal, Itagaki then turned to dispersion to check the concentration of power, which now appeared to have been pursued successfully by all the members but himself.

More generally put, the root of the disagreements among the Restoration leaders lay in their differing assessments of the impact upon the government of the two political dynamics that had brought all of them to their current prominence. Some, like Itagaki, believed that the balance had been upset by the political development that led to the concentration of power by only a few while excluding the others. Others, including Ōkubo and Kido, were more disturbed by the fact that *both* dynamics had broken down, leading to a general inability of the members in the government to attain even a minimum consensus on a given issue.

These opposing assessments underlay the Korean expedition dispute. The members of the Imperial government were irreconcilable. After all, the *Sei-in*, or the Imperial government as a whole, was primarily a body of men who had risen to political significance through their conscious exploitation of the two political dynamics. Such a body could claim no overriding power to settle disputes among themselves or to enforce the decisions of some over those of the others. Their opposing assessments were the undercurrents, also, of what the leaders wished to realize by either leaving the government or remaining in it, and of what they saw in the others' actions of leaving or remaining.

For Saigō Takamori, the two years since the *Haihan chiken* attested to a decay in political life and in the moral integrity the Restoration had seemed to inject into the old nation. For him, the issue was not the ideal balance between the two political dynamics, but who was even qualified to discuss either of the two. Accordingly, his approach was to treat the deteriorating body in its entirety; he thus remarked, once at the *Haihan chiken* and again at the end of the Korean dispute, "We need more wars."[53] His stratagem was to exploit or even create, if necessary, a crisis that would remind the Restoration leaders of the years when the tension between the two types of political thrust was the driving force for the entire new regime and had transcended the petty struggles among them.[54]

For the petitioners for a National Assembly, such as Itagaki, the Korean issue was telling evidence of a detrimental trend within the Imperial government: the locus of power was gradually shifting into the hands of a few and away from the whole, allowing the few to usurp even the formal governing authority. In taking this view, Itagaki was of one mind with those such as Otagi Michiakira, cited earlier, who saw the problem of the Meiji government as the "unjust intrusion of officials" into the emperor's rule. Itagaki's Petition, using the more general language of popular participation, was thus highly consistent in its demand to restore the dispersion of power. His attack upon the "oligarchical few" was more of a denunciation of the concentration of power among the few within the government than a plea to make the government as a whole more open to those outside it.

## The Petitioners and the Idea of Government

The opening words of the Petition for a National Assembly that Itagaki and others submitted to the *Sei-in* on January 17, 1874, revealed the document's main purpose—the denunciation of the consolidation of power that seemed to be taking place in the central government:

> When we humbly reflect upon the quarter in which the governing authority rests, it rests not with the emperor nor with the people, *but solely with the oligarchical few*.... Hundreds of government decrees are issued in the morning and are changed by the evening. The conduct of the administration is arbitrary; rewards and punishments are administered through partiality. The people's access to the government is cut off, and their grievances have no way to reach the government.... We fear that the state will collapse unless reforms are implemented to undo these evil habits. Unable to resist compelling patriotic feelings, we have sought measures to prevent this from going any further. There can be only one measure, that is, the promotion of public discussion. In order to promote public discussion, the establishment of a national assembly by popular election is the only means. *Only then will limits be placed upon the power of the oligarchical officials* and will security as well as prosperity be enjoyed by governors and governed alike....[55] (Emphasis mine)

This general defense of popular political participation, however, was based on a more specific interest on the part of Itagaki and his followers, that is, the reinstatement of their own places in the central arena of politics. A reply prepared by Itagaki and others to the criticism of the Petition raised by Katō Hiroyuki (to be discussed shortly) reveals this motive:

> The establishment of a national assembly does not mean universalizing the right of representation among the populace. It means simply that the right will be granted for the time being to the former samurai, the rich merchants, and the rich farmers. *For they are the ones who have produced men of distinct contributions to the Restoration.*[56] (Emphasis mine)

Mindful both of the need to protect these specific interests and of the problems of power sharing, the petitioners viewed their own brand of limited political participation as the only solution.[57]

The Petition continues, pointing out the numerous objectives the popularly elected assembly could achieve:

> Those who object to the establishment of a national assembly by popular election insist: our people are still uneducated and wanting in intelligence, and are far from reaching the level of enlightenment. ... [However,] waiting for the people to develop their knowledge and intelligence so as to lead themselves to a level of enlightenment is like allowing a hundred years for a muddy river to clear.... Between despotic decisions by a few officials and decisions guided by public discussion, where could one find the choice of wisdom or folly? We hold that the wisdom of these officials itself must have evolved since before the Restoration. It must be so because the intelligence of human beings develops as it is practiced. Therefore, the establishment of a national assembly by popular election is the way to advance the intelligence of the people, hence quickly leading them also to reach the level of enlightenment.

> The goal that our government ought to serve is the establishment of a national assembly by popular election, thereby inspiring the people with an enterprising spirit, teaching them the duty of sharing the responsibilities of the nation, and inducing them to participate in the affairs of the state. Only then will the people of the country be of one mind.

> How is the government to be made solid? It is by the people of the country becoming of one mind.... The establishment of a national assembly will promote a community of understanding between the government and the people; they will become one unified body; only then will the nation become strong and the government solid....[58]

Despite its strong words, this Petition by the defected Councilors seemed to affect Ōkubo Toshimichi and others still in the government only marginally. Some of its specific allegations against the government made little sense to men like Ōkubo and Kido Kōin. Indeed, allegations such as "hundreds of government decrees are issued in the morning and changed by the evening" could apply more to the defected Councilors who had managed the government during the two years of constant reform policies than to Ōkubo and Kido, who had been abroad most of that time.[59]

Further, the submission of the Petition was not exactly a well-prepared venture systematically followed up by organized activities, nor was it a final rejection by the petitioners of their one-time associates in the government. Itagaki and a few others often frequented Kido's residence, even on the day of the submission of the Petition. All of this had convinced Kido that their concerns might have less to do with the general affairs of the government than with the perception that their share of power was denied them.[60]

Moreover, there was a more fundamental distance between the petitioners and some of the remaining leaders, which to the latter made the petitioners' denunciation of the government's arrogance toward the "immature" populace seem irrelevant. On the one hand, the petitioners were concerned primarily with the reinstatement of the balance between the concentration and dispersion of power and, by extension, with the maintaining of the two political dynamics by including some of the public who had been peripheral to the early Meiji politics. On the other hand, for Ōkubo Toshimichi, there was a far more disturbing problem in the government, the solution of which would have to precede the issue of balancing the two political dynamics. The Korean dispute, for him, was evidence that the Imperial government as a whole still lacked any authority of its own to command, first and foremost, the powerful proxies of the emperor. Ōkubo's "Opinion on Constitutional Government," prepared in 1873, clearly outlines his assessment of the problem plaguing the Imperial government:

As a way of government, each country tailors its constitution to the old customs and sentiments of its people. Monarchical despotism, joint government by the monarch and the people, and republicanism certainly differ from each other. *However, in making decisions and conducting the affairs of state, there must always be a quarter that holds firm and uncontested power.* Without a resolve thus assured, the affairs of state invite a great deal of argument and undisciplined opinion leading only to confusion. Everyone will support and entertain his own ideas and make his own decisions as he pleases, and there will be no order in the conduct of the administration. We may wish to rush forward, yet wind up retreating; wish to rush ahead,

yet wind up remaining at a standstill. Government will grow stag-
nant and rest upon no foundation.[61] (Emphasis mine)

In this light, Ōkubo characterized the Imperial government as
resting "upon no foundation":

> In the quarter that issues decrees, no power exists. . . . [The govern-
> ment] resembles a human body whose arms and legs go in different
> directions and move as they desire and which has no center of co-
> ordination and cooperation.[62]

For Ōkubo, the problem of the formal governing authority did
not come from its abuse by any particular individuals. He attributed it, instead, to those who exercised power to the neglect of
everyone else and of the whole government, of which ideally they
were parts and to which ideally they were responsible. The problem for him was that the Imperial government had become the
instrument of its individual members' self-expression and self-
assertion. In contrast to the petitioners' preoccupation with the
dispersion principle, therefore, Ōkubo's concern was the question
of how to protect the formal governing authority from what appeared to be its unlimited exploitation by all of the emperor's
proxies. Accordingly, Ōkubo's plea for a "quarter that holds firm
and uncontested power" could not be achieved either by simply
eliminating rivals or by surrounding its formal holder with mystery, be it the emperor or anyone else. His idea was to liberate
that quarter entirely from the particular political dispositions of
any individuals through reliance on political institutions above
the individuals, whether the formal holders of power or those
who sought access to them.

From this perspective, the antithesis to Ōkubo's ideal was a
"benevolent rule" that relied upon the attributes of a particular
individual for its persistence, integrity, justice, and even capacity
for change.[63] Therefore, Ōkubo's ideal government was not in
accord with the prevailing belief that held the emperor with all
of his personal attributes to be identical with the formal governing
authority. However, Ōkubo was not alone on this matter. Iwakura
Tomomi, a year after the Restoration, had come to articulate a

similar view that sought the creation of the kind of "political institutions that could support the state even in the absence of a sagacious emperor or an intelligent chancellor."[64]

Ōkubo's resistance to the pressure to make the government a more open system found allies in a small group of intellectuals, the *Meirokusha*, who offered still another line of criticism against the use of political participation to solve the problems of Japan's new regime. The enthusiasm of the *Meirokusha* (named after the sixth year of the Meiji emperor, when the idea for the group was first conceived) for all varieties of knowledge, from political economy to science, and for social experimentation came from their earlier (pre-Restoration) travel to the West, which had also removed them from the intrigues of Restoration politics. Their eagerness may also be attributed to their political ambitions, which were not entirely fulfilled by their peripheral significance in a government run by the Restoration activists. As Uete Michiari points out, many of the *Meirokusha* members were formerly bakufu officials and in the same age group as the Restoration activists now in the central government.[65] Whether or not bound by a sense of repressed ambition, they shared a common orientation best characterized by their tolerance of pluralism both in the forms that political and social problems could take and in the approaches to solve them. By that same token, they had much less inclination to be preoccupied with politics per se.

One of their members, Fukuzawa Yukichi, succinctly summarized this aspect of the group's outlook. His stress upon the various forms that human activities could and should take within society inevitably defined politics as only part of the whole fabric of social life, and thus something that owes its distinctiveness to the particular functions it performs for the whole.

> Politics is after all one of the threads interwoven into human interactions. . . . Politics is not the sole source of civilization. It is but one part of civilization, like literature, commerce, and other things that mature and decay as civilization does.[66]

One important outgrowth of this view was the theoretical reconstruction of an ideal government by Nishi Amane, another *Meirokusha* member:

One corporation is instituted for profit-making, another for industrial ventures, and still another for religious needs. All are one in
their nature. There is always a head at the top; the administrative
system is integrated in order to serve the common purposes of its
constituent members; the division of labor among the managers is
generated and defined by the amount of business and its direction.
The form and nature of a government are of the type of such cor-
porations in the society and claim no difference.[67]

Nishi argued that a government was a highly purposeful organ;
its nature was fundamentally the same as that of other social
organizations of specified functions; together, they served to
achieve the "three treasures" of social life—health, knowledge,
and wealth. This defining of an ideal government by the purposes
it served led back to Ōkubo's instrumental view of political power
that did not vary according to the particular personal attributes
of its holder(s), and to the need for a stable and credible governing
authority before the government could be made more open. Admittedly, as William Braisted points out,[68] some among the *Mei
rokusha* members were sympathetic to popular political
participation. Yet, with the exception of Kanda Kōhei, who prac-
ticed his belief in popular political participation in his own Hyōgo
ken when he was governor, the group kept its distance from the
petitioners, who stressed political participation as the solution to
a multitude of problems ranging from "despotic government" to
the "enlightening" of the immature populace.

Ōkubo's and Iwakura's projections of an ideal government were
echoed by another *Meirokusha* member, Katō Hiroyuki. As early
as 1861, through observation of the neighboring Confucian state
of Ch'ing China, Katō theorized an ideal government that "ena-
bles even an imbecile to conduct an administration no less benevolent than that of a sagacious emperor or an enlightened
monarch."[69] Katō later became an arch enemy of the petitioners
and their followers for his frontal attack on the Petition.[70] But
he, and for that matter many of the other *Meirokusha* members,
by no means categorically opposed the notion of political participation or incorporation of public opinion. Their criticism was
directed primarily at the petitioners' exclusive emphasis upon
political participation. For the *Meirokusha*, who treasured the

power of knowledge and learning, any "public opinion" that ideally embodied "common sense and knowledge"(*tsūgi*)[71] could not develop simply through one particular type of action, political participation. Their passive attitude toward the Petition and negative attitude toward the populace as socially immature were not based, therefore, on an authoritarian bent. These attitudes were rather the result of their own politically isolated advancement into their self-designated "realm of enlightenment."[72] In any case, Ōkubo Toshimichi, and for that matter some of the other remaining leaders, did not face the petitioners alone and did not confront their critics without an array of counterarguments.

## The End of the Restoration Coalition

The ultimate significance of the parting of the Restoration leaders does not lie in the intensity of the criticisms they leveled against one another. One could prepare a neat typology that would place Saigō's attempt to resurrect an almost theocratic rule on the far right and Itagaki's plea for a more open political system on the far left, with the government hostile to both. Yet the divergence in their real actions does not fit into such a neat typology, nor was each leader particularly effective in influencing the others. As noted earlier, what initially prompted the Restoration leaders to take these diverging courses of action was their common awakening to the inability of the central governing authority to command. The divisions the ensuing debates brought about among the leaders were the result of a unique dynamic: precisely because each justified his position by attributing the cause of this problem to the others, each was unreceptive to the others' perceptions of the problem and of constitutional improvements in general.

Such heedlessness of the others' positions, therefore, did not mean that each leader was blind to alternative measures of constitutional development. Viewed in this light, it is not surprising that the Imperial government, or its leading members, responded to the pressures for a more open political system. The individual attempts of the central officials, as well as the collective attempts of the *Sa-in* (Left Chamber), to produce some constitutional means to make the government more responsive were indeed extensive. Much of the constitutional language subsequently used by the petitioners, in fact, would have been unthinkable without them.[73] The number of constitutional improvements authorized by the central government itself suggests that the pressure on it by the petitioners was quite indirect. These instances include the Imperial Rescript of 1875, which proposed concrete measures for the drafting of a constitution and for the opening of the Prefectural Governors' Conference; the establishment of the popularly elected Prefectural Assemblies in 1879; and the history of limited popular representation in various localities preceding the Petition of 1874. These instances indicate that the government's policy of, or its basic predisposition in favor of, constitutional improvements coincided with, rather than was shaped by, the popular pressure the petitioners often claimed to have organized.[74]

The real significance of the parting of the Restoration leaders lies in the fact that the Korean expedition dispute, while terminating the tenuous Pledge of 1871, signified an end to something far more central to the politics of the Restoration. The two political dynamics of dispersion and consolidation of the governing power could no longer be sustained among their principal "beneficiaries," the Restoration leaders, without leading them to contradict each other or making the formal governing authority unable to command. Any further exploitation of these two dynamics would have had to presuppose two things: one, the realization among the Restoration leaders that they were no longer the proxies of the emperor; and, two, the realization that the dispersion of political power would mean the inclusion of new political forces outside their original nexus and that any subsequent consolidation of political power would have to be based on that inclusion. It is in this sense that the Korean dispute marked the end of the Restoration coalition and the beginning of a new phase in the politics of the Restoration.

In this light, Itagaki's adoption of the popular rights movement is an intriguing indication of just how much he and his followers were aware of the coming of a new stage of Restoration politics. From the very beginning, the petitioners were not a well-organized opposition to the government, distinguished by virtue of solid membership or a definite and stable political orientation. The petitioners fashioned the symbols of "Popular Rights" and of the "Popular Rights movement" in order to stress their stance as visionaries. Yet, in fact, they also harbored an unmistakable resentment toward their estrangement from the central arena of politics. In addition, during the attempts to gather momentum for their movement, they immediately developed the very same view that had led Ōkubo and others in the government to choose a much more gradual approach to the question of popular representation. What was perceived as the "low level of political maturity" of the populace retarded Itagaki's own attempt to popularize his position through yet another instrument, his Society of Patriots, or the *Aikokusha*:

> Their minds still being governed by the remnants of the feudalistic way of life, with the exception of a few who were knowledgeable, the people were convinced that support for popular rights was the act of rebels and tended to detest it. Accordingly, there were no men of wealth or of status among those who participated in the meeting [of the *Aikokusha*], but only those from the rank of samurai who pledged their loyalty to their country in the name of their swords and with nothing but their lives to offer.[75]

In fact, because of this view of the general populace, the members of the *Aikokusha* were slow to accommodate themselves to the new political generation emerging precisely from among the men "of wealth or of status" with their characteristically different type of political orientation.

The breakup of the community of the Restoration leaders thus raises the important question of whether Ōkubo's plea for the reinforcement of political power and Itagaki's pressure for a more open political system were sustained by their awareness that the Restoration politics was entering a new period: in other words, that the two principles of dispersion and consolidation of political power were universal, rather than limited only to those who had risen to political prominence through their specific application in the bakumatsu politics. As Meiji politics moved to a new stage, the Restoration leaders were now confronted by the questions of (1) how to free themselves from their specific experiences in the past as samurai activists and as proxies of the emperor, and (2) how to protect the emperor from the recurrence of a destabilizing competition among his proxies.

# 7

# Limits of the Restoration

OUR CONCERN in this final chapter is to probe the ways in which the key Restoration leaders prepared themselves for the coming of a new stage in Restoration politics. As examined in the previous chapter, the divisive Korean dispute was to all these men, but for different reasons, the betrayal of what they had hoped the Restoration would bring about. Their hopes for correction and improvement were based on an idealized, if simplified, image of a Restoration sustained by a perfectly balanced development of both dispersion and consolidation of power.

Such an image of the Restoration was most vivid among those who now had the most acute sense of disillusionment—the Councilors who had decided to leave the Imperial government and had returned home. While the remaining government leaders observed this new development with rising apprehension and suspicion, those who had resigned from the government found it perfectly logical to return to their home "domains" where they had begun their careers as Restoration activists. Saigō Takamori left for Satsuma a few days after his resignation. According to an account by one of his former followers, Saigō's hasty return was prompted by the need to pacify the Satsuma soldiers, who were allegedly angered by the reversal of the Korean decision.[1] But his return also seemed to reflect his conflicting desires: to withdraw from the politics of the Imperial government altogether, and to implement his stratagem for political reform by conducting "more wars." Satsuma appeared to provide an opportune distance for both plans, but in reality the distance kept him from realizing that the political climate was changing to his disadvantage. Etō Shimpei, too, returned to his home in Saga the month after he had signed the Petition for a National Assembly. There it became clear, as Ōkuma and Itagaki had warned, that the disgruntled samurai and their organizations would not leave him much choice except to become the unwilling leader for their uprising.[2] Finally, Itagaki Taisuke himself returned from Tokyo to Tosa in March 1874, leaving the first attempt at a political party, his Public Party of Patriots, stranded in Tokyo.

The course of action taken by Itagaki and his associates was particularly crucial. Their Petition for a National Assembly brought them close to recognizing the ideological thrust of the popular rights movement toward a new stage of Restoration politics in which the governing authority should have become progressively more responsive to the public. Their use of a new political cause, popular rights, could have convinced them that the further application of the principles of dispersion and consolidation meant the opening of the central arena of politics to more diverse political actors than themselves. However, their emphasis upon popular political participation was at least partly motivated by the sense that, despite their past contribution to the Restoration, their "rightful" place in the central arena of politics had been unduly slighted by the concentration of power among a few in the Imperial government. Thus, the concern to correct the unjust neglect of their "rightful" place in the government, in their eyes, obscured the real ideological thrust of the popular rights movement.

### The Samurai in the "New" Localities and the Return of the Councilors

The most obvious allies for the returning Councilors were the former samurai in the localities, who had faced profound changes since the *Haihan chiken* in particular and since the Restoration in general. Although they appeared to share the Councilors' dissatisfactions with the government, however, they would soon prove the most elusive of allies, making the return of the Councilors more symbolic than substantial. The deceptive similarity in outlooks on political action between the local samurai and the defected Councilors, strengthened by the latter's sympathy for the samurai's economic plight, prevented the former leaders from being more realistic about their idealized Restoration. It thus also kept them from systematically seeking expanded support from the new political forces in society in their attempt to reconsolidate power.

One problem the returning Councilors grasped quite accurately was that by 1874 the financial status of the former samurai had considerably worsened. Among other things, two policies adopted by the government toward the end of 1873 had placed the former samurai under severe strain of further impoverishment. One of these measures was a tax on the hereditary samurai pension that the government imposed for the sake of creating the funds necessary to strengthen the national army. To halt the constant drain on the central treasury, the government also encouraged certain samurai to give up their pensions in return for the cash value of a six-year terminal pension.[3] These samurai, who were in the majority, received under 100 *koku*, and the net outcome was the retrieval of otherwise nonproductive funds for the central treasury. However, given both the small income of the typical samurai and the unstable local economies of the transitional society, these measures quickly reduced most samurai to an uncertain life at a subsistence level.[4]

Amid this economic deterioration, the *Haihan chiken* also had an adverse impact on the samurai. There were no more daimyo houses to provide them with provincial identities and a psychological sense of stability.[5] This psychological void could have relieved the samurai of their rigid domain identities and allowed them to form a more broadly based social and political identity transcending their localities. However, in these years of acute uncertainty, the impoverished samurai needed a sense of stability based on the familiar domain identity more than a sense of liberation based on a new consciousness of their all being former samurai under the same strains of adjustment. In addition, there was little objective basis for the formation of a national samurai identity, because at its core was primarily the absence of other tangible sources of orientation. Without specific domains, the class identity of samurai bound together, only by default, some of those who would otherwise have disappeared in the new egalitarian society. As such, it could not generate a positive replacement for the old source of social identity, thus leaving most samurai highly susceptible to schemes to revive their old domain or provincial identity. It mattered little whether the schemes were invented by the government or by those who sought to change it.

For certain domains, this vulnerability to diverse overtures had another dimension that kept the samurai from overcoming their residual domain identities. Among those outside the four major southwestern domains, there was a strong sense that they had never really been instrumental to the new regime since the early years of the Restoration and had certainly fallen out of the main orbit since the *Haihan chiken*. These samurai combined their lingering domain identities with the hope of redeeming their past inaction by rendering the new government some service and thereby regaining at least some of their past prestige. By 1874, that hope was made even more urgent by the realization that opportunities for such a redemption were becoming more and more scarce. The Kanazawa samurai are an excellent case in point. On the occasion of the Korean dispute, they desperately sought permission to send voluntary forces of their own: "Due to our own lack of competence we were unable to render our services to the state when it faced its most profound transformation. We have not yet been able to return the infinite debts that we owe to the state and perform our duty of cooperating with the people."[6] Thus prefaced, their petition demonstrates perfectly their hope of participating in national affairs as prompted by their sense of alienation from the mainstream of Restoration politics. The petition reads in part:

While our years of aspiration [to render our services to the state] have failed to meet with a single opportunity, the state has become

increasingly stable, and men like us, having no assignments to perform, simply wind up useless.... We have heard recently that the
Imperial government, vexed by the Koreans' discourteous statements
and incivility, has already decided to send a punitive mission to that
country. We can hardly suppress our joy and excitement, for this
must be the occasion for us to contribute our small part to the state
and fulfill our long-standing aspirations.[7]

Even when the Korean expedition did not materialize, the Kanazawa samurai's hopes for action did not end. They formed a
samurai society in Kanazawa, the *Chūkokusha*, whose angry
expression combined frustration with the indecisiveness of the
Imperial government, bitter denunciation of others' rebellion
against it (especially Etō Shimpei's rebellion), and criticism of the
government's plans for internal improvements, which appeared
to them to place an excessive burden on the populace. On yet
another occasion, that of the punitive expedition to Formosa six
months after the Korean dispute, they again tried to seize the
opportunity to redeem themselves as samurai, by offering almost
an exact replica of the petition cited above.[8]

Similar associations and societies were formed during these
years among the samurai of Morioka, Tottori, Nagoya, and other
areas outside the four-domain nexus of Satsuma, Chōshū, Tosa,
and Saga. These developments reflected a complex perception of
the Imperial government on the part of the former samurai. On
the one hand, they were convinced that the government was fully
capable of devising means by which they could redeem themselves from past inaction and regain their old influence. On the
other hand, however, they were perfectly aware that such a conviction was rarely held by the government itself. In fact, in their
view, the Imperial government often appeared to be simply toying
with them. This was the reason that the samurai societies' responses vacillated between bitter opposition to and uncritical
support of the new regime.

It was also in this context that the former samurai were likely
to bring up the term *"minken,"* or popular rights. Their use of
the term did not merely designate a demand for wider popular
participation in government, however. Rather, the emotional tone

of the slogan was resonant with the frustration attendant upon their own obsolete desire to participate in the making of a new state. Their apparent interest in *minken* really stemmed from their hope of escaping into national participation from the confines of their local settings, which were suffocating them financially and psychologically.[9]

Given these circumstances among the former samurai throughout Japan, the political chemistry created among those in the southwestern domains by the return of the former Councilors was especially complex. There, the local samurai were not uniformly receptive to these powerful individuals' challenge to the central government, however high the samurai's hopes might initially have been raised by their return. Likewise, the returned Councilors never completely reciprocated the samurai's expectations, nor did all the local samurai feel the same about these leaders or about each other. The samurai in these localities might have been unified in relation to outsiders just as elsewhere, but internally they were far from one. The greatest internal division existed between those who had gone to serve in the Imperial government and those who had remained at home.

Such a division was particularly acute in these southwestern domains because they had been the backbone of the new regime. In Tosa, a government informant reported, there were three groups of samurai: one that rigidly maintained its feudalistic loyalty to the bygone daimyo; another that still tried to promote the cause of "Expel the Barbarians"; and a third that was loyal to Itagaki. The past careers of their returning fellows, Itagaki, Gotō, and others from the central government, and their publicized challenge to that government simply did not sit well with the first two groups of samurai, and deepened the hostility among all three.[10] A similar division was reported to exist even in Satsuma, where Saigō's popularity among the samurai had once been uncontested.[11]

The problem with the most profound consequence for the next phase of politics, however, was that the majority of samurai in these regions could not escape the economic and moral degradation plaguing samurai everywhere. Itagaki, when still in Tokyo, had already felt the impact of this economic plight upon his new political venture as he tried to assemble his Public Party of the Patriots in Tokyo. From the very beginning of its short life, the Party had depended upon Itagaki and a few others to raise the necessary funds for its operation, including travel expenses for some of the participants.[12] The urgent need for the economic rehabilitation of the samurai in their own domains, before any national political action could be taken, greatly inhibited the initial actions of the returning Councilors.

Under these circumstances, the former Councilors' first step was to establish local societies of their own followers, which then devoted much of their energies to seeking economic relief for their own samurai members. Such measures for economic and psychological relief diffused the political impact of the Councilors' return on the popular rights movement. The *Risshisha* (the Society of High Aspiration), established in Kōchi prefecture (formerly Tosa) in April 1874, is a case in point. Formally a local arm of Itagaki's popular rights campaign, the Society also engaged in a number of relief programs, including the founding of a tea-processing establishment and the acquisition of mountain and forest land for reclamation and for the harvest of natural resources. These programs not only largely failed,[13] but they also diluted the Society's stated *political* concern, the promotion of the popular rights movement. One *Risshisha* prospectus stated its general position that the state would prosper only when people knew how to discipline themselves, to help themselves, to govern themselves, and would thus depend *less* on the government.[14] This manifesto, with its criticism of the oligarchical few and belief in the importance of independent individuals, could easily be interpreted as an assertion of the need for "popular" political participation. But another prospectus prepared for circulation indicated the Society's more urgent preoccupation, which belied its supposedly popular orientation:

Unable to maintain their long-held positions, the former samurai are falling backward into the track of the servile and bigoted populace. The former samurai alone among the four classes [samurai, farmers, artisans, and merchants] possess knowledge and intelligence as well as free minds. As yet the other three classes are unable to mature, and the samurai have lost their former positions.... This means that the only people capable of fostering the state are losing their intelligence and spirit altogether.[15]

Therefore, the prospectus continued, the other three classes with stable livelihoods must come to the aid of the samurai, who could promote independent minds and advance the others into a more enlightened stage. Only then could all four classes be truly united, promoting the welfare of the nation.[16] In other words, the Society never clearly distinguished between the promotion of popular rights and the economic protection as well as social salvation of the samurai.

The preoccupation of such societies with the samurai relief also had an ironical consequence. Because measures such as purchasing mountain and forest lands for reclamation by the samurai members invariably involved approval from their prefectural governments, these societies became politically aligned with the local governing authorities. The Councilors' supporters were not hesitant about exploiting the national prominence of the returning Councilors in order to forge such alignments; this leverage even brought about their own appointments to administrative positions within the hierarchy of the prefectural governments. In Satsuma, a group that drew on Saigō's prominence and influence created a political alignment that reached all the way from the governor of the prefecture to the appointments of Saigo's own protégés to the *ku* posts of *kuchō* and *kochō*. Despite opposing samurai contingents, the resulting political machine could not have been stopped by anything short of large-scale central government interference. The irony was that the gains made through such alignments might have solidified their own select constituencies, but deepened factional distance with other local samurai groups who did not benefit from the alignments, and led the beneficiaries of the successful alignments to confuse their exclusivity for cohesiveness and effectiveness.

A strong alignment of Itagaki's followers, too, was forged to the neglect of other samurai contingents within Tosa.[17] This group, the *Risshisha*, tried to do everything expected of similar samurai associations elsewhere. In addition to instituting programs for economic relief, the members—like the Kanazawa samurai— sought opportunities for redemption. On the occasion of the Formosan punitive expedition, the *Risshisha* campaigned throughout Kōchi prefecture to enlist 5,000 volunteers and petitioned unsuccessfully to the central government and prefectural authority to be sent to Formosa. The personal tie between Itagaki, at the head of the *Risshisha*, and the Kōchi governor, Iwasaki Nagatake (also of Tosa origin), provided the political leverage to promote the welfare of the Society's members, including their administrative appointments in the ken government. The *Risshisha* at times even managed the finances of the Kōchi ken administration.[18] The central government, alarmed by the simultaneous development of such alignments in Tosa and Satsuma, first tried to weaken the Tosa alignment by replacing Iwasaki, only to learn of the strength of the interdependence between the ken administration and the *Risshisha*. The new governor, Koike Kunitake (from Nagano), facing an imminent protest from the *Risshisha* members, had no choice but to turn to them for consultation.[19] By 1877, the important posts in the ken administration of Kōchi were all occupied by *Risshisha* members.[20] The growth of the *Risshisha's* political, as opposed to simply economic usefulness, thus consisted in large measure of the increasing ability of its key members to use it as a source of power in Tosa. With such growth came reinforcement of the *Risshisha's* promotion of the interest of its samurai members under the aegis of popular rights. The *Risshisha's* achievements were thus tied to its members, and its "popular rights" did not expand to a wider group.

Therefore, although this lobbying for concessions might have created a solid constituency, it could not contribute to the expansion of that constituency as promised in the stated platforms of the popular rights movement. This inherent limit to the impact of the *Risshisha* action became even more apparent when removed from the local political arena. Two events in early 1875 illustrate this problem, to which Itagaki and his followers remained oblivious. One was the Osaka Conference (January through February), which Ōkubo Toshimichi, Kido Kōin, and Itagaki attended to discuss the return of Kido and Itagaki to the

Imperial government. The other was the formation of the *Aiko-kusha*, the Society of the Patriots, also in Osaka, on February 22. Itagaki and his followers held these two events to be a testament to their capability for collective action, initiated in the *Aikoku-kōtō* and tested against the Tosa background of the *Risshisha*. They believed that they had wrested concessions from the government for constitutional improvements and thereby forged a central link in a coalition of wider constitutional forces across the localities.[21] Careful investigation of these months in early 1875, however, does not support their view.

Despite claims to the contrary, the Osaka Conference was not a direct result of Itagaki's or his followers' pressure upon the government. Rather, the Conference was designed and promoted by Itō Hirobumi as Ōkubo's proxy and Inoue Kaoru as Kido's, primarily to bring Kido back to the government from his home, where he had retreated in protest over the military expedition to Formosa a year earlier. The government was also alarmed by the loss of personnel, given the departure within a year and half of Saigō Takamori, Etō Shimpei, Kido Kōin, and Itagaki Taisuke, among others. Also worrisome for Ōkubo, as Andrew Fraser points out, were signs that his managerially gifted lieutenants were quarreling among themselves in the central government.[22] Despite these problems, however, none of the participants—including Kido— betrayed a particularly urgent sense of crisis at the Conference. Nor did any show a recognition of the particular parliamentary initiative in constitutional development that Itagaki and his followers claimed to have engineered through the formation of the *Aikokusha*.

The results of the Conference were the return of Kido and Itagaki to the central government and the establishment of a four-point, government reform program. These measures were the separation of the administrative and deliberative responsibilities that previously had been performed indistinguishably by the Councilors; the establishment of the *Genrō-in* as a more autonomous alternative to the *Sa-in*; the creation of the *Daishin-in* as a step toward a more modern, autonomous judicial system; and the promotion of a prefectural governors' conference. These measures, however, were implemented because Kido insisted upon the creation of harmony among the branches, and were devised really to placate him.

Thus the significance of Itagaki's presence was at best secondary, [23] and even the "concession" Itagaki gained from the Conference was none other than his own return to the Imperial government. Furthermore, Itagaki's own creation had begun to inhibit his political action in the months preceding and following the Osaka Conference. Just as the need for the *Risshisha* to provide economic relief for its members had prompted the exploitation of Itagaki's prominence with the Kōchi prefectural government, the subsequent failure of these relief programs pressed Itagaki to exploit his prominence again, this time with the central government, in asking for funds to salvage his rehabilitation projects.[24] And just as the *Risshisha's* politically critical purpose gradually shifted in Kōchi to the dispensing of administrative posts, the *Aikokusha*, its national version, also diluted its critical stance toward the Imperial government. A cynical observer described the *Aikokusha's* operation: "The shortest cut to acquiring government posts is to join the *Aikokusha*."[25]

The government's initiative in arranging the Osaka Conference has given the misleading impression that the central authority was under strong pressure from the popular rights protest movements. However, it should be noted that these protest movements did not all share the desire to open the central arena of politics to progressively more diverse and wider forces in society. In fact, the protesters ranged from those demanding popular representation at the prefectural level to those samurai to whom the "popular rights" movement was primarily a vehicle for redeeming themselves by regaining their lost political visibility. As seen above, Itagaki's activities hardly made him representative of all of these voices. As the nucleus for expanding the constituency of the Petitioner tradition, his *Risshisha-Aikokusha* nexus had begun to reveal its inherent limits.

Itagaki went back to the central government after a little over a year's absence, again leaving one of his societies stranded, this time the *Aikokusha*. Etō Shimpei and Saigō Takamori died as rebels in their domains in 1874 and 1877, respectively. The return of these former Councilors to their home domains had seemed to promise a turning point in early Meiji constitutional development toward popular participation or a more open political system. Yet in retrospect, the return of the Councilors did not realize the kind of change that, in the eyes of the government or of those who had expected constitutional improvement, it may have seemed to support.

### The Popular Rights Movement and the Rebellious Samurai

The prevailing belief retained by all of these samurai, even among the leading activists of populist persuasion, was the residual certainty of samurai superiority over the populace they seemingly wished to represent. As noted earlier, this attitude was indicated in a *Risshisha* prospectus suggesting class limits on the samurai-sponsored popular rights movements and the government opposition. The closed, political, patron-clientele relationships between the former Councilors and their followers, to the exclusion even of other samurai in the same domains, certainly seemed to contradict wider political participation. In addition to this arrogance and exclusivity, a greater hindrance to the political impact of the return of the Councilors was the view of local politics among those southwestern samurai who had once played significant roles in bringing about the Restoration. They saw prefectural politics as a resource to be exploited both to resurrect their own political influence and to make it felt *nationally*.

Samurai consciousness of their "rightful" place proved especially obstructive to the popular rights movements when linked with its other expression, domain identity. Identity based upon domain evoked the dynamics of pre–*Haihan chiken* politics, in which it had guaranteed access to the governing authority, and even of pre-Meiji politics, in which it had provided an entry to the national theater of the Restoration movement. An example of this continuing preoccupation with domain identity occurred in 1874. When approached by the Saga rebels regarding a simultaneous uprising in Tosa, Hayashi Yūzō, Itagaki's associate, stuck by his own Tosa plan: "I am a Shikoku man. Unless the uprising commenced in Shikoku and aimed at taking over the Osaka Garrison Station of the government, any organizing of supporters on our part would be unlikely."[26] The central government had no aversion to exploiting this provincial pride of the former samurai to its own advantage. When confronted with the Satsuma Rebellion, the government called upon former daimyo and vassals of high standing, now serving in the Imperial government, to enlist their former retainers to fight the rebels. Interestingly, the local samurai, like their former daimyo, responded to this call to arms as regional groups of men and not as individuals.[27] Hayashi Yūzō agreed to fight but requested that Tosa samurai volunteers be separated from those of the other domains and placed under Tosa officers.[28] The irony of the return of the Councilors was, thus, that it inspired a reenactment of the pre-Restoration political dynamics that had lifted them to national prominence; only this time, the central government was not the Tokugawa bakufu, and the slogan of "Expel the Barbarians" was replaced by "popular rights."

Viewed in this light, the *Risshisha* members' seemingly contradictory actions—their attempt to forge a coalition with Saigō to challenge Ōkubo, Kido, and others in the central government at one point, and their alliance with Kido at another, as evident at the Osaka Conference—were actually consistent. Their aim was to keep the central arena of politics open while promoting their old domain identity. Thus, in the case of the Satsuma Rebellion, the *Risshisha* members on the one hand appeared willing to cooperate with the government by agreeing to send their Tosa volunteers, as we have just seen, provided that they remained under the Tosa officers and separate from the national troops. On the other hand, they still tried to retain the option of challenging the central government: some of their members, including Hayashi Yūzō, were arrested for purchasing weapons to attack a target of their own, the government garrison station in Osaka castle, and for plotting to assassinate some of the key government leaders.[29] In all of these actions, one important feature of the samurai's behavior remained unchanged: the desire to influence the government without compromising their domain identity.

In this light, too, the lessons of the Satsuma Rebellion of 1877 and its failure need to be reexamined. The failure meant far more than the subsequent marked disappearance of samurai armed revolts. Tōyama Shigeki has taken the view that the Rebellion by its failure compelled the groups opposing the government to drop one type of method, direct action, and to adopt the indirect method of influencing the course of constitutional development.[30] Political developments, however, were not as linear as Tōyama portrays. First, the growth in the use of nonviolent methods did not even coincide with the end of the Satsuma Rebellion. An uneasiness about samurai-led or samurai sponsored government protests had already been in the air for some time. Activists such as Kōno Hironaka of Fukushima, who had been close to the *Risshisha*, had warned all along of the drawbacks of a coalition between Itagaki and the others in the event of a successful Satsuma Rebellion—a government by militaristic and anachronistic samurai that would include Saigō and his provincial lieutenants.[31] But more importantly, there was no single, coherent organizational opposition to the government, nor was there a single set of opposition goals. Thus the failure of one type of action could not lead to a change in methods even within one group, because no method or goal could elicit consensus internally, let alone externally. Furthermore, the residual domain identities discouraged the various samurai opposition groups' interest in each other. Thus even an obvious failure in one group's method would not necessarily lead to the elimination of that same method by the others.[32] The Satsuma Rebellion was thought to be largely the act of Satsuma alone, even though it attracted many supporters from the neighboring domains, just as the petitioners' earlier act had appeared to Saigō to be mostly that of Tosa. The real lesson of the Rebellion was that domain identity, which before the *Haihan chiken* had facilitated action for political change, now could only impede it.

The limits of samurai leadership of the popular rights movement, however, did not dawn immediately on its founders because the movement continued to expand rapidly. After the Satsuma Rebellion, the *Risshisha* leaders resurrected the *Aikokusha* in September 1878 in Osaka, where it had begun in 1875. This first attempt at revival drew participants little different from those in the original *Aikokusha*.[33] But the second meeting of the new *Aikokusha*, held in March 1879, again in Osaka, brought in some eighty participants from eighteen prefectures. Later in the same year, the third meeting witnessed the beginning of an expansion in geographical representation among the participants that included, for the first time, those from the northeastern regions. In March 1880, the *Aikokusha* meeting gathered 114 delegates representing 87,000 members of some 80 associations and societies in 24 prefectures. From this gathering emerged the *Kokkai kisei dōmeikai* (the League for Opening a National Assembly), whose second meeting in November of the same year had delegates representing 135,000 members of local associations and societies.[34] This rapid growth in the number of participants and geographical representation in the movement led to qualitative changes in it that began to discredit the *Risshisha* leaders' claim to have led the expansion.

At the first meeting of the resurrected *Aikokusha* in September 1878, the samurai's objective remained conspicuously that of regaining their own political influence. Some samurai representatives from Saga and Kanazawa even demanded that the word *"minken"* be either deemphasized or replaced by another, *"kin'nō"* ("Revere the Emperor").[35] At the same time, however, the samurai hegemony of the *Risshisha-Aikokusha* was being increasingly threatened. For example, non-*Risshisha* and non-Tosa members attempted to open a branch office of the *Aikokusha* in Tokyo. These attempts soon developed into a more direct challenge to the claim of the *Risshisha-Aikokusha* nexus to dictate the course of the popular rights movement. At the third meeting in late 1879, the proposal by the chairman, a Tosa samurai, that a petition to the Imperial government for a national assembly by popular election be prepared and submitted in the name of the *Aikokusha*, provoked strong protests from many participants. The protesters' demand was to emphasize the legitimacy of their petition as coming from the "people" rather than just from the *Aikokusha*.[36]

The period of the Satsuma Rebellion was also a turning point in the popular rights movement, and Kōno Hironaka's dissatisfaction with the Rebellion was very much an expression of it. The popular rights cause was beginning to move beyond its original form of diffused government opposition embracing many different forms of samurai protest and self-expression. The new developments showed two contrasting results: the increase in the conscious promotion of the *minken* ideals, as well as its symbols, by those who had been subtly critical of samurai-led protests; and the disappearance from the movement of those samurai formerly active in it. The samurai protesters were beginning to feel the difficulty of reconciling themselves with this new, nonsamurai phase of the overall popular rights movement.

The gradual and general decline in the degree of commitment by local samurai associations to the movement and the government protest in general even included the *Jijosha* of northern Shikoku and others that had come to the original *Aikokusha* meeting. Some of this withdrawal can be attributed to the continued influence of factors mentioned earlier, such as the samurai's financial difficulties, their realization of the limited use of the *minken* to sustain their associations, and dissatisfaction with the fact that leading figures in the associations seemed to regard them as a springboard for gaining government posts. More significant, however, was their long-standing animosity toward alignment with the nonsamurai strata.[37] On this last count even the *Risshisha* members were no exception. In 1879, prefectural assemblies by popular election were established by thirty-eight prefectures to implement the Regulations for the Fu-Ken Assemblies (*Fu-Ken kai kisoku*, July 22, 1878), and the Kōchi prefectural assembly was opened in October 1879. However, with electoral eligibility based on a ten-yen land-tax payment, the majority of the local samurai, who were still impoverished, did not become enfranchised. The condescending reaction of the *Risshisha* leaders to the resulting nonsamurai representation in the prefectural assembly revealed an important holdover from the past in their attitudes: "The assembly consists mainly of rich farmers," and hence their public deliberations "require no particularly outstanding intelligence and knowledge. . . ."[38]

In the meantime, a new course of action independent of the *Risshisha-Aikokusha* initiatives began to emerge in the movement. Led primarily by the prefectural assembly men, the majority of whom were not samurai, this new development was more than just a historical accident coinciding with the decline of samurai visibility in the movement. As a point of reference for the collective actions of these new actors, their shared experiments with various elective bodies at village, township, *ku* and finally prefectural levels took the place of the old attraction to national affairs that had been typical of many samurai activists. This emergence of new political actors brought into the movement more concrete, local concerns, such as the problems of prefectural taxation policies or expenditures. Thus, inevitably, as the movement was used as a tool of political expression by these newcomers, it became explicitly as well as implicitly disassociated from the 1874 Petitioner tradition.

An example of this new attitude can be found in a prospectus by Sakurai Shizuka of Chiba prefecture. In June 1879 he proposed a coalition among the prefectural assemblymen throughout the localities to seek a form of representation at the national level quite different from that of the former samurai:

> The people's right to be represented in the prefectural assemblies and the efficient promotion of the people's welfare by means of their power of approval or disapproval of tax legislation [at the assemblies] are indeed severely limited. It is obvious that the true benefit [of these measures] cannot be realized until a national assembly opens.[39]

The proposal was sent to prefectural assemblymen throughout Japan.[40] In response to Sakurai's proposal, a few representatives of the Okayama assembly sought to organize a regional coalition of neighboring prefectures. Even though this regional version did not materialize, the attempt showed that the *a priori* fascination with national affairs typical of many samurai activists was gone, giving way to proposals for bringing *local* concerns to a *national* body.

This new trend produced many petitions requesting the government to open up a national assembly by popular election. Some preceded and were independent of the one prepared by the *Aikokusha*.[41] In one petition, prepared in December 1879 and submitted to the government the following month by representatives from Fukuoka ken, the usual *Risshisha-Aikokusha* condemnation of "despotism by the oligarchical few" was now deemphasized. Instead, the experiment in political participation in the prefectural assemblies was hailed as the model for participation at the national level. Another, prepared in the same month by the members of the Okayama assembly mentioned above, did even more to counter the *Risshisha-Aikokusha* tradition.

This petition by the Okayama assemblymen projected its own identity by virtue of its repudiation of the self-righteousness of the samurai ingrained in that tradition: "We, the commoners, are implied to be still ignorant and immature, [but] how can we, having some intelligence, not be incited and appalled [by these signs of condescension]?" Although it referred to the 1874 Petition by the former Councilors as the origin of the movement, the Okayama petition departed from that source in important ways. It went on to blame the problems plaguing the nation, such as the recurrence of the samurai revolts or Japan's unequal treaty status, on the absence of true communication between the upper and lower orders of society. Such communication, the petition emphasized, must be real and positive rather than merely symbolic. "[We learn from the West that] the people's rights are not something that the rulers grant to the people, but something that the people willfully acquire...." Most importantly, the Okayama petition distinctly departed from the 1874 Petition in a passing remark revealing its nonsamurai orientation: "Those who aspire to the opening of a national assembly are not only learned men and activists of high birth but also ordinary people of the middle and lower classes across the nation...."[42] Not surprisingly, at the meeting before the drafting of the petition, a move to elect representatives to the rally from the ranks of the samurai was soundly defeated by the participants, more than 80 percent of whom were of nonsamurai origin.[43] This was only the logical outcome of an action that really owed very little to the 1874 Petitioner tradition and even less to the samurai estrangement from Restoration politics.

The groups opposing the government in the early Meiji period thus paradoxically combined attempts to direct rapid changes in political life and to resist those changes. Some simply wanted to reverse them; others hoped the changes would be either faster or slower. Differences in preferred directions, however, were often not as important to those opposing the government as were differences in their degree of commitment to the act of opposition. It is primarily in this specific context that the popular rights movement was frequently identical with the opposition to the government in general; the platforms of popular rights were sufficiently ambiguous to embrace the varied reasons for strong aversion to a government that appeared unresponsive. However, even from the start, the ideological thrust of the popular rights movement was also sufficiently specific to cause internal differentiation among those critical of the government. The expansion in number and diversity of participants in the movement inevitably made it difficult for it to maintain any sort of unity and cohesiveness, while at the same time accommodating to its diverse constituents. When differentiation did develop, it was the former samurai who began to see the movement as less and less instrumental in expressing their sentiments and hopes. The popular rights cause opened politics to at least some of that local populace to whom the Restoration had been a remote event. But for the majority of the samurai in the movement, it became yet another lost opportunity for redemption.

## Limits on the Future

The diversity of the groups opposing the government, then, demonstrates that, by the end of the first decade after the demise of the bakufu, Restoration politics was indeed moving into a new stage. To recall briefly, the center-local linkages in politics had changed most fundamentally in the nature of their authority relationship just before and after the *Haihan chiken*. Before it, even after the Restoration, such linkages had operated on the basis that the Imperial government was the "central" government but one which was barely more powerful than such feudal governments as Satsuma, Chōshū, Tosa, or Saga individually. The threat thus existed that these "peripheries" collectively could overwhelm the authority of the "central" government. The two seemingly contradictory dynamics of the dispersion and concentration of power were sustained, albeit more consciously after the Restoration, on the basis of both the confidence and the fear that corresponded to the central government's basing its authority on the domains.

Against this background, the post–*Haihan chiken* developments brought about some changes and also revealed what could not be so easily changed. On the one hand, the primarily hegemonial relationship of the Imperial government to the feudal domains lost its institutional framework. It was replaced by another more functional type of relationship, a division of political labor, which began to regulate both the central and the local, that is, the prefectural governments. This shift, as we saw in Chapter 6, was the catalyst for the increasing administrative reliance on the *ku* officials which in effect enfranchised the nonsamurai strata and in turn facilitated their more general political participation. On the other hand, these developments also required an abrupt shift in political orientation on the part of those who had based their actions on the pre–*Haihan chiken* authority relationship between the central government and the domains. These were the Restoration leaders whose domain identity had provided guaranteed access to the central arena of politics and whose loss of political influence during the Saigō administration had led them to return home. Their failure or refusal to accommodate to the shift, or the realization that the cost of the shift would exceed its benefits for themselves and their preferred political development, had led these men to defect from the government. The resulting climate of government opposition initially found its most ready allies in the former samurai, who all along had least benefited from the post–*Haihan chiken* reforms. But one factor had remained unchanged and actually was reinforced by these leaders and their samurai followers: their belief in the dispersion-concentration dynamics which had surfaced in the forming of the Restoration coalition and had been strengthened by the process of maintaining it.

The attempts during the second half of the 1870s to exploit these dynamics against a background in which the promptings of the Restoration coalition were now largely inactive, however, inevitably made the defected Councilors' actions uniquely reactionary. Saigō's and Etō's resorting to violence and Itagaki's turning to constitutional measures were identical in one way. They all operated on the assumption, or hope, that the hegemonial authority relationship between the central government and the domains, now submerged within the new localities, could be reinstated—with themselves back at the hegemonial center. For Saigō and Etō this attempt ended abruptly, as they died leading local rebellions. But even for Itagaki the shift was no less difficult. Most of his organizational activities were slowed by preoccupations such as samurai relief that were not directly relevant to his constitutional campaign. More importantly, his action had to rely on his samurai followers, who, as the formerly dominant social class, resisted the passing of the old authority relationship and the coming of the new, as embodied in the nonsamurai strata who were gaining firmer footholds in prefectural politics.

The transition to a new stage of Meiji politics did not, obviously, mean complete discontinuity for these individuals and for society. Itagaki remained a central figure in the popular rights movement and shuttled back and forth between government leaders and his lieutenants in the movement. Yet it is unlikely that he had come to a clear realization that further dispersion of power had to hinge on the progressive inclusion of more new actors, since this would have provoked even more resistance from his samurai followers. It seems more likely that he was exploiting both his prominence as a former Restoration leader and his newly acquired status as a spokesman for the government opposition to supplement his political influence. In his case it would never be clear just how far the principle of dispersion could have been pressed. Since his criticism of the government arose more from the sense that his "rightful" prominence as a Restoration leader had been slighted by the others than from a belief that wider political participation was genetically needed to make the government more accountable to the populace, Itagaki's opposition was bound to cease when he was accepted back into the central government.

The sense that the change in Restoration politics was profound was not widespread. The popular rights movement itself had as yet facilitated the enfranchisement of only a very small fraction of the nonsamurai strata. Beyond the mobilization of those in prefectural politics, the inclusion of new political actors was slow and limited. The coming of a new stage of Meiji politics was thus only gradually evolving from an even more gradual recognition of it.

In another sense, the transition was incomplete. The popular rights movement had been employing an inductive sort of reasoning to support the increase in political participation: participation in politics at one level (village, township, or *ku*) justified participation at another, higher level of *fu* and *ken*, which in turn justified the demand for participation at the still higher national one. This argument by the newly enfranchised generated pressure leading to a government response at progressively higher levels, but not in a manner that added a wider range of political actors. There were, in other words, two conservative trends in the popular pressures for political participation: the promotion and preservation of the status only of those *already* enfranchised, and their participation at a level lower than the one they sought.

Even as the government limited its response to these pressures, the newly enfranchised were bound to become less and less critical of the central authority's limited accountability to only a small segment of the populace. Thus, when the government issued the imperial decree in 1881 announcing the opening of a national assembly in 1890, the popular rights movement actually ceased to promote further constitutional debates. Those already enfranchised used the nine years between 1881 and 1890 to ensure that they would still be the major beneficiaries of participation at this new, highest level. The newly established national assembly, which would secure their presence in the central arena of politics, was thus not to become a means of expanding government accountability even further. It would instead be used to dispense the benefits of institutionalized access to governing power to those who had already been enfranchised.[44]

The failure of the former Councilors' attempts to make the Imperial government once again responsive to them also left an important mark on the political thinking of some of those leaders who remained in the government. As dramatized by the dispute over the Korean expedition, the paralysis of the central authority

led Ōkubo Toshimichi to revamp the government, minus its defected Councilors. He managed to retain for its pivotal posts men
such as Itō Hirobumi and Ōkuma Shigenobu, who seemed to him
the least prone to the anachronistic view that their place in the
government was ensured by their past contributions to the Restoration. Ironically, Ōkubo's life came to a premature end on May
14, 1878, at the hands of a band of samurai assassins who saw in
his actions an outright violation of his own belief in the invincible
authority of the emperor. Ōkubo, according to one of his admiring
biographers, is quoted as having said on the morning of his death:
"The era of creation is now over, and the second decade will be
devoted to internal improvements and development."[45] Had he
lived, he would have seen this prediction realized to a large extent.
However, he also would have seen, in the new but limited trend
toward a more open political system, an unexpected twist to his
efforts to extricate the governing authority from the self-ap-
pointed proxies of the emperor.

After Ōkubo's death, his plea for a detached authority was transformed by the following generations of government leaders. It
became simply a proposition about the formal holder of the governing authority, the emperor in particular, rather than about the
governing authority in general. The protection of the locus of
authority from personal exploitation began to mean the protection
of the emperor from excessive exposure to those who sought his
sanction. Even more strikingly, the protection of the government
from the accidents of personality became the insulation of the
emperor from political responsibility.

Another consequence of this uniquely paternalistic view of the
formal holder of the governing authority was an ambivalent attitude on the part of the leaders toward Japan's constitutional
development. The receptiveness of the government leaders to political participation was checked by the consideration that the
emperor himself must remain immune to such pressures. The
writing of the Constitution of 1889, which was to define explicitly
the role of the emperor and his prerogatives, also indicated implicitly the ways in which the emperor's exposure could be minimized. In other words, the Constitution was designed so as not
to impede the insulation of the emperor from political respon-

sibility. He was no longer clearly to be the final arbiter of disputes, or "the repository of the will to achieve agreement and maintain order among the various interests which compete for power under him."[46] The emperor could not be held so readily responsible, at least not until occasions arose that might be deemed critical enough to warrant his action.

This protective orientation toward the emperor fostered one paradox of serious political consequence. The continued need for access to the ultimate holder of the governing authority, which had to be satisfied without violating his insulation, led to the tolerance of extraconstitutional channels through which the emperor's authority—and his prerogatives— could be called upon in order to legitimize the decisions made *within* the confines of the constitutional framework. The *Genrō*, elder statesmen of undefined political status,[47] formed just such a channel, whose legitimacy originally did not come from the Constitution or from any explicit stipulations of their role. Their access to the emperor was ensured by their personal credentials, which included distinct records of service in the Restoration movement and in a central government that had survived the first decade of its precarious existence. In other words, it was the Restoration enshrined and preserved in these men that assured them, as well as the government as a whole through them, of a special relationship to the emperor. However, to the extent that the government relied on this extraconstitutional channel for its authority, it, too, was never held responsible for its actions. In addition, to the extent that the authority of the emperor remained accessible to extraconstitutional actors, the government remained vulnerable to the competing voices of those, within and without the constitutional framework, who might claim to have his sanction.

The perpetuation of the *Genrō* saw a further paradox in the following decades. The generations changed and the Restoration "preserved" in these men, as well as in society, began to fade. The *Genrō*, however, did not disappear; new *Genrō* replaced the old. They became an institution whose legitimacy was based in that limbo where the Constitution was least clear. Also, the *Genrō's* exploitation of their access to the emperor never developed into a systematic practice, and instead, they were often routinely called upon to solve political disagreements such as the appointment of prime ministers or the formation of cabinets. Thus, the use of their proximity to the emperor by the *Genrō* became routinized and integrated into the formal political process, thereby further weakening the fundamental basis for the government's authority.

Such routinization of access to the emperor resulted in another paradox. The *formal* protection of the emperor from political responsibility continued to be reinforced, even though it began to erode in practice. Eventually, the occasions critical enough to warrant the involvement of this final arbiter became undefinable—in effect making those occasions nonexistent. Much later, toward the end of World War II, the central government leaders categorically rejected the idea of forming a government under a member of the Imperial family, despite the fact that the deterioration of Japan's position in the war warranted extraordinary measures. In other words, the routinization of the use of the authority entrusted to the emperor left only the most extreme contingency as, paradoxically, the ultimate occasion for the emperor and his family to remain politically irresponsible.[48] Ōkubo's original plea to strengthen the government by placing the governing authority above the entanglements of the proxies of its formal holder, having undergone many twists in its evolution, ended by resulting in the weakening of the political system at its very core.

# Notes

## Introduction

1. See Hall, "A Monarch for Modern Japan," in Ward, ed., *Political Development in Modern Japan*, especially pp. 19–59.

2. For an excellent analysis of this peculiar feature of Tokugawa feudalism, see Hall, "Feudalism in Japan," in Hall and Jansen, eds., *Studies in the Institutional History of Early Modern Japan*, pp. 15–51.

3. This term from Carl J. Friedrich, "Nation-Building?" in Deutsch and Foltz, eds., *Nation-Building*, p. 31, stresses the stage of political development in which the populace achieved the sense of both nationhood and a common "central" governing authority.

4. Bolitho, *Treasures among Men.*

5. Among the works in English, see, for example, McLaren, ed., "Japanese Government Documents"; Beckmann, *The Making of the Meiji Constitution*; and Wilson, "Genesis of the Meiji Government." A number of Japanese works cover this decade, and some of these works will

be listed as this study proceeds. A particularly useful reference work is Tōyama Shigeki and Adachi Shizuko, eds., _Kindai Nihon seijishi hikkei_.

6. Tōyama Shigeki, _Meiji ishin_, and Norman, _Japan's Emergence as a Modern State (1940)_, in Dower, ed. and comp., _Origins of the Modern Japanese State_, pp. 109–316. William G. Beasley, although distant from the critical language of these two historians, still adopts the basic pattern of political development presented by them for bakumatsu politics and the Meiji Restoration in his _Meiji Restoration_.

7. Tanaka Akira, _Meiji ishin seijishi kenkyū_, and _Kindai tennōsei eno dōtei_; Shibahara Takuji, _Meiji ishin no kenryoku_.

8. Beasley, _The Meiji Restoration_, p. 326.

9. The exceptions are Sakata Yoshio and John W. Hall, both of whom place far more significance than others upon the threat of Western encroachment as the cause for the Restoration movement. Consequently, the role of the period preceding the 1850s becomes less decisive. See Sakata Yoshio, "Meiji ishin no mondaiten," in Sakata Yoshio, ed., _Meiji ishin no mondaiten_, and Sakata and Hall, "The Motivation of Political Leadership in the Meiji Restoration," _Journal of Asian Studies_ 16 (1956): 31–50.

10. Ōe Shinobu, _Meiji kokka no seiritsu_, p. 39.

11. Norman, _Japan's Emergence_, p. 115.

12. Inoue Kiyoshi, _Nihon gendaishi_, and Haraguchi Kiyoshi, _Nihon kindai kokka no keisei_.

13. Shimoyama Saburō, _Kindai tennōsei kenkyū josetsu_, pp. 79–116.

14. See, for example, Jansen, "The Meiji State," in Crowley, ed., _Modern East Asia_, especially pp. 97–103, and Beasley, _The Meiji Restoration_, especially Chapter 12.

15. See, for example, Akita, _Foundations of Constitutional Government_.

16. Norman, _Japan's Emergence_.

17. For the notion of the dispersion and concentration of political power facilitating political change, see Maruyama Masao, "Meiji kokka no shisō," in Rekishi gakkai, ed., _Nihon shakai no shiteki kyūmei_, Tokyo, 1949 pp. 181–236.

## 1. Restoration

1. See Smith, _Agrarian Origins of Modern Japan_, Chapter 11, for the disequilibrated class distinctions. See also Aoki Kōji, _Hyakushō ikki sōgō nempyō_, for the regional distribution and the frequency of rural disruptions throughout the Tokugawa period.

2. Huber, *Revolutionary Origins of Modern Japan.*

3. Totman, *Collapse of the Tokugawa Bakufu,* especially pp. 331–72.

4. Two representative works on the shogunal bureaucracy are Kitajima Masamoto, *Edo bakufu no kenryoku kōzō,* especially Chapters 3 and 4, and Totman, *Politics in the Tokugawa Bakufu,* Chapters 3 and 4.

5. For the cases of transfers and confiscations of the daimyo fiefs by the bakufu throughout the Tokugawa period, see Fujino Tamotsu, *Bakusei to hansei,* Appendix.

6. The best description of the *sankin kōtai* is Tsukahira, *Feudal Control of Tokugawa Japan.*

7. Smith, "Japan's Aristocratic Revolution," Bendix and Lipset, eds., *Class, Status, and Power,* pp. 135–40.

8. Huber, *Revolutionary Origins,* pp. 226–27 and passim.

9. See, for example, the travel diary of a Chōshū activist, Takasugi Shinsaku, while he was in Shanghai in 1862. *Tōgyō sensei ibun,* pp. 72–124.

10. *Saimukiji,* vol. 1, pp. 141–43, 183, and *Zoku saimukiji,* vol. 1, pp. 121–22, 421–23. See also Honjō Eijirō, *Bakumatsu no shinseisaku,* in *Honjō Eijirō chosakushū,* vol. 9, pp. 92–112.

11. Totman, *Collapse of the Tokugawa Bakufu,* p. xv.

12. See, for example, the behavior of Shimazu Hisamitsu, a Satsuma lord, in Tokutomi Iichirō, *Kinsei Nihon kokuminshi,* vol. 86, pp. 224–26; and Katsuta Magoya, *Ōkubo Toshimichi den,* vol. 1, pp. 183–271.

13. On this formula, known as the Union of the Court and the Military or the Camp, see Totman, *Collapse of the Tokugawa Bakufu,* pp. 269–304, and Beasley, *The Meiji Restoration,* Chapter 11.

14. Nakaoka Shintarō, "Dōshi ni okuru no sho," (1866) in Watanabe Yosuke, comp., *Kinnō shishi ibunshū,* vol. 1, pp. 429–36.

15. Ōkubo Toshimichi's letter to a Satsuma domain official on 9/23/1865, *Ōkubo Toshimichi monjo,* vol. 1, p. 293. For the use of the notion by a Chōshū activist, see also Takasugi Shinsaku, *Tōgyō sensei ibun,* pp. 136, 184.

16. Dajōkan, ed., *Fukkoki,* vol. 1, pp. 111–36 and passim.

17. See *Iwakurakō jikki,* vol. 2, pp. 203–22, for an eyewitness account of developments during and after the Kogosho Conference.

18. Kido Kōin's letter to Shinagawa Yajirō, a Chōshū activist, on 12/17/1867, *Kido Kōin monjo,* vol. 2, pp. 336–40.

19. *Iwakurakō jikki,* vol. 2, p. 209. Nakane Yukie, a retainer of Fukui han, was the most articulate spokesman of this position. See

also *Teibō nikki*, in *KIN*, vol. 7, book 1, passim. Although Iwakura Tomomi was considered one of the militants, more often than not he appeared quite susceptible to Nakane's persuasion. *Iwakurakō jikki*, vol. 2, p. 204.

20. For an interview with Tokugawa Yoshinobu, which revealed a great deal of his strong conviction that the removal of Satsuma from Kyoto could reverse the turn of events to the Tokugawa's advantage, see Shibusawa Eiichi, ed., *Sekimukai hikki* (1915), pp. 71–72.

21. For Ōkubo's proposal to move the capital to Osaka, see Sashihara Yasuzō, *Meiji seishi*, in *MBZ*, vol. 9, pp. 25–26; Shimoyama Saburō, *Kindai tennōsei kenkyū*, pp. 80–81.

22. See, for example, Ōkubo Toshimichi's letter of 1/22/1868 to Minoda Denbei, a Satsuma official, for Ōkubo's frustration. *Ōkubo Toshimichi monjo*, vol. 2, pp. 128–45.

23. *Ishin nisshi*, vol. 5, p. 125, and Dajōkan, ed., *Fukkoki*, vol. 1, p. 416.

24. Haraguchi Kiyoshi, *Boshin sensō*, provides the most succinct account of the War of the Restoration, whereas Ishii Takashi synthesizes many interpretations of the war in his richly documented *Boshin sensōron*.

25. *Fuken shiryō*, Chiba, book 3; Dajōkan, ed., *Fukkoki*, vol. 3, p. 207; and Kimura Motoi and Sugimoto Toshio, eds., *Fudai hansei no tenkai to Meiji ishin*, pp. 310–12.

26. *Shinshū Shimanekenshi*, vol. 2, pp. 12–15; "Sanindō chimbushi shimatsusho," in *Fuken shiryō*, Shimane, book 1.

27. Dajōkan, ed., *Fukkoki*, vol. 1, p. 486.

28. Ibid., pp. 581–82, 689, and Shidankai, comp., *Shidankai sokkiroku*, vol. 18, pp. 392–96.

29. Dajōkan, ed., *Fukkoki*, vol. 1, pp. 747–48.

30. Ibid., p. 759.

31. Ibid., vol. 2, pp. 557–58; vol. 4, p. 348; and *Dajōkan nisshi*, no. 12, 1868, in *KIN*, vol. 1, book 1, pp. 22–23.

32. It is not clear how the figure of 700,000 *koku* was arrived at for the new fief of the Tokugawa mainhouse. Iwakura Tomomi believed that "even if the fief was to be set at 2,000,000 *koku*, the resistance of the *hatamoto* would be unavoidable." *Iwakura Tomomi kankei monjo*, vol. 3, pp. 513–17. See also Ishii Takashi, *Boshin sensōron*, pp. 152–61, for a discussion of different alternatives aired among the Restoration leaders before the final decision.

33. *Chinshōfu nisshi*, nos. 1 and 7, 1868, in *KIN*, vol. 6, pp. 162, 238.

34. Katsu Kaishū, *Suijinroku*, in *Kaishū zenshū*, vol. 4, pp. 130–48.

35. Totman, *Politics in the Tokugawa Bakufu*, p. 74.

36. Katsu Kaishū, "Daikanron," in *Suijinroku*, in *Kaishū zenshū.*, vol. 3, pp. 104–5, and Ogyū Sorai, "Seidan," in Bitō Masahide, comp., *Nihon no meicho*, pp. 465–66.

37. Katsu Kaishū, *Kainanroku*, in *Kaishū zenshū.*, vol. 2, p. 325.

38. Dajōkan, ed., *Fukkoki*, vol. 1, p. 516.

39. On Sagara Sōzō and other self-styled "pacification missions," see *Sagara Sōzō kankei shiryō* (Chiba, 1975), and Kurihara Ryūichi, *Bakumatsu shotai hyakusen*.

40. *Nagasaki kenshi*, p. 633, and *Ōkumakō hachijūgononshi*, vol. 1, p. 162.

41. Ōkubo Toshiaki, "Meiji shinseikenka no Kyūshū," in Ōkubo, ed., *Meiji ishin to Kyūshū*, pp. 399–402.

42. Tsuda Shigemaro, *Sasaki rōkō sekijitsudan*, p. 581.

43. However, the contingent of samurai from a score of the nearby domains in Nagasaki was hardly a unified and coherent group. Yanai Kenzō of Chōshū, who drafted the pledge, for example, was not convinced that the Saga han would join the Restoration camp. See Ichijima Kenichi, Ōkumakō hachijūgononshi, vol. 1, p. 164.

44. Dajōkan, ed., *Fukkoki*, vol. 1, pp. 629–47.

45. On the eve of *Haihan chiken* in the summer of 1871, there were forty-three fu and ken covering lands worth roughly 8,000,000 *koku*. Inoue Kiyoshi, *Nihon gendaishi*, p. 360.

46. Wilson, "Genesis of the Meiji Government," p. 44.

47. Dajōkan, ed., *Fukkoki*, vol. 3, p. 515.

48. Sashihara Yasuzō, *Meiji seishi*, p. 44, and McLaren, "Japanese Government Documents," pp. 9–10.

49. See Shidankai, comp., *Shidankai sokkiroku*, vol. 23, book 159, pp. 357–64, for the background and the text of the Himeji han proposal.

50. "Itōko seidan," in *Itōkō zenshū*, vol. 3, pp. 54–57, and Shumpokō tsuishōkai, *Itō Hirobumiden*, vol. 1, pp. 380–81.

51. Itō Hirobumi, "Jikiwa," in *Itōkō zenshū*, vol. 3, pp. 6–7. Another account of the meeting between Iwakura and Tamamatsu does not say anything about the topic. *Iwakurakō jikki*, vol. 2, p. 60.

52. Itō, "Jikiwa," p. 189.

53. Cited in Nakane Yukie, *Teibō nikki*, in *KIN*, vol. 7, p. 48. See also Asai Kiyoshi, *Gunken shisō*, pp. 60–76, which lists more evidence that the *gunken* system as a form of actual government gained little support among the leaders.

54. *Kōgisho nisshi*, in *KIN*, vol. 7, book 1, pp. 195–200.

55. *Nanki Tokugawashi*, vol. 4, p. 570.

56. Ishizuka Hiromichi, "Meiji ishin," Rekishigaku kenkyū, 181 (1955): 13–27.

2. The Constitutional Politics of the Restoration

1. Beasley, The Meiji Restoration, pp. 329–30.

2. Kido Kōin nikki, the entry for 6/1/1868, vol. 1, p. 23.

3. See, for example, the entry for 6/18/1868 in Katsu, Kaishū nikki, in Kaishū zenshū, vol. 9, p. 143.

4. Chūgai shimbun, vol. 1, no. 13, sometime in early summer of 1868, in MBZ, vol. 17, pp. 342–43.

5. See, for example, Kido Kōin's letter to Ōkubo Toshimichi on 7/23/1868, Kido Kōin monjo, vol. 3, pp. 113–16.

6. McLaren, "Japanese Government Documents," p. 8, for the Oath, and Fukuoka Takachika, "Gokajō goseimon," in Kokka gakkai, ed., Meiji kensei keizaishiron, pp. 1–45 for the Outline and Pledge.

7. Date Munenari zaikyō nikki, the entries for 12/7/1867, 1/17/1868, and 1/25/1868, pp. 617–19, 651, and 668; Higashikuze Michitomi, Chikutei kaikoroku, p. 255; and Yuri Masamichi, Shishaku Yuri Kimimasaden, pp. 200–222.

8. The best account of the incidents and of the developments that followed is Ishii Takashi, Zōtei Meiji ishin, pp. 757–69 for the Kobe Incident, and pp. 799–809 for the Sakai Incident. See also Oka Yoshitake, Reimeiki no Meiji Nihon, Chapters 1 and 2.

9. Higashikuze Michitomi, Chikutei kaikoroku, pp. 254–55.

10. Sakazaki Takeshi, "Ishin gokajō goseimon happu no yurai," in Shidankai, comp., Shidankai sokkiroku, vol. 207.

11. Fukuoka Takachika, "Gokajō goseimon," and Ōkubo Toshiaki, "Gokajō no seimon," Rekishi chiri, 88 (1957): 65–91.

12. Hōrei zensho, Dajōkan no. 603, 9/19/1868.

13. Sashihara Yasuzō, Meiji seishi, p. 118. For a general discussion of the kōshi, see Ogata Hiroyasu, "Kōshisei no kōsatsu," Shakaigaku tōkyū, 2 (1957): 301–34.

14. Shumpokō, ed., Itō Hirobumi den, vol. 1, pp. 442–44.

15. Sashihara Yasuzō, Meiji seishi, p. 118.

16. Kido Kōin monjo, vol. 8, pp. 25–26.

17. Kido Kōin's letter to Ōmura Masujirō, another Chōshū activist, in mid-February of 1869, Kido Kōin monjo, vol. 3, p. 231.

18. See the entries for 6/4/1868 and 8/6/1868, Kido Kōin nikki, vol. 1, pp. 26, 56–57.

19. The entry for 9/9/1868, ibid., p. 73.

20. Suematsu Kenchō, comp., *Bō-Chō kaitenshi*, vol. 6, book 2, pp. 505–6.

21. Ibid.

22. *Chūgai shimbun*, no. 5, 1869, in *MBZ*, vol. 17, p. 379.

23. *Dajōkar nisshi*, no. 9, 1869, in *KIN*, vol. 2, book 1, p. 26.

24. Ibid., pp. 24–25. See also *Iwakurakō jikki*, vol. 2, p. 678 for the same line in Iwakura's letter to Kido Kōin before the four-domain Petition.

25. A good example may be found in a letter of Tani Tateki, a Tosa retainer, to Sanjo Sanetomi after the four-domain Petition. *Tani Tateki ikō*, vol. 2, p. 38.

26. *Dajōkan nisshi*, no. 12, 1869, in *KIN*, pp. 38–39.

27. The entry for 3/11/1869, *Kido Kōin nikki*, vol. 1, p. 183.

28. See, for example, Inoue Kaoru's letter to Kido Kōin on 11/10/1869, which urged the reduction in the size of Chōshū's irregular armies. Inoue Kaorukō denki hensankai, *Segai Inouekō den*, vol. 1, pp. 389–90.

29. *Iwakurakō jikki*, vol. 2, pp. 728–30.

30. A letter to Sanjō Sanetomi on 9/15/1870, *Kido Kōin monjo*, vol. 4, pp. 103–4.

31. Sasaki Takayuki, *Hogohiroi*, vol. 4, p. 36, the entry for 8/2/1869.

32. Quoted in Tsuda Shigemaro, *Meiji seijō to shin Takayuki*, pp. 184–85.

33. Quoted in *Soga Sukenoriō jijoden*, p. 207.

34. The entry for 7/22/1869, Sasaki Takayuki, *Hogohiroi*, vol. 4, pp. 93–94.

35. *Iwakurakō jikki*, vol. 2, pp. 747–50. See also a letter from Iwakura Tomomi to Ōkubo Toshimichi on 3/10/1869 and another on the same day from Okubo to Iwakura, in *Iwakura Tomomi kankei monjo*, vol. 4, pp. 212–13, *Ōkubo Toshimichi monjo*, vol. 3, pp. 59–61, and Katsuta Magoya, *Ōkubo Toshimichi den*, vol. 2, pp. 684–85.

36. Ōkubo Toshimichi's letter to Shin'nō Tateo on 10/25/1869, *Ōkubo Toshimichi monjo*, vol. 3, pp. 304–5.

37. *Ōkubo Toshimichi monjo*, vol. 1, pp. 259–60. See also Masumi Junnosuke, *Nihon seitōshiron*, pp. 11–18.

38. See for example, Ōkubo Toshimichi, "Kihan no sai dōshi ni waka-chishi ikensho," on 1/19/1870, in *Ōkubo Toshimichi monjo*, vol. 3, pp. 348–58.

39. Masumi Junnosuke, *Nihon seitōshiron*, pp. 19–38.

40. *Ōkubo Toshimichi nikki*, vol. 2, p. 124, the entry for 9/27/1870.

41. See note 10 of Chapter 4.

42. Ōkubo Toshimichi's letter to Iwakura Tomomi on 9/29/1870 and another on 10/29/1870, in *Ōkubo Toshimichi monjo*, vol. 4, pp. 10–11, 45–46.

43. See note 38 of this chapter.

44. *Ōkuma bunsho*, vol. 1, pp. 5–7.

45. *Kido Kōin nikki*, vol. 1, pp. 443–44.

46. Sasaki Takayuki, *Hogohiroi*, vol. 4, pp. 265–67.

47. Shimauchi Toshie, *Tani Tateki ikō*, vol. 1, p. 209.

48. *Iwakura Tomomi kankei monjo*, vol. 5, pp. 88–89.

49. See, for example, the exchange between Iwakura Tomomi and Sasaki Takayuki sometime in June 1871, in Sasaki, *Hogohiroi*, vol. 5, pp. 88–89.

50. Kido Kōin's letter to Sanjō Sanetomi and Iwakura Tomomi on 4/15/1871, *Kido Kōin monjo*, vol. 4, pp. 196–97.

51. *Iwakurakō jikki*, vol. 2, pp. 916–17.

52. See, for example, note 28 of this chapter. Also see Inoue Kaorukō denki hensankai, *Segai Inouekō den*, vol. 1, pp. 447–54.

53. Tokutomi Iichirō, *Kōshaku Yamagata Aritomo den*, vol. 2, pp. 124–36.

54. Suematsu Kenchō, comp. *Bō-Chō kaitenshi*, vol. 6, book 2, pp. 545–46.

55. Tokutomi Iichirō, *Kōshaku Yamagata Aritomo den*, vol. 2, pp. 124–125; *Segai Inouekō den*, pp. 448–49.

56. *Kido Kōin nikki*, vol. 2, p. 69, and *Ōkubo Toshimichi nikki*, vol. 2, p. 179, in both the entry for 8/27/1871.

57. Asai Kiyoshi, *Gunken shisō*, pp. 288–89.

58. See William Griffis's observation of samurai reaction to the arrival of the news of the *Haihan chiken* in Fukui han, *The Mikado's Empire*, p. 526.

59. Tōyama Shigeki, *Meiji ishin*, p. 249.

60. Beasley, *The Meiji Restoration*, p. 326.

## 3. *The Demise of Feudal Politics*

1. Itō Hirobumi's speech in San Francisco on 12/14/1871, while he was on the Iwakura mission. Shumpokō tsuishōkai, *Itō Hirobumi den*, vol. 1, p. 626.

2. Tsuchiya Takao, *Hōkenshakai hōkai katei no kenkyū*, pp. 391–483.

3. Bolitho, *Treasures among Men*, pp. 215–21.

4. Smith, *Political Change and Industrial Development*, Chapter 1.

5. Beasley, *The Meiji Restoration*, pp. 63–73; Craig, *Chōshū in the Meiji Restoration*, pp. 58–84; and Huber, *Revolutionary Origins*, Chapter 8.

6. Allen, *Economic History of Modern Japan*, pp. 30–46.

7. Smith, *Political Change and Industrial Development*, pp. 26–31.

8. See a memorandum submitted by Mutsu Munemitsu, Governor of Settsu ken, urging the integration of tax practices in order to help modernize and streamline the fiscal policy of the central government. *Gijōkan nichiroku*, in *KIN*, vol. 7, book 1, pp. 115–16.

9. Sashihara Yasuzō, *Meiji seishi*, p. 122.

10. Sawada Akira, *Meiji zaisei*, pp. 109–203.

11. Kido Kōin's letter to Iwakura Tomomi on 5/28/1869 and another to Ōkubo Toshimichi on 6/3/1869, *Kido Kōin monjo*, vol. 3, pp. 312–17, 331–33.

12. Sawada Akira, *Meiji zaisei*, pp. 307–22.

13. Bendix, "Preconditions of Development," in Dore, ed., *Aspects of Social Change in Modern Japan*, pp. 27–68.

14. See a short but perceptive essay on this point, Dowdy, "Aspects of Tokugawa Bureaucracy," *Australian Journal of Politics and History*, 16 (1970): 375–89.

15. Issued on 2/9/1868. *Iwakurakō jikki*, vol. 2, pp. 273–74.

16. A detailed description of the institutional changes in the central government can be obtained from Wilson, "Genesis of the Meiji Government." See also Haraguchi Kiyoshi, "Meiji shonen," Hara, *Taikei Nihon kokkashi*, vol. 4, pp. 65–135, and Tōyama Shigeki, "Yūshi sensei no seiritsu," *Jiyū minkenki no kenkyū*, vol. 1, pp. 1–44.

17. Only six were categorized as *heimin*, or commoners. At least two of the six were originally samurai, one from Owari han and the other from bakufu.

18. Sashihara Yasuzō, *Meiji seishi*, pp. 41–43, 76–80, 123–27.

19. Ibid., pp. 24–27. There seemed to be no coherent relationship between the Home Affairs Department and the fu-ken offices before the *Haihan chiken*, when the former was supposed to be the head office for the latter. Interesting evidence is an announcement made by the central government in the summer of 1870, pleading the governors of fu and ken to report to the Home Affairs Department when they were in Tokyo. *Dajōkan nisshi*, in *KIN*, vol. 2, book 2, p. 118.

20. See, for example, a four-point pledge exchanged among high-ranking officials in September 1869, *Ōkubo Toshimichi monjo*, vol. 3, pp. 247–49.

21. Osatake Takeki, *Ishin zengo*, pp. 397–99.

22. *Hōrei zensho*, no. 98, 1868.

23. Ibid., no. 1063, on 1/22/1869.

24. Sashihara Yasuzō, *Meiji seishi*, pp. 19–22, and Ōkubo Toshimichi's memorandum to Iwakura Tomomi on 1/27/1868, *Ōkubo Toshimichi monjo*, vol. 2, pp. 154–58.

25. *Okubo Toshimichi monjo*, vol. 2, pp. 154–58.

26. A letter to Kido Kōin on 5/23/1868, ibid., pp. 257–62.

27. Nihon keieishi kenkyūjo, comp., *Godai Tomoatsu denki shiryō*, vol. 1, p. 113.

28. *Boshin senkō shōtenhyō*, in *MZZKSS*, vol. 8, pp. 462–75. Any recognition of merit awarded to individuals could prove a source of embarrassment in a society in which the daimyo's house was at the epicenter of political action. Such was the case for Saigō Takamori, who received a court rank higher than that of his Satsuma lord, Shimazu Tadayoshi. See Saigō Takamori's reaction in his letter to Ōkubo Toshimichi on 4/23/1870, *Dai Saigō zenshū*, vol. 2, pp. 471–74.

29. On the depletion of the domain treasuries, see Niwa Kunio, *Meiji ishin to tochi henkaku*, pp. 9–47; Beasley, "Feudal Revenue in Japan," *Journal of Asian Studies*, 19(1960): 255–72.

30. Niwa Kunio, *Meiji ishin*, pp. 16–17.

31. *Ishin nisshi*, no. 114, 1869, in *KIN*, vol. 2, book 1, p. 304.

32. A few members of the Finance Department, notably Inoue Kaoru and Ōkuma Shigenobu, insisted that 5 percent of the domain revenue should be enough for the daimyo house, thereby allowing the domain's public expenditure to have a larger share of the revenue. See a letter from Inoue Kaoru to Ōkuma Shigenobu on 7/29/1869, *Ōkuma Shigenobu kankei monjo*, vol. 1, pp. 92–93. Also Fukaya Hakuji, *Kashizoku chitsuroku shobun*, pp. 170–72.

33. *Hōrei zensho*, no. 902, 1868.

34. *Chitsuroku shobun enkaku gaihyō*, in *MZZKSS*, vol. 8, pp. 310–87, for the cases of thirty-seven domains.

35. See *Dajōkan nisshi* in *KIN*, especially for the period between July 1869 and March 1871.

36. *Dajōkan nisshi*, no. 9, 1871, in *KIN*, vol. 3, book 1, p. 139.

37. *Dajōkan nisshi*, no. 38, 1870, in *KIN*, vol. 2, book 2, pp. 125–26. This was one of rare occasions when the deliberative chamber for the domain representatives (*Shūgiin*) performed some noticeable function in the promotion of what they deemed feudal interest, defending the allocation of 81 percent of the revenue for public expenditure (against the government's proposal of 72 percent) and 9 percent (against the govern-

ment's 18 percent) for military expenditures. *Shūgiin nisshi,* in *MBZ,* vol. 4, pp. 176–212.

38. *Ishin shiryō kōyō,* vol. 10, passim, especially for 1870 and 1871 before the *Haihan chiken.*

39. *Ōkurashō enkakushi,* in *MZZKSS,* vol. 2, p. 374.

40. Kumamoto han initiated this series of appeals by the feudal domains to the central government in late 1870, which lasted until as late as July of 1871. For the Kumamoto han appeal, see *Dajōkan nisshi,* no. 38, 1870, in *KIN,* vol. 2, book 2, pp. 124–25.

41. The memorandum of the lord-governor of the Gujō han, *Dajōkan nisshi,* no. 2, 1871, in *KIN,* vol. 3, book 1, p. 115.

42. *Dajōkan nisshi,* no. 82, 1869, in *KIN,* vol. 2, book 2, p. 223.

43. *Dajōkan nisshi,* no. 39, 1870, no. 66, 1870, and no. 39, 1871, in *KIN,* vol. 2, book 2, pp. 129, 198, and vol. 3, book 1, p. 247.

44. *Dajōkan nisshi,* no. 113, 1869, in *KIN,* vol. 2, book 1, pp. 301–2.

45. Kido Kōin's letter on 9/27/1871 to Shinagawa Yajirō, *Kido Kōin monjo,* vol. 4, pp. 267–69.

## 4. The Emperor's Government

1. For a general account of the mission's formation and function, see Mayo, "Iwakura Embassy," and "Rationality in the Meiji Restoration," Harootunian and Silberman, eds., *Modern Japanese Leadership: Transition and Change,* pp. 323–69. Also consult Ōkubo Toshiaki, *Iwakura shisetsu no kenkyū,* especially pp. 53–107.

2. Shumpokō tsuishokai, *Itō Hirobumi den,* vol. 1, p. 573. See also Mioka Takeo, *Yuri Kimimasa den,* pp. 129–37, and Yuri Masamichi, *Shishaku Yuri Kimimasa den,* pp. 72–60 and 343–56.

3. During the early days of the new regime, the Foreign Affairs Department had to face the foreign powers' criticisms and protests directed against the Finance Department. Date Munenari, a daimyo from Uwajima and the head of the Foreign Affairs Department, resigned in the crossfire of criticism and protests from the foreign representatives which often included personal denunciation of Date for his mediocrity. See Date's letter to Iwakura Tomomi on 6/10/1869, *Iwakura Tomomi kankei monjo,* vol. 4, p. 257, and Terajima Munenori's letter to Ōkuma Shigenobu on 9/7/1869, *Ōkuma Shigenobu kankei monjo,* vol. 1, pp. 123–24.

4. See the sections for these individuals in *Hyakkan rireki,* vol. 1, for their transfers and promotions.

5. *Ōkurashō enkakushi,* in *MZZKSS,* vol. 2, p. 69; *Itō Hirobumi den,*

vol. 1, pp. 47–48; and Inoue Kaorukō denki hensankai, *Segai Inouekō den*, vol. 1, p. 411.

6. *Hōrei zensho*, nos. 67, 148, 152 and 727, 1869. See also note 32 of Chapter 3.

7. Ichijima Kenichi, *Ōkumakō hachijūgonenshi*, vol. 1, pp. 317–18, and Tokutomi Iichirō, *Kōshaku Matsukata Masayoshi den*, vol. 1, pp. 324–29.

8. Ishizuka Hiromichi, *Nihon shihonshugi seiritsushi kenkyū*, pp. 28, 107–8.

9. Kido Kōin's letter to Itō Hirobumi on 7/15/1870, *Kido Kōin monjo*, vol. 4, pp. 67–68.

10. Kido's complaint quoted in Iwakura Tomomi's letter to Ōkubo Toshimichi, on 8/2/1870, *Ōkubo Toshimichi monjo*, vol. 4, pp. 255–56.

11. *Ōkurashō enkakushi*, in *MZZKSS*, vol. 2, p. 4.

12. The appointments in the central government first seemed to be made primarily through the exchange of letters and conversations. The names of candidates for the positions were circulated among the high-ranking leaders only to obtain formal approvals. See, for example, *Ōkubo Toshimichi monjo*, vol. 3, pp. 38–57.

13. Sashihara Yasuzō, *Meiji seishi*, p. 185. It was so rare for the individual departments to make the reports on their budgetary planning to the Finance Department that no review was possible on how much was actually used for different projects by the other departments.

14. Aware of his increasing weight in the central government, Ōkuma was willing to promote himself further to the point that he did not seem to be reluctant to exploit to his advantage a special support extended to him by Harry Parkes, who, it is claimed, warned the government officials from Satsuma and Chōshū not to tamper with Ōkuma's administrative responsibility. Ichijima Kenichi, *Ōkumakō hachijūgoneshi*, vol. 1, p. 180.

15. Haraguchi Kiyoshi, "Hantaisei no kaitai," in *Iwanami kōza Nihon rekishi*, vol. 15, pp. 33–34.

16. For Ōkubo Toshimichi's shrewd way of surviving many adverse circumstances, see a short but highly perceptive commentary by Satō Seizaburō, "Ōkubo Toshimichi," in Kamishima Jirō, ed., *Kenryoku no shisō*, pp. 35–37.

17. Tsuda Shigemaro, *Meiji seijō*, p. 81.

18. See Kido's letter to Itō Hirobumi on 7/29/1870, *Kido Kōin monjo*, vol. 4, pp. 77–81. See also Masumi Junnosuke, *Ninhon seitōshiron*, pp. 40–45.

19. Inoue Kaorukō denki hensankai, *Segai Inouekō den*, vol. 1, p. 537.

20. Enjoji Kiyoshi, *Ōkumahaku sekijitsutan*, p. 458.

21. See Haga Noboru, *Meiji kokka to minshū*, pp. 96–108, and Tanaka Akira, *Kindai tennōsei*, pp. 221–24. See also note 24 of Chapter 1.

22. Dajōkan, ed., *Fukkoki*, vol. 11, p. 186.

23. *Gifukenshi*, vol. 8, pp. 18–50.

24. See note 7 of this chapter.

25. Yamanaka Einosuke, "Meiji shoki kanryōsei," in Miyamoto Mataji, ed., *Osaka no kenkyū*, pp. 73–112. For the case of Bōjō Toshiakira, the governor of Yamagata ken, who was penalized and eventually dismissed because of his attempt to remove surtaxes as a measure of poor relief without the central office's permission, see *Yamagatashi shi*, vol. 3, pp. 127–28.

26. *Ōkurashō enkakushi*, in *MZZKSS*, vol. 2, p. 292.

27. *Fuken shiryō*, Hiroshima, book 12. See also Tsuchiya Takao and Ono Michio, comps. and eds., *Meiji shonen nōmin sōjōroku*, for the cases of peasant protest directly and indirectly caused by the departure of the daimyo.

28. Tsuchiya and Ono, *Meiji shonen nōmin sōjōroku*, pp. 215–20.

## 5. Politics of Integration and Local Order

1. A good illustration may be obtained from Fukuzawa's "Kyūhanjō," in *Fukuzawa Yukichi zenshū*, Tokyo, 1959. Fukuzawa describes feudal life in his home at Nakatsu, where the local community of the domain as a whole had been isolated from the outside, modes of life differed from one social class to another within the domain, and life even within one social class was fragmented to the extent that the different strata spoke different languages.

2. For example, *Fuken shiryō*, Gumma, books 22 and 23.

3. *Chiso kaisei hōkokusho*, in *MZZKSS*, vol. 7, p. 3. Also see *Fuken shiryō*, Ibaraki, book 15. Ibaraki ken incorporated under its jurisdiction villages from more than fifteen different feudal authorities.

4. Griffis, *Mikado's Empire*, p. 526.

5. *Ōkuma Shigenobu kankei monjo*, vol. 1, pp. 506–9.

6. See for example, Yamanaka Einosuke, *Nihon kindai kokka*, pp. 22–35; Ōshima Tarō, *Nihon chihō gyōzaiseishi josetsu*, pp. 16–29; and Ōishi Kaichirō, *Nihon chihō zaigyōseishi josetsu*, pp. 54–58. Also Mikiso Hane, *Peasants, Rebels, and Outcasts*, pp. 13–16.

7. Calculated from Naikaku kampōkyoku, *Chihō enkaku ryaku-fu*.

8. *Kōbunsho ruijū,* vol. 7, book 3, 5/9/1883.

9. See note 7 of this chapter.

10. Jichi shinkōkai, comp., *Fuken seido shiryō,* vol. 1, pp. 31–43. Consider, for example, Shizuoka ken before the first wave of amalgamation in the fall of 1871, where there were still 2,126 officials receiving some form of allowance from the ken government for their various services in the administration. *Fuken shiryō,* Shizuoka, book 1.

11. *Hōrei zensho,* Dajōkan no. 350, 1871.

12. A report by a high-ranking official in the Finance Department after a tour of investigation in regions northeast of Tokyo. *Ōkuma bunsho,* vol. 1, pp. 181–86.

13. Ibid., vol. 1, pp. 186–87.

14. *Dajōruiten,* vol. 2, book 95.

15. *Fuken seido shiryō,* vol. 2, pp. 14–16.

16. Fukushima Masao, "Meiji shoki no chihōkan," *Chihōshi kenkyū,* 24 (1956): 2–14.

17. *Fuken seido shiryō,* vol. 2, pp. 16–23.

18. See, for example, *Chiso kankei shorui shūsan,* in *MZZKSS,* vol. 7, p. 352.

19. *Kōno Banshū den,* vol. 1, pp. 181–94.

20. Kikegawa Hiroshi, *Jichi gojūnenshi,* p. 19.

21. *Hōrei zensho,* Dajōkan no. 170, 1871.

22. See Fukushima Masao, ed., *Koseki seido to 'iye' seido,* Chapters 3, 4, 5, and 7, for a discussion of the political and social consequences of the Household Residence Registry, which had the effect of institutionalizing a patriarchy as a key mode of social relationships, from the smallest social institution — a family — to the state.

23. *Hōrei zensho,* Dajōkan no. 170, 1871.

24. See, for example, *Fuken shiryō,* Akita, book 4; *Fuken shiryō,* Ishikawa, book 1; and *Okayama kenseishi,* pp. 104–8.

25. *Hōrei zensho,* Dajōkan nos. 416, 437, and 654, 1871 and 1872.

26. Ibid., the Finance Department notification, no. 118, 1872.

27. Norman, *Japan's Emergence,* p. 180; Tsuchiya and Ono, comps. and eds., *Meiji shonen nōmin sōjōroku,* passim.

28. *Ōkurashō enkakushi,* in *MZZKSS,* vol. 2, pp. 275–76, 289–90. See also Fukushima Masao, *Chiso kaisei no kenkyū,* pp. 20–22.

29. The Finance Department report (9/8/1871), *Meiji nenkan beika chōsetsu enkakushi,* in *MZZKSS,* vol. 11, no. 2, p. 613.

30. Fukushima Masao, *Chiso kaisei no kenkyū,* pp. 81–82.

31. *Ōkurashō enkakushi,* p. 339.

32. *Chiso kankei shorui shūsan,* p. 302.

33. One was prepared by Ōkubo Toshimichi (then the minister of Finance) and Inoue Kaoru before the departure of the Iwakura mission on 11/9/1871, and the other by Inoue Kaoru and Yoshida Kiyonari around the same time. Ibid., pp. 306–9.

34. *Hōrei zensho*, Finance Department, no. 25, 4/1/1872 and no. 83, 8/7/1872.

35. Quoted in Fukushima Masao, *Chiso kaisei no kenkyū*, p. 52. Also, Matsukata Masayoshi, *Matsukatahaku zaisei ronsakushū*, in *MZZKSS*, vol. 1, pp. 388–91.

36. To some, such as Iwakura Tomomi, the commercialization of agriculture was nothing but a threat to agrarian values and order for an ideal Japan, as the farmers might develop a new inclination toward consumerism rather than production per se. Such a shift, Iwakura argued, would contradict the traditional work ethic. Inoue Kaorukō denki hensankai, *Segai Inouekō den*, vol. 3, pp. 157–58.

37. This measure, of course, necessitated a new system of penalties for delinquent taxpayers. See Niwa Kunio, "Chiso kaisei to nōgyō kōzō no henka," in *Nihon keizaishi taikei*, vol. 5, pp. 253–55.

38. For authoritative studies on the Land Tax Reform, see Fukushima Masao, *Chiso kaisei no kenkyū*; Seki Junya, *Meiji ishin to chiso kaisei*; and Niwa Kunio, *Meiji ishin no tochihenkaku*. See also Appendix A in Nakamura, *Agricultural Production and Economic Development*. Fukushima Masao, "Meiji rokunen," *Tōyō bunka kenkyūjo kiyō*, 18(1959): 1–47, gives a detailed account of the discussion among the fu-ken and the central (Finance) officials shortly before the beginning of the Reform.

39. Seki Junya, *Meiji ishin to chiso kaisei*, pp. 152–56, and Fukushima Masao, *Chiso kaisei no kenkyū*, pp. 103–15.

40. First on 7/15/1872, in a letter to Ōkubo Toshimichi and Itō Hirobumi on the Iwakura mission, Inoue Kaoru explained the need to strengthen the central control over the fu-ken offices in order to minimize misunderstandings of the purposes of the Reform by the local offices and the local populace. Then, on 9/4/1872, this need was put into a formal proposal of the Finance Department. The proposal recommended that the fu-ken governors remain in the same localities for at least four years and that two kinds of taxes (*keiso* for the central government and *iso* for the fu-ken governments) be distinguished from each other in order to allow the governors a degree of autonomy in the management of local expenditure for efficient implementation of the Reform. *Chiso kaisei shorui shūsan*, pp. 313–14.

41. *Meiji zaiseishi*, vol. 5, pp. 378–82.

42. *Fuken shiryō*, Ishikawa, book 1.

43. For example, *Fuken shiryō*, Ibaraki, books 1 and 7.

44. For example, *Akita kenshi, shiryō, Meijihen*, vol. 1, p. 355.

45. *Ishin irai chōson enkaku*, p. 44, and *Hōrei zensho*, Dajōkan no. 117, 5/15/1872.

46. For example, *Fuken shiryō*, Tochigi, book 20, and Yamanashi, book 24.

47. See Steiner, "Popular Political Participation," in Ward, ed., *Political Development in Modern Japan*, pp. 213–47.

48. *Hōrei zensho*, Dajōkan no. 88, 8/23/1872, and no. 109, 9/19/1872.

49. *Fuken shiryō*, Akita, book 4; *Fuken shiryō*, Ibaraki, book 7; and *Fuken shiryō*, Ōita, book 26.

50. Fukushima Masao, *Chiso kaisei no kenkyū*, pp. 318–19.

51. Tsuchiya and Ono, comps. and eds., *Meiji shonen nōmin sōjōroku*, pp. 1 and 428, and *Fuken shiryō*, Ōita, book 18.

52. *Fuken shiryō*, Ibaraki, books 14 and 15; Kondō Tetsuo, "Chiso kaisei to kisei jinushi," *Tochi seido shigaku*, 11(1961): 16–30, for the case of Aichi ken governor; and Arimoto Masao and Ōta Kenichi, "Chiso kaisei to jinushi gōnō," *Tochi seido shigaku*, 11(1961): 31–44.

53. *Fuken shiryō*, Wakayama, books 1 and 44; *Fuken shiryō*, Mie, book 6; and Kondō, "Chiso kaisei to kisei jinushi."

54. Tsuchiya and Ono, comps. and eds., *Meiji shonen nōmin sōjōroku*, passim.

55. *Hōrei zensho*, Dajōkan no. 440, 12/4/1873.

56. *Hōrei zensho*, Dajōkan no. 28, 3/8/1874.

57. *Hōrei zensho*, Finance Department, no. 130, 10/17/1876. See also Kikegawa Hiroshi, *Meiji chihō seido*, pp. 22–23.

58. See, for example, *Okayama kenseishi*, vol. 1, p. 108, and Fukushima Masao and Tokuda Ryōji, "Meiji shonen no chō-sonkai," in *Chiso kaisei to chihōjichisei*, pp. 158–264, for various forms of similar practices in ten localities.

59. *Fuken shiryō*, Hyōgo, book 25.

60. *Okayama kenseishi*, vol. 1, pp. 68–70; Arimoto Masao, "Chiso kaisei to chihōseiji," in *Iwanami kōza Nihon rekishi*, vol. 14, pp. 190–94.

61. *Chihōkan kaigi nisshi*, in *MBZ*, vol. 4, p. 313.

62. Ibid., p. 314.

63. Ibid., p. 315.

64. Ibid., p. 317.

65. Ibid., p. 322.

66. Ibid., p. 316.

67. Watanabe Takaki, "Chihō minkai," *Chihōshi kenkyū*, 19(1969): 32–33.

68. Shōji Kichinosuke, *Nihon seisha seitō hattatsushi*, pp. 236–41.

69. Quoted in Sashihara Yasuzō, *Meiji seishi*, pp. 284–89.

70. Consult the works listed on note 6 of this chapter for the new local government system, known as the Three-New-Law system.

71. Quoted in Tokyo shisei chōsakai, ed., and comp., *Jichi gojūnenshi*, p. 46.

## 6. *The End of the Restoration Coalition*

1. Quoted in Norman, *Feudal Background of Japanese Politics*, in Dower, *Origins of the Modern Japanese State*, p. 398.

2. A letter to Shinagawa Yajirō on 9/27/1871, *Kido Kōin monjo*, vol. 4, p. 267.

3. *Dai Saigō zenshū*, vol. 2, pp. 591–92.

4. A letter to Nakai Hiroshi on 7/20/1875, *Kido Kōin monjo*, vol. 6, p. 194.

5. A letter to Matsumoto Kanae sometime in January 1874, ibid., vol. 5, p. 201.

6. See a recollection by Soejima Taneomi quoted in Ōtsu Junichirō, *Dai Nihon kenseishi*, vol. 1, p. 786.

7. Itagaki Taisuke, "Wagakuni kensei no yurai," in Kokka gakkai ed., *Meiji kensei keizai shiron*, pp. 186–87. Also see Ukita Kazutami, "Seitōshi," in Soejima Yasoroku, ed., *Kaikoku gojūnenshi*, vol. 1, p. 325.

8. See the entries for 8/6/1868 and 1/26/1869 in *Kido Kōin nikki*, vol. 1, pp. 55–57, 159–61; Kido's letters to Ōmura Masujirō early in January 1869, and to Sanjō Sanetomi and Iwakura Tomomi on 3/13/1869, in *Kido Kōin monjo*, vol. 3, pp. 203–4, 237–42.

9. A letter from Saigō Takamori to Itagaki Taisuke on 8/17/1873, *Dai Saigō zenshū*, vol. 2, p. 755.

10. Kido Kōin left the government in protest at this expedition. For the development of the events leading to Kido's resignation from the government, see Miyake Setsurei, *Dōjidaishi*, pp. 402–14.

11. Tōyama Shigeki, "Seikanron, jiyūminkenron, hōkenron," in Meiji shiryō kenkyū renrakukai, ed., *Kindai shisō no keisei*, pp. 35–119.

12. See an excellent analysis of the partisan politics following the Korean dispute by Banno Junji, "Seikanronsō go no 'naijiha,' to 'gais-

eiha,'" in *Nempō kindai Nihon kenkyū*, pp. 245–62. Beasley in his *Meiji Restoration*, pp. 369–371, attributes Ōkubo's and Kido's opposition to the military expedition to their awakening to Japan's backwardness compared to the West during their mission abroad. Beasley thus sees the partisan politics within the central government in this period as originating in the tension between those who placed a higher priority on domestic improvements and those who were concerned more with the problem of the disgruntled samurai. See also Fujimura Michio, "Seikan ronsō," *Kokusai seiji* 37(1967): 1–22.

13. Saigō Takamori's letter to Katsura Shirō on 9/4/1871, *Dai Saigō zenshū*, vol. 2, p. 530.

14. Sashihara Yasuzō, *Meiji seishi*, p. 123, and Inada Masatsugu, *Meiji kempō seiritsushi*, pp. 98–104.

15. Those who signed the pledge were Iwakura Tomomi, Kido Kōin, Ōkubo Toshimichi, Sasaki Takayuki, and Itō Hirobumi (all on the mission); and Sanjō Sanetomi, Saigō Takamori, Itagaki Taisuke, Ōkuma Shigenobu, Inoue Kaoru, Gotō Shōjirō, Yamagata Aritomo, and Soejima Taneomi. Gaimushō, *Dai Nihon gaikō monjo*, vol. 4, pp. 102–3.

16. Ichijima Kenichi, *Ōkumakō hachijūgonenshi*, vol. 1, p. 430.

17. Enjōji Kiyoshi, *Ōkumahaku sekijitsutan*, p. 400.

18. Quoted in Tokutomi Iichirō, *Kinsei Nihon kokuminshi*, vol. 84, pp. 15–16.

19. See, for example, Tamamuro Taijō, *Saigō Takamori*, pp. 119–28.

20. Yamada Seisai, comp., *Saigō Nanshū ikun*, pp. 11–13. These statements were recorded by samurai from the Shōnai han, one of the few strong supporters of the Tokugawa during the Boshin War, who developed a unique friendship with Saigō and his supporters, formerly their arch foes. They visited Satsuma with the lord Sakai Tadaatsu late in the summer of 1870.

21. Tokutomi Iichirō, *Kōshaku Yamagata Aritomo den*, vol. 2, pp. 148–203.

22. For a succinct account of this development, see Someno Yoshinobu, "Saiban seido," in *Kōza Nihon kindaihō hattatsushi*, vol. 6, pp. 60–76, and also Matono Hansuke, *Etō Nampaku*, vol. 1, pp. 648–63.

23. *Ōkubo Toshimichi monjo*, vol. 4, pp. 483–84.

24. Tokutomi Iichirō, *Kōshaku Yamagata Aritomo den*, vol. 2, pp. 200–205.

25. Niwa Kunio, *Meiji ishin*, pp. 120–21, 189–236.

26. *Hachiburitsuki gaikoku kōsai hakkō nikki*, in *MZZKSS*, vol. 10, p. 63.

27. The entry for 5/14/1872 in *Kido Kōin nikki*, vol. 2, pp. 174–75.

28. *Hachiburitsuki gaikoku kōsai hakkō nikki*, p. 71.

29. Fukaya Hakuji, *Kashizoku chitsuroku shobun*, pp. 254–97.

30. *Ōkubo Toshimichi monjo*, vol. 4, p. 438.

31. *Ōkuma bunsho*, vol. 5, p. 106.

32. On 5/29/1872, *Ōkuma Shigenobu kankei monjo*, vol. 1, pp. 469–70.

33. Quoted in Inoue Kaorukō denki hensankai, *Segai Inouekō den*, vol. 1, pp. 520–21.

34. Ibid., p. 523.

35. Etō Shimpei, a legal specialist from Saga, seemed obsessed with the idea that all evils were coming from the usurpation of Imperial authority by the members of the government from the two most powerful domains, Satsuma and Chōshū. It is said that Etō had vowed to separate the two groups of men and to cause internal divisions within each. Matono Hansuke, *Etō Nampaku*, vol. 2, pp. 284, 301–2 and Tokutomi Iichirō, *Kinsei Nihon kokuminshi*, vol. 84, pp. 6–7. See also Mōri Toshihiko, *Meiji rokunen seihen*, pp. 41–43.

36. *Itō Hirobumi kankei monjo*, vol. 5, p. 265; another letter from Inoue Kaoru to Itō Hirobumi on 1/22/1873, in ibid., pp. 129–31. See also a letter from Shibusawa Eiichi on 1/27/1873 to Yoshida Kiyonari, in Shibusawa Seien kinenzaidan, comp., *Shibusawa Eiichi denki shiryō*, vol. 3, p. 634.

37. *Iwakura Tomomi kankei monjo*, vol. 5, pp. 292–96.

38. See a letter from Saigō Takamori to his brother Tsugumichi on 5/19/1873, *Dai Saigō zenshu*, vol. 2, pp. 717–19; Miyake Setsurei, *Dōjidaishi*, pp. 323–26.

39. Quoted in Matono Hansuke, *Etō Nampaku*, vol. 2, pp. 48–49.

40. For detailed analysis and account of the event, see Conroy, *The Japanese Seizure of Korea*, pp. 1–77, and Mōri Toshihiko, *Meiji rokunen seihen*.

41. A letter from Saigō to Itagaki Taisuke on 7/28/1873, *Dai Saigō zenshū*, vol. 2, p. 737.

42. See letters Saigō sent to Itagaki on 8/4, 8/17, 8/19, and 8/23/1873, ibid., pp. 751–52, 754–56, 758, and 760–61.

43. Katsuta Magoya, *Ōkubo Toshimichi den*, vol. 3, p. 93.

44. Ōkubo Toshimichi's letter to Murata Shimpachi and Ōyama Iwao on 8/13/1873, *Ōkubo Toshimichi monjo*, vol. 4, pp. 521–22.

45. Saigō's letter to Sanjō Sanetomi on 10/11/1873, *Dai Saigō zenshū*, vol. 2, p. 787.

46. Masumi Junnosuke, *Nihon seitōshiron*, pp. 145–48; "Chōsenkoku kenshi ni tsuki kakugi bunretsu jiken," in *MBZ*, vol. 22, pp. 404–22.

47. Masakazu Iwata, Ōkubo Toshimichi, pp. 173–76; Beasley, The Meiji Restoration, p. 403; and Tokutomi Iichirō, Ōkubo Kōtō sensei, p. 247.

48. Beasley, The Meiji Restoration, p. 376. See also Oka Yoshitake, Kindai Nihon seijishi, p. 70.

49. Iwakurakō jikki, vol. 3, pp. 90–92; Hirao Michio, Shishaku Tani Tateki den, pp. 353–54.

50. The belief that the Korean dispute and the ensuing polarization in the government could be exploited to organize former samurai into a strong government opposition turned out to be an illusion. The idea tended to be stronger among those who had at one point or another served in the Imperial government. For example, Maebara Issei, who led an abortive local revolt of Chōshū samurai in 1876, kept his hopes high that his attempt would find a similar and simultaneous response in other localities. Seinan kiden, vol. 1, book 2, p. 606.

51. Itagaki Taisuke, "Wagakuni kensei no yurai," p. 183.

52. Miyajima Seiichirō, Kokken hensan kigen, p. 344.

53. Konuki Shūichirō, Sei-en kaikoroku, vol. 1, pp. 266–70.

54. See the entry for 10/24/1873 of Sasaki Takayuki's, Hogohiroi, vol. 5, pp. 404–5. Sasaki attributed Saigō's insistence on the military expedition to Korea to his hope of instilling a sense of crisis by which to generate the kind of moral excitement known among the Restoration leaders during the Boshin War.

55. For the text of the entire Petition, see Itagaki, ed., Jiyūtōshi, vol. 1, pp. 87–93, and McLaren, "Japanese Government Documents," pp. 427–32.

56. Itagaki, ed., Jiyūtōshi, vol. 1, p. 107.

57. Matsuo Shōichi, Jiyū minken shisō, pp. 39–43, and Tōyama Shigeki, "Seikanron, jiyūminkenron, hōkenron," pp. 76–95.

58. Itagaki, ed., Jiyūtōshi, vol. 1, pp. 90–91.

59. See Kido Kōin's letter to Matsumoto Kanae, in January 1874, Kido Kōin monjo, vol. 5, pp. 201–2.

60. Kido's letter cited in note 59 and another to Itō Hirobumi on 1/4/1874, ibid., pp. 175–77, and the entries for 1/17 and 1/18/1874 in Kido Kōin nikki, vol. 2, pp. 480–81. See also Ōkubo Toshiaki, Meiji kempō no dekirumade, pp. 65–71.

61. Ōkubo Toshimichi monjo, vol. 5, pp. 189–211.

62. Ibid.

63. See, for example, a letter to Iwakura Tomomi on 2/6/1869, ibid., vol. 2, p. 498.

64. Iwakurakō jikki, vol. 2, p. 685.

65. Uete offers a pointed analysis of the political thoughts of this group in his *Nihon kindai shisō no keisei*, especially pp. 111–96. For a brief account of the members' careers and views, consult William R. Braisted, *Meirokusha: Journal of the Japanese Enlightenment*, pp. xvii–xlviii, and Havens, *Nishi Amane and Modern Japanese Thought*, pp. 164–69.

66. Fukuzawa Yukichi, "Bunmeiron no gairyaku" (1875), in *Fukuzawa Yukichi zenshū*, vol. 4, pp. 48–49.

67. Nishi Amane, *Jinsei sampōsetsu*, (1875), in Uete Michiari, ed. and comp., *Nihon no meicho, Nishi Amane, Katō Hiroyuki*, p. 244.

68. Braisted, *Meirokusha*, pp. xxxiii–xl.

69. Katō Hiroyuki, *Tonarigusa*, in Uete Michiari, *Nihon no meicho, Nishi Amane, Katō Hiroyuki*, pp. 309–12.

70. Itaguki, ed., *Jiyūtōshi*, vol. 1, pp. 97–102.

71. Ibid.

72. See Matsumoto Sannosuke, "Keimō shisō no tenkai," in Hashikawa Bunsō and Matsumoto Sannosuke, eds., *Kindai Nihon seiji shisōshi*, pp. 171–72.

73. Inada Masatsugu, *Meiji kempō seiritsushi*, pp. 210–12.

74. Akita, *Foundations of Constitutional Government*, Chapter 2.

75. Itagaki, ed., *Jiyūtōshi*, vol. 1, p. 190.

## 7. Limits of the Restoration

1. Suzuki Takashige, *Daikeishi Kawaji Toshiyoshikun den*, p. 181.

2. Ichijima Kenichi, *Ōkumakō hachijūgonenshi*, vol. 1, pp. 539–40; Matono Hansuke, *Etō Nampaku*, vol. 2, pp. 408–14.

3. *Chitsuroku shobun sankōsho*, in *MZZKSS*, vol. 8, pp. 439, 443–44.

4. By 1876, the majority of samurai who received the cash had by and large used it up. As a result, "eight out of ten" were barely maintaining some measure of livelihood. *Iwakurakō jikki*, vol. 3, p. 544.

5. Maeda Masana made an interesting remark about the impact of the transition in political order upon local life following the *Haihan chiken*. Deeply motivated by the idea of reconstructing locally based industrial, commercial, and cultural activities, Maeda traveled widely in Japan toward the close of the nineteenth century, first as a government official and later as a private citizen: "[In various localities] many enterprises had once flourished. Who had given the incentives? The daimyo had. However, after the *Haihan chiken*, all localities suddenly lost these catalysts. The artisans were driven by daily needs and manufacturing

activities rapidly deteriorated." Maeda Masana, *Kōgyō iken*, in *MZZKSS*, vol. 18, book 1, p. 90.

6. Kanazawa shishi hensaniinkai, comp. *Honkō Kanazawa shishi*, vol. 9, pp. 86–87.

7. Ibid., p. 87.

8. Ibid., p. 88, 94–100.

9. Shimada Kazuyoshi, who assassinated Ōkubo Toshimichi in 1878, also flaunted the word *minken* to justify his extreme action. Shimada was at one time closely associated with the *Chūkokusha*. *Honkō Kanazawashishi*, pp. 95–97, 191–204.

10. Cited in Hirao Michio, *Risshisha to minken undō*, p. 13.

11. *Ichiko Shirō nikki*, in *Seinankiden*, vol. 2, book 1, passim.

12. Itagaki, ed., *Jiyūtōshi*, vol. 1, p. 134.

13. Ueki Emori, "Risshisha shimatsu kiyō," *Shigaku zasshi* 65 (1956): 66–67.

14. Ibid., p. 67.

15 .Ibid., p. 68.

16. Hirao Michio, *Risshisha to minken undō*, pp. 33–35.

17. The entry for 3/30/1875 in Sasaki Takayuki's *Hogohiroi*, vol. 6, pp. 227–37.

18. Ueki Emori, "Risshisha shimatsu kiyō," p. 65.

19. For these developments, see a letter from Ōkubo Toshimichi to Iwakura Tomomi on 9/10/1876 and another from Itō Hirobumi to Ōkubo on 10/13/1876. *Ōkubo Toshimichi monjo*, vol. 7, pp. 245–46, 297.

20. Kawada Mizuho, *Kataoka Kenkichi sensei den*, pp. 378–79.

21. Itagaki, ed., *Jiyūtōshi*, vol. 1, pp. 158–68. See also Beckmann, *The Making of the Meiji Constitution*, pp. 34–38.

22. Fraser, "The Osaka Conference of 1875," *Journal of Asian Studies*, 26(1967): 593–95. See also Shumpokō tsuishōkai, *Itō Hirobumi den*, vol. 2, pp. 889–913; a letter from Ōkubo Toshimichi to Kuroda Ryōsuke on 1/26/1875, *Ōkubo Toshimichi monjo*, vol. 6, pp. 255–56, for Ōkubo's general indifference to the activities of Itagaki and his group.

23. Komatsu Midori, ed. and comp., *Itōkō zenshū*, vol. 3, p. 19; Akita, *Foundations of Constitutional Government*, p. 23; and Sashihara Yasuzō, *Meiji seishi*, p. 254, for Kido Kōin's proposal for constitutional improvements.

24. For example, Itō Hirobumi's letter to Kido Kōin on 1/14/1875, cited in Miyake Setsurei, *Dōjidaishi*, p. 426, and the entry for 3/30/1875 in Sasaki's *Hogohiroi*, vol. 6, pp. 227–31.

25. An editorial of the first issue of *Hyōron shimbun* in *MBZ*, vol. 18, p. 378.

26. Hayashi, *Hayashi Yūzō kyūmudan*, p. 59.

27. See the letters exchanged among Iwakura Tomomi, Sanjō Sanetomi, Itō Hirobumi, Kido Kōin, and Ōkubo Toshimichi, discussing various methods of recruiting former samurai. *Iwakura Tomomi kankei monjo*, vol. 7, pp. 39–43; *Kido Kōin monjo*, vol. 7, pp. 393–95; and *Ōkubo Toshimichi monjo*, vol. 8, pp. 114–15, 116–19.

28. Hayashi, *Hayashi Yūzō kyūmudan*, p. 68.

29. Ibid., pp. 70–71, 74–75, 79–80.

30. Tōyama Shigeki, *Meiji ishin*, pp. 331–36.

31. *Kono Banshū den*, vol. 1, p. 234; Kōno Hironaka, "Nanyū nisshi," in Shōji Kichinosuke, *Nihon seisha seitō hattatsushi*, pp. 115–49.

32. When Ōkubo Toshimichi died in 1878, direct actions against the government were again aired among the disillusioned samurai sympathizers of the Satsuma rebels. Itagaki Taisuke was suggested as their possible leader. For the meeting of Tōyama Mitsuru, a Fukuoka samurai sympathetic to Saigō's rebellion, with Itagaki during the months of uncertainty following the death of Ōkubo Toshimichi, see Genyōsha, *Genyōsha shashi*, pp. 205–7.

33. Sashihara Yasuzō, *Meiji seishi*, p. 305.

34. Itagaki, ed., *Jiyūtōshi*, vol. 1, pp. 296–97, 320–22, 356–77, 443–55.

35. "Mittei hōkokusho," *Rekishi hyōron* 80 (1956): 73.

36. "Aikokusha ketsugiroku," in Shōji Kichinosuke, *Nihon seisha seitō hattatsushi*, pp. 89–90, 102–4.

37. See "Aikokusha saikō gijiroku," *Rekishi hyōron* 86 (1957): 72–75, for the problem of financing the samurai associations.

38. Cited in Iyenaga Saburō, *Ueki Emori kenkyū*, p. 151.

39. Sakurai Shizuka, "Kokkai kaisetsu konsei kyōgian," in *Ōkuma bunsho*, vol. 1, pp. 165–66.

40. Suzuki Yasuzō, *Jiyū minken, kempō happu*, pp. 52–55.

41. Ibid., pp. 64–89, and Sashihara Yasuzō, *Meiji seishi*, pp. 355–56.

42. Meiji shiryō kenkyū renrakukai, comp., *Meiji jūsannen zenkoku kokkai kaisetsu genrōin kempakusho shūsei*, p. 95.

43. Suzuki Yasuzō, *Jiyū minken, kempō happu*, p. 95.

44. Two works in English on prewar Japanese party politics offer excellent analyses of the consequences of this tendency among the parliamentarians: one, Najita, *Hara Kei in the Politics of Compromise, 1905–1915*, deals with the height of Japan's prewar party development, often referred to as Taishō democracy, and the other, Berger, *Parties Out of Power in Japan, 1931–1941*, focuses on the conditions for the rise of the Imperial Rule Assistance Association, *Taisei yokusankai*, in the 1940s.

45. Quoted in Tokutomi Iichirō, *Kinsei Nihon kokuminshi*, vol. 100, pp. 27–28.

46. Hall, "A Monarch for Modern Japan," pp. 27–28.

47. See Hackett, "Political Modernization and the Meiji Genrō," pp. 65–97.

48. For example, the debate among the leaders on who would succeed Premier Tōjō Hideki, who was facing the deterioration of Japan's position in the Pacific War. See the entry for 7/18/1944 in *Kido Kōichi nikki*, pp. 1122–28.

# Glossary and Biographical Notes

Words set in SMALL CAPS are defined elsewhere in the Glossary

AIKOKU KŌTŌ (Public Party of Patriots): A political party founded in January 1874 by ITAGAKI TAISUKE in Tokyo to promote popular political participation.

AIKOKUSHA (Society of Patriots): A political association founded in February 1875 in Osaka by ITAGAKI TAISUKE and his followers in his RISSHISHA to step up the movement to promote parliamentary government.

BAKUFU: Military government headed by the shogun as the overlord of all military houses.

BAKUMATSU: The term used to refer to the closing years of the TOKUGAWA shogunate.

BOSHIN SENSŌ: The War of the Restoration between January 1868 and July 1869.

CHIHŌKAN KAIGI: The prefectural governors' conference.

CHIKEN: Certificate of land ownership.

CHISO KAISEI: The Land Tax Reform, begun in 1873 and completed in 1881, aimed at monetarization of tax payment in order to stabilize the MEIJI government's revenue. The reform also provided the momentum for commercialization of agriculture.

CHŌSHI: An Imperial government official created immediately after the Restoration in order to allow daimyo's retainers to serve the Imperial government. Many well-known samurai activists joined the government initially as Chōshi.

DAJŌKAN: The system of government in operation from 1868 to 1885. Throughout early MEIJI, the term was used to refer both to the Imperial government generally and to the highest executive organ in the government specifically.

DAJŌKANSATSU: Government paper notes issued following the restoration of Imperial rule; originally irredeemable but soon made redeemable following its disastrous impact on economy.

DATE MUNENARI (1818–1892): Daimyo of Uwajima in Shikoku, played a key role in BAKUMATSU politics in Kyoto and subsequently served in a number of government posts after the Restoration.

ETŌ SHIMPEI (1834–1874): Samurai activist from Saga, helped modernize Japan's judicial system; later died following the unsuccessful Saga Rebellion.

FU: The name of local government units reserved especially for large metropolitan areas such as Tokyo, Kyoto, and Osaka. Before the HAI-HAN CHIKEN of 1871, the name was used for local government units in the former Tokugawa territories.

FUDAI: The vassal daimyo.

FU-KEN KAI KISOKU: The Regulations for the Fu-Ken Assemblies, July 1878.

FU-KEN KANSEI: The System of Ranks for the Fu-Ken Officials, December 1871.

FUKOKU KYŌHEI (Enrich the Country and Strengthen the Nation): The national slogan of the early MEIJI era to launch and sustain westernization policies.

FUKUOKA TAKACHIKA (1835–1919): Samurai activist from Tosa; helped draft the Oath of 1868 and later served the Restoration government in a number of posts.

GENRŌ (Elder Statesmen): A group of men with considerable political power serving as liaison between the Emperor and the government throughout Japan's pre-World War II period; they usually had distinguished records as Restoration activists.

GIJŌ: Senior Councilor of the Imperial Government, from 1868 to 1869, under the DAJŌKAN system.

GOKAJŌ NO GOSEIMON: The Five Charter Oath of 1868.

GUNKEN: A general term referring to the centralized control of local government on the basis of the prefectural system.

HACHIKYOKU: The Eight-Department System of the Imperial Government, 1868.

HAIHAN CHIKEN: The abolition of feudal domains and the creation of prefectures, 1871.

HANSEKI HŌKAN: The return of fiefs to the Emperor, 1869.

HATAMOTO: The direct retainer of the shogun.

HEIMIN: Commoner.

HŌKEN: The feudal system of political control.

INOUE KAORU (1835–1915): Chōshū activist; played a key role in the Imperial government by occupying a number of posts.

ITAGAKI TAISUKE (1837—1919): Samurai activist from Tosa; helped organize and lead the Tosa military forces in the wars against the TO-KUGAWA. Subsequently, he joined the Restoration government only to withdraw and launch the movement for parliamentary government in 1874.

ITŌ HIROBUMI (1841–1909): Samurai activist from Chōshū; later architect of the MEIJI Constitution; served in various posts in the Imperial government following the Restoration.

IWAKURA MISSION: The mission formed and sent to the United States and Europe in 1871 initially for the purpose of treaty revision negotiations; following the unsuccessful negotiations with the United States, the mission's purpose shifted to that of investigating Western civilization. The key members of the mission included IWAKURA TO-MOMI, KIDO KŌIN, ŌKUBO TOSHIMICHI, and ITŌ HIROBUMI.

IWAKURA TOMOMI (1825–1883): Court noble who emerged as a key contact of samurai Restoration activists especially from Satsuma. Along with SANJŌ SANETOMI, Iwakura was one of the leading Court nobles who guided the Imperial government in its formative years.

KATŌ HIROYUKI (1836–1916): Samurai from Tajima, studied Western learning during the BAKUMATSU period; a key member of MEIROKUSHA who grew critical of ITAGAKI TAISUKE's popular rights movement.

KATSU KAISHŪ (1823–1899): A TOKUGAWA retainer, trained in military science and Dutch studies; climbed up steadily the BAKUFU's hierarchy during the BAKUMATSU period, and played a key role in engineering the peaceful surrender of Edo to the Emperor's forces in 1868.

KAZOKU: New nobility, instituted in 1869, to consist until 1884 of the Court nobles and daimyo. Later it became the equivalent of a Western-style peerage.

KEN: Prefectures.

KENJI JŌREI: The Prefectural Government Ordinance, January 1872.

KIDO KŌIN (1833–1877): Chōshū activist leader worked closely with ŌKUBO TOSHIMICHI of Satsuma throughout the final days of the TO-KUGAWA and the formative years of the Imperial government. He was also a writer of the Oath of 1868, opposed the plan to send military expedition to Korea in 1873, and died during the Satsuma Rebellion.

KOKKAI KISEI DŌMEIKAI: The League for Opening a National Assembly, created in 1880.

KOKU: The unit for the measurement of rice and other grains. One koku is approximately five bushels.

KŌMEI, EMPEROR (1831–1867): Succeeded to throne in 1846, and stimulated the fanatic "anti-barbarian" campaign among the Restoration activists.

KŌNO HIRONAKA (1849–1923): A native of Fukushima, active in the popular rights movement from its formative stage.

KOSEKI: The Household Residence Registry.

KŌSHI: Domain representatives, usually the ranking retainers of the domain, sent to the Imperial government before the HAIHAN CHIKEN of 1871, participated in various policy discussion at the Kōgisho; later called, Kōginin.

KUCHŌ (kochō): Official of the districts, *ku*, created for the purpose of taking census for the Household Residence Registry.

MATSUDAIRA YOSHINAGA (1828–1890): Daimyo of Fukui (Echizen), one of the daimyo active in BAKUMATSU politics who had a moderating effect on the demise of the TOKUGAWA; held various posts in the Imperial government.

MEIJI, Emperor (1852–1912): Succeeded to throne in 1867; oversaw the creation of Japan's modern state from its very beginning, and wielded considerable influence over the course of Japan's political and economic modernization.

MEIROKUSHA: A society of Japanese scholars and practitioners who had received training in Western studies, founded in 1874, the sixth year of MEIJI. The members included Fukuzawa Yukichi, Kanda Kōhei, KATŌ HIROYUKI, and NISHI AMANE, among others.

MINKAI: Popularly elected assemblies.

MINKENKA: The popular rights activists.

NISHI AMANE (1829–1897): Samurai from Tsuwano, a key member of the MEIROKUSHA.

ŌKUBO TOSHIMICHI (1830–1878): One of the most influential samurai activists from Satsuma throughout BAKUMATSU and early MEIJI politics; served the Imperial government in a number of important domestic posts. He was assassinated by a group of disgruntled former samurai in the aftermath of the Satsuma Rebellion.

ŌKUMA SHIGENOBU (1838–1922): Samurai activist from Saga; served the

Imperial Government in its formative years in various diplomatic and domestic affairs posts.

RISSHISHA (Society of High Ambition): A local association for former samurai, established in Tosa in 1874 by ITAGAKI TAISUKE. It also promoted parliamentary government. The leading members included Ueki Emori, among others.

SAIGŌ TAKAMORI (1928–1877): Samurai activist from Satsuma and one of the most influential military leaders of the Imperial government; headed the Imperial government from 1871 to 1873, but left it following the Korean military expedition dispute and launched an unsuccessful revolt against it in 1877.

SA-IN: The Left Chamber of the Three-Chamber System of government.

SAMPAN KEMPEI: An agreement in 1871 among the three principal Restoration domains, Satsuma, Chōshū, and Tosa, to contribute their troops to the Imperial Court.

SANGI: Councillor of the Imperial government, 1869–1885, under the DAJŌKAN system.

SAN'IN SEI: The Three-Chamber System of government, 1869–1875.

SANJŌ SANETOMI (1837–1891): Court noble who, like IWAKURA TOMOMI, acquired political prominence in BAKUMATSU politics as contact of samurai activists; served the Imperial government during its turbulent formative years in a number of posts including that of prime minister.

SANKIN KŌTAI: Alternate residence requirement.

SANYO: Junior Councillor of the Imperial government, 1868–1869, under the DAJŌKAN system.

SASAKI TAKAYUKI (1830–1910): Tosa samurai activist who rose in political prominence through a number of posts in the infant Imperial government after the Restoration.

SEI-IN: The Central Chamber of the Three-Chamber System of government.

SEIKAN RONSŌ: The dispute over the question of military expedition to Korea in 1873, which divided the Imperial government.

SEIKANTŌ: Political associations and parties formed following the divisive dispute in the Imperial government over the military expedition to Korea in 1873. Most of the members of these associations and parties were former samurai.

SHIBUSAWA EIICHI (1841–1931): A rich farmer's son who later became a TOKUGAWA retainer toward the close of the BAKUFU; served the Imperial government and helped INOUE KAORU in the Department of Finance. He later became an immensely successful businessman.

SHICHIKA: The Seven-Department System, 1868.

SHIMAZU HISAMITSU (1817–1887): Father of Satsuma daimyo, Shimazu Tadayoshi, for whom he served as regent; consistently critical of the Imperial government and its modernization policies. He practically ruled the Satsuma domain politics during the BAKUMATSU and early MEIJI period.

SHISHI (Men of High Purpose): The term usually refers to the pro-Restoration activists in BAKUMATSU politics.

SHIZOKU: A new class designated for former samurai after 1869.

SONNŌ JŌI (Revere the Emperor and Expel the Barbarians): Anti-BAKUFU and anti-foreign slogan adopted by the Restoration activists in the closing decades of the TOKUGAWA BAKUFU.

TAKASUGI SHINSAKU (1839–1867): A protégé of Yoshida Shōin, a Chōshū ideologue of the restoration of Imperial rule, organized Chōshū's irregular armies which, together with the Satsuma and Tosa forces, constituted the backbone of the Imperial forces during the Boshin war.

TANI TATEKI (1837–1911): A Tosa military leader during the Boshin war, and proceeded to serve the Imperial government in various military posts.

TOKUGAWA YOSHINOBU (1837–1913): A son of Tokugawa Nariaki of Mito and the last of the fifteen Tokugawa shoguns, to which he succeeded in 1866. His return of the governing power to the Emperor late in 1867 opened the final phase of the Restoration movement culminating in the Boshin war.

U-IN: The Right Chamber of the Three-Chamber System of government.

YAMAGATA ARITOMO (1838–1922): A samurai activist from Chōshū and a key military leader of the Imperial forces during the Boshin war; along with the other two Chōshū activists, INOUE KAORU and ITŌ HIROBUMI, he helped to maintain the prominence of men from Chōsū in the Imperial government even after the death of their senior leader, KIDO KŌIN.

YURI KIMIMASA (1829–1909): A samurai activist from Echizen, who earlier served as aid to MATSUDAIRA YOSHINAGA before the Restoration; participated in drafting the Oath and served the Imperial government in various posts.

# Bibliography

## Abbreviations

KIN     Hashimoto Hiroshi, comp., *Kaitei ishin nisshi*, vols. 1–7. Tokyo: Meicho kankōkai, 1966.

MBZ     Meiji bunka kenkyukai, ed. and comp., *Meiji bunka zenshū*, vols. 1, 2, 4, 8, 17, 18, and 22. Tokyo: Nihon hyōron shinsha, 1929.

MZZKSS     Ōuchi Hyōe and Tsuchiya Takao, eds. and comps., *Meiji zenki zaisei keizai shiryō shūsei*, vols. 1–4, 7–11, and 18. Tokyo: Meiji bunken shiryo kankōkai, 1962–64.

## Primary Sources

Andō Hiroshi, comp. *Tokugawa bakufu kenji yōryaku*. Tokyo: Kashiwa Shobō, 1965.

Aoki Shūzō. *Aoki Shūzō jiden*. Tokyo: Heibonsha, 1970.

Bitō Masahide, ed. and comp. *Nihon no meicho, Ogyū Sorai*. Tokyo: Chūōkoronsha, 1974.

*Chihōkan kaigi nisshi*, in *MBZ*, vol. 4.

*Chindai nisshi*, in *KIN*, vol. 6.

*Chinshōfu nisshi*, in *KIN*, vol. 6.

*Chiso kaisei hōkokusho*, in *MZZKSS*, vol. 7.

*Chiso kaisei shorui shūsan*, in *MZZKSS*, vol. 7.

*Chitsuroku shobun temmatsuryaku*, in *MZZKSS*, vol. 8.

*Chūgai shimbun*, in *MBZ*, vol. 17.

Dai Saigō zenshū kankōkai, comp. *Dai Saigō zenshū*, 3 vols. Tokyo: Heibonsha, 1926–27.

Dajōkan, ed. (Tokyo daigaku shiryō hensanjo, comp.). *Fukkoki*, 15 vols. Tokyo: Naigaishoseki, 1929–32.

*Dajōkan nisshi*, in *KIN*, vols. 1–5.

*Date Munenari zaikyō nikki*. Tokyo: Nihon shiseki kyōkai, 1916.

*Fuken shiryō* (Kokuritsu kōbunshokan microfilm): Akita; Chiba; Ehime; Fukushima; Gifu; Gumma; Hiroshima; Hyōgo; Ibaraki; Ishikawa; Mie; Miyagi; Nagasaki; Ōita; Shimane; Shizuoka; Tochigi; Tottori; Wakayama; Yamagata; Yamaguchi; and Yamanashi.

Fukuoka Takachika. "Gokajō goseimon to seitaisho no yurai ni tsuite," in Kokka gakkai, ed., *Meiji kensei keizaishiron*. Tokyo: Kokka gakkai, 1919.

Fukushima kenshi hensan iinkai, comp. *Fukushima kenshi*, vols. 11 and 15. Fukushima: Fukushima ken, 1964 and 1968.

Fukuzawa Yukichi. *Fukuzawa Yukichi zenshū*, vols. 4 and 7. Tokyo: Iwanami shoten, 1959.

——. "Bunmeiron no gairyaku," in *Fukuzawa Yukichi zenshū*, vol. 4.

——. "Kyūhanjō," in *Fukuzawa Yukichi zenshū*, vol. 7.

Gaimushō. *Dai Nihon gaikō bunsho*, vol. 4. Tokyo: Nihon kokusai kyōkai, 1938.

——. *Dai Nihon gaikōbunsho, bessatsu, kindai inyōreki taishōhyō*. Tokyo: Nihon kokusai kyōkai, 1910.

*Gijōkan nichiroku*, in *KIN*, vol. 7.

*Hachiburitsuki gaikoku kōsai hakkō nikki*, in *MZZKSS*, vol. 10.

*Hansai shobunroku*, in *MZZKSS*, vol. 9.

*Hansai shūroku*, in *MZZKSS*, vol. 9.

Hayashi Yūzō. *Hayashi Yūzō kyūmudan*, in *MBZ*, vol. 22.

Higashikuze Michitomi. *Chikutei kaikoroku, Ishin zengo*. Tokyo: Hakubunkan, 1911.

*Hōrei zensho*, 1868–1883. Tokyo: Naikaku kanpōkyoku, 1887–1890.

*Hyakkan rireki*, 2 vols. Tokyo: Nihon shiseki kyōkai, 1927–28.

*Hyōron shimbun*, in *MBZ*, vol. 18.

Ibaraki ken, comp. *Ibaraki kenshiryō, kindai seiji shakaihen*, vols. 1 and 2. Ibaraki: Ibaraki ken, 1974.

*Ishin irai chōson enkaku*. Tokyo: Meiji shiryo kenkyū renrakukai, 1957.

*Ishin shiryō kōyō*, vol. 10. Tokyo: Tokyo daigaku shuppankai, 1984 (1939).

Itagaki Taisuke. "Wagakuni kensei no yurai," in Kokka gakkai, ed., *Meiji kensei keizaishiron*, Tokyo: Kokka gakkai, 1919.

Itō Hirobumi kankei monjo kenkyūkai, comp. *Itō Hirobumi kankei monjo*, vols. 1–5. Tokyo: Hanawa shobō, 1976–77.

*Iwakura Tomomi kenkei monjo*, 8 vols. Tokyo: Nihon shiseki kyōkai, 1929–35.

Jichi shinkōkai, comp. *Fuken seido shiryō*, 2 vols. Tokyo: Jichi shinkōkai, 1973.

*Kaku-han senkō-roku*, in *KIN*, vol. 6.

Kanazawa shishi hensaniinkai, comp. *Honko Kanazawa shishi*, vol. 1. Kanazawa: Kanazawa shiyakusho, 1933.

Katsu Kaishū. *Kaishū zenshū*, vols. 2–4, and 9. Tokyo: Kaizosha, 1927–29.

———. *Kainanroku*, in *Kaishū zenshū*, vol. 2.

———. *Kaishū nikki*, in *Kaishū zenshū*, vol. 9.

———. *Suijinroku*, in *Kaishū zenshū*, vols. 3 and 4.

*Kido Kōichi nikki*, vol. 2. Tokyo: Tokyo daigaku shuppankai, 1966.

*Kido Kōin monjo*, 8 vols. Tokyo: Nihon shiseki kyōkai, 1929–31.

*Kido Kōin nikki*, 2 vols. Tokyo: Nihon shiseki kyōkai, 1932–33. (Volume 1 is also available in English, translated by Sidney D. Brown and Akiko Hirota, *The Diary of Kido Takayoshi, Volume I: 1868–1871*, Tokyo, University of Tokyo Press, 1983.)

*Kōgisho nisshi*, in *MBZ*, vol. 4.

Komatsu Midori, ed. and comp. *Itōkō zenshū*, 3 vols. Tokyo: Showa shuppansha, 1928.

Konuki Shūichiro. *Seien kaikoroku*, 2 vols. Tokyo: Seien kaikoroku kankōkai, 1927.

Maeda Masana. *Kōgyō iken*, in *MZZKSS*, vol. 18.

Matsukata Masayoshi. *Matsukatahaku zaisei ronsakushū*, in *MZZKSS*, vol. 1.

Meiji bunka kenkyūkai ed. and comp. *Meiji bunka zenshū*, vols. 1, 2, 4, 18, and 22. Tokyo: Nihon hyōron shinsha, 1929.

*Meiji jūichinen shigatsu chihōkan kaigi bōchōroku*. Tokyo: Meiji shiryō kenkyū renrakukai, 1958.

*Meiji jūsannen zenkoku kokkai kaisetsu genrōin kempaku shūsei*. Tokyo: Meiji shiryō kenkyū renrakukai, 1956.

*Meiji nenkan beika chōsetsu enkakushi*, in *MZZKSS*, vol. 11, book 1.

*Meiji zenki fukenkai giin meibo*, 3 vols. Tokyo: Meiji shiryō kenkyū renrakukai, 1960.

*Meiroku zasshi*, in *MBZ*, vol. 18. (See also *Meiroku zasshi: Journal of the Japanese Enlightenment*, William R. Braisted, trans., Tokyo, University of Tokyo Press, 1976.)

Miyajima Seiichirō. *Kokken hensan kigen*, in *MBZ*, vol. 4.

Naikaku kampōkyoku. *Chihō enkaku ryakufu*. Tokyo: Naimushō toshokyoku, 1882.

Nakane Yukie. *Saimu kiji*. Tokyo: Nihon shiseki kyōkai, 1922.

———. *Zoku saimu kiji*. Tokyo, 1921–22.

———. *Teibō nikki*, in *KIN*, vol. 7.

*Nanki Tokugawashi*, vol. 4. Wakayama: Nanki Tokugawashi kankōkai, 1931.

Nihon keieishi kenkyūjo, comp. *Godai Tomoatsu denki shiryō*, 4 vols. Tokyo: Tōyō keizaishimposha, 1970–73.

*Ōkubo Toshimichi monjo*, 10 vols. Tokyo: Nihon shiseki kyōkai, 1927–31.

*Ōkubo Toshimichi nikki*, 2 vols. Tokyo: Nihon shiseki kyōkai, 1927.

*Ōkuma Shigenobu kankei monjo*, 6 vols. Tokyo: Nihon shiseki kyōkai, 1932–35.

*Ōkurashō enkakushi*, in *MZZKSS*, vols. 2 and 3.

*Otedome nikki* (Date Munenari), in *KIN*, vol. 7.

Ōuchi Hyōe and Tsuchiya Takao, eds. and comp. *Meiji zenki zaisei keizai shiryō shūsei*, vols. 1–4, 7–11, and 18. Tokyo: Meiji bunken shiryō kankōkai, 1962–64.

Rikkyō daigaku Nihonshi kenkyūkai, comp. *Ōkubo Toshimichi kankei monjo*, vols. 1–5. Tokyo: Yoshikawa kōbunkan, 1965–71.

*Saishutsunyū kessan hōkokusho*, in *MZZKSS*, vol. 4.

Sasaki Takayuki. *Hogohiroi: Sasaki Takayuki nikki*, 8 vols. Tokyo: Tokyo daigaku shuppankai, 1970–76.

Shibusawa Eiichi, ed. *Sekimukai hikki*. Tokyo: Heibonsha, 1967.

Shibusawa Seien kinenzaidan ryūmonsha, comp. *Shibusawa Eiichi denki shiryō*, vol. 3. Tokyo: Shibusawa Eiichi denki shiryō kankōkai, 1955.

Shidankai, comp. *Shidankai sokkiroku*, vols. 18, 23, and 207. Tokyo: Shidankai, 1973.

Shimauchi Toshie, comp. *Tani Tateki ikō*, 2 vols. Tokyo: Seikensha, 1912.

*Shūgiin nisshi*, in *MBZ*, vol. 4.

*Soga Sukenoriō jijoden*. Tokyo: Soga Sukenori denki kankōkai, 1930.

Suematsu Kenchō, comp. *Bō-Chō kaitenshi*, vol. 6. Tokyo: Tokyo kokukōsha, 1921.

Tōgyō gojūnensai kinenkai. *Tōgyō sensei ibun*, Tokyo: Gojunensai kinenkai, 1916.

Tsuchiya Takao and Ono Michio, eds. *Meiji shonen nōmin sōjōroku.* Tokyo: Keisō shobō, 1953 (1931).

Tsuda Shigemaro, ed. *Kinnō hishi Sasaki rōkō sekijitsudan.* Tokyo: Nikkōkan, 1915.

Ueki Emori. "Risshisha shimatsu kiyō," *Shigaku zasshi* 65, no. 1 (1956).

Uete Michiari, ed. and comp. *Nihon no meicho, Nishi Amane, Katō Hiroyuki.* Tokyo: Chuō kōronsha, 1972.

Waseda daigaku shakaikagaku kenkyūjo, comp. *Ōkuma bunsho,* 5 vols. Tokyo: Waseda daigaku shakaikagaku kenkyūjo, 1958–62.

Watanabe Yosuke, comp. *Kinnō shishi ibunshū,* vol. 1. Tokyo: Dai Nihon bunko kankōkai, 1941.

*Zokuroku shobunroku,* in *MZZKSS,* vol. 8.


## Secondary Sources

*Aichiken gikaishi.* Nagoya: Aichiken gikai jimukyoku, 1953, vol. 1.

Akita, George. *Foundations of Constitutional Government in Modern Japan, 1868–1900.* Cambridge, Mass.: Harvard University Press, 1967.

*Akita kenshi,* vol. 4. Akita: 1961.

Allen, G. C. *A Short Economic History of Modern Japan, 1867–1937.* London: George Allen and Unwin, 1962.

Aoki Kōki. *Hyakushō ikki sōgō nempyō.* Tokyo: Sanichi shobō, 1971.

———. *Hyakushō ikki no nenjiteki kenkyū.* Tokyo: Shinseisha, 1966.

Arimoto Masao. "Chiso kaisei to chihō seiji," in *Iwanami kōza Nihon rekishi,* vol. 14, pp. 167–208. Tokyo: Iwanami shoten, 1975.

Arimoto Masao and Ōta Kenichi. "Chiso kaisei to jinushi gōnō," *Tochi seido shigaku,* no. 11 (1961): 31–44.

Asai Kiyoshi. *Meiji ishin to gunken shisō.* Tokyo: Ganshōdō shoten, 1939.

Banno Junji. "Seikanronsō go no 'Naijiha' to 'gaiseiha,' " in *Nempō kindai Nihon kenkyū,* vol. 3, pp. 245–62. Tokyo: Yamakawa shuppan, 1981.

Beasley, William G. "Feudal Revenue in Japan," *Journal of Asian Studies,* 19, no. 3 (1960): 255–72.

———. *The Meiji Restoration.* Stanford, Cal.: Stanford University Press, 1972.

———. *The Modern History of Japan.* New York: Praeger, 1973.

Beckmann, George M. *The Making of the Meiji Constitution: The Oligarchs and the Constitutional Development of Japan, 1868–1891.* Lawrence, Kans.: University of Kansas Press, 1957.

Bendix, Reinhard. "Preconditions of Development: A Comparison of Japan and Germany," in Dore, ed., *Aspects of Social Change in Modern Japan*, pp. 27–68. Princeton, N.J.: Princeton University Press, 1967.

Berger, Gordon M. *Parties Out of Power in Japan, 1931–1941*. Princeton, N.J.: Princeton University Press, 1977.

Blacker, Carmen. *The Japanese Enlightenment: A Study of the Writings of Fukuzawa Yukichi*. Cambridge: Cambridge University Press, 1969.

Bolitho, Harold. *Treasures among Men: The Fudai Daimyo in Tokugawa Japan*. New Haven, Conn.: Yale University Press, 1974.

Bowen, Roger W. *Rebellion and Democracy in Meiji Japan*. Berkeley and Los Angeles: University of California Press, 1980.

Conroy, Hilary. *The Japanese Seizure of Korea: 1868–1910. A Study of Realism and Idealism in International Relations*. Philadelphia: University of Pennsylvania Press, 1960.

Craig, Albert M. *Chōshū in the Meiji Restoration*. Cambridge, Mass.: Harvard University Press, 1961.

Crowley, James B. ed. *Modern East Asia, Essays in Interpretation*. New York: Harcourt, Brace and World, 1970.

Deutsch, Karl W. and William Foltz, eds. *Nation-Building*. New York: Atherton, 1963.

Dore, Ronald P., ed. *Aspects of Social Change in Modern Japan*. Princeton, N.J.: Princeton University Press, 1967.

Dowdy, Edwin. "Aspects of Tokugawa Bureaucracy and Modernization." *Australian Journal of Politics and History* 16, no. 3 (1970): 375–89.

Dower, John W., ed. *Origins of the Modern Japanese State: Selected Writings of E. H. Norman*. New York: Pantheon Books. 1975.

Eisenstadt, S. N. *Modernization: Protest and Change*. Englewood Cliffs, N.J.: Prentice-Hall, 1966.

Emerson, Rupert. *From Empire to Nation: The Rise to Self-Assertion of Asian and African Peoples*. Boston: Beacon Press, 1962.

Enjōji Kiyoshi. Ōkumahaku sekijitsutan. Tokyo: Shinchōsha, 1938.

Fraser, Andrew. "The Osaka Conference of 1875." *Journal of Asian Studies* 26, no. 4 (1967): 589–611.

Fujimura Michio. "Seikan ronsō ni okeru gaiin to naiin," *Kokusai seiji* 37 (1967): 1–22.

Fujino Tamotsu. *Bakusei to hansei*. Tokyo: Yoshikawa kōbunkan, 1979.

Fukaya Hakuji. *Kashizoku chitsuroku shobun no kenkyū*. Tokyo: Takayama shoin, 1941.

Fukushima Masao. *Chiso kaisei no kenkyū*. Tokyo: Yūhikaku, 1962.

——. "Meiji rokunen no chihōkan kaidō to chiso kaisei." *Tōyō bunka kenkyūjo kiyō*, no. 18 (1959): 1–47.

——. "Meiji shoki no chihōkan to gunseikaikaku." *Chihōshi kenkyū*, no. 24 (1956): 2–14.

——, ed. *Koseki seido to 'iye' seido*. Tokyo: Tokyo daigaku shuppankai, 1959.

Fukushima Masao and Tokuda Ryōji. "Meiji shonen no chō-sonkai," in Meiji shiryō kenkyū renrakukai, ed., *Chiso kaisei to chihōjichi*, pp. 121–286. Tokyo: Ochanomizu shobō, 1956.

Genyōsha shashi hensankai. *Genyōsha shashi*. Tokyo: Genyōsha shashi hensankai, 1918.

Gotō Yasushi. "Hansei kaikaku, tokuni Tempō kaikaku ni tsuite." *Rekishigaku kenkyū*, no. 176 (1954): 38–42.

——. *Jiyū minken*. Tokyo: Chuō kōronsha, 1972.

——. *Shizoku hanran no kenkyū*. Tokyo: Aoki shoten, 1967.

Griffis, William E. *The Mikado's Empire*, 2 vols. New York: Harper, 1883.

Hackett, Roger F. "Political Modernization and the Meiji Genrō," in Ward, ed., *Political Development in Modern Japan*, pp. 65–97. Princeton, N.J.: Princeton University Press, 1968.

——. *Yamagata Aritomo in the Rise of Modern Japan, 1838–1922*. Cambridge, Mass.: Harvard University Press, 1971.

Haga Noboru. *Meiji kokka to minshū*. Tokyo: Yūzankaku, 1974.

Hall, John W. "Feudalism in Japan—A Reassessment," in Hall and Jansen, eds., *Studies in the Institutional History of Early Modern Japan*, pp. 15–51. Princeton: N.J.: Princeton University Press, 1968.

——. "A Monarch for Modern Japan," in Ward, ed., *Political Development in Modern Japan*, pp. 11–64. Princeton, N.J.: Princeton University Press, 1968.

Hall, John W. and Marius B. Jansen, eds. *Studies in the Institutional History of Early Modern Japan*. Princeton, N.J.: Princeton University Press, 1968.

Hane, Mikiso, *Peasants, Rebels, and Outcasts: The Underside of Modern Japan*. New York: Pantheon Books, 1982.

Hara Hidesaburō et al., eds. *Taikei Nihon kokkashi*, vol. 4. Tokyo: Tokyo daigaku shuppankai, 1975.

Haraguchi Kiyoshi. *Boshin sensō*. Tokyo: Hanawa shobō, 1963.

——. "Hantaisei no kaitai," in *Iwanami kōza Nihon rekishi*, vol. 15, pp. 1–51. Tokyo: Iwanami shoten, 1962.

——. "Meiji shonen no kokka kenryoku," in Hara et al., eds., *Taikei Nihon kokkashi*, vol. 4, pp. 65–135. Tokyo: Tokyo daigaku shuppankai, 1975.

——. *Meiji zenki chihōseijishi josetsu*, 2 vols. Tokyo: Hanawa shobō, 1972.

——. *Nihon kindai kokka no keisei*. Tokyo: Iwanami shoten, 1968.

Harootunian, Harry D. "The Economic Rehabilitation of the Samurai in the Early Meiji Period." *Journal of Asian Studies* 19 (1960): 433–44.

Harootunian, Harry D. and Bernard S. Silberman, eds. *Modern Japanese Leadership: Transition and Change*. Tucson, Ariz.: University of Arizona Press, 1966.

Hashikawa Bunsō and Matsumoto Sannosuke, eds. *Kindai Nihon seiji shisōshi*, vol. 1. Tokyo: Yūhikaku, 1971.

Havens, Thomas R. H. *Nishi Amane and Modern Japanese Thought*. Princeton, N.J.: Princeton University Press, 1970.

Hirao Michio. *Jiyū minken undō no keifu*. Kōchi shimin toshokan, 1970.

——. *Risshisha to minken undō*. Kōchi: Kōchi shimin toshokan, 1956.

——. *Shishaku Tani Tateki den*. Tokyo: Tozanbō, 1935.

Hirschmeier, Johannes, S.V.D. *The Origins of Entrepreneurship in Meiji Japan*. Cambridge, Mass.: Harvard University Press, 1964.

Honjō Eijirō. *Honjō Eijirō chosakushū*, vol. 9. Tokyo: Seibundō, 1973.

Horie Eiichi, ed. *Hansei kaikaku no kenkyū*. Tokyo: Ochanomizu shobō, 1955.

Horie Eiichi and Tōyama Shigeki, eds. *Jiyū minkenki no kenkyū*, 4 vols. Tokyo: Yūhikaku, 1959.

Huber, Thomas. *The Revolutionary Origins of Modern Japan*. Stanford, Cal.: Stanford University Press, 1982.

Ichijima Kenichi. *Ōkumakō hachijūgonenshi*, 3 vols. Tokyo: Ōkumakō hachijūgonenshi hensankai, 1926.

Ike, Nobutaka. *The Beginnings of Political Democracy in Japan*. Baltimore: Johns Hopkins University Press, 1950.

Inada Masatsugu. *Meiji kempō seiritsushi*, vol. 1. Tokyo: Yūhikaku, 1960.

Inoue Kaorukō denki hensankai. *Segai Inouekō den*, 5 vols. Tokyo: Naigai shoseki, 1933–34.

Inoue Kiyoshi. *Nihon gendaishi*, vol. 1. Tokyo: Tokyo daigaku shuppankai, 1954.

Ishii Takashi. *Boshin sensōron*. Tokyo: Yoshikawa kōbunkan, 1984.

——. *Gakusetsu hihan Meiji ishinron*. Tokyo: Yoshikawa kōbunkan, 1961.

——. *Zōtei Meiji ishin no kokusaiteki kankyō*. Tokyo: Yoshikawa kōbunkan, 1966.

Ishizuka Hiromichi. "Meiji shoki ni okeru Kishūhan hansei kaikaku no seijishiteki kōsatsu." *Rekishigaku kenkyū*, no. 182 (1955): 13–25.

——. *Nihon shihonshugi seiritsushi kenkyū*. Tokyo: Yoshikawa kōbunkan, 1973.

Itagaki Taisuke, ed. *Jiyūtōshi*, 3 vols. Tokyo: Iwanami shoten, 1957.

Iwakurakō kyūseki hozonkai. *Iwakurakō jikki*, 3 vols. Tokyo: Iwakurakō kyūseki hozonkai, 1927.

Iwata, Masakazu. *Ōkubo Toshimichi, The Bismarck of Japan*. Berkeley and Los Angeles: University of California Press, 1964.

Iyenaga Saburō. *Ueki Emori kenkyū*. Tokyo: Iwanami ohotcn, 1960.

Jansen, Marius B. "The Meiji State: 1868–1912," in Crowley, ed., *Modern East Asia*, pp. 95–121. New York, Harcourt, Brace and World, 1970.

——. *Sakamoto Ryōma and the Meiji Restoration*. Princeton, N.J.: Princeton University Press, 1961.

——, ed. *Changing Japanese Attitudes toward Modernization*. Princeton, N.J.: Princeton University Press, 1965.

Jansen, Marius B. and Gilbert Rozman, eds. *Japan in Transition: From Tokugawa to Meiji*, Princeton, N.J.: Princeton University Press, 1986.

Kamishima Jirō, ed. *Kenryoku no shiso*. Tokyo: Chikuma shobō, 1965.

Katsuta Magoya. *Ōkubo Toshimichi den*, 3 vols. Tokyo: Dōbunkan, 1910.

Kawada Mizuho. *Kataoka Kenkichi sensei den*. Kyoto: Ritsumeikan daigaku shuppanbu, 1940.

Kikegawa Hiroshi. *Meiji chihō seido no seiritsu katei*. Tokyo: Tokyo shisei chōsakai, 1955.

Kimura Motoi and Sugimoto Toshio. *Fudai hansei no tenkai to Meiji ishin: Shimoosa Sakura han*. Tokyo: Bungadō ginkō kenkyūsha, 1963.

Kitajima Masamoto. *Edo bakufu no kenryoku kōzō*. Tokyo: Iwanami shoten, 1964.

Kokuryūkai ed. *Seinankiden*, vols. 1 and 2. Tokyo: Kokuryūkai honbu, 1908.

Kondō Testuo. "Chiso kaisei to kisei jinushi." *Tochi seido shigaku*, no. 11 (1961): 16–30.

*Kōno Banshū den*, 2 vols. Tokyo: Kōno Banshū den hensankai, 1924.

*Kumamotokenshi, kindai*, vol. 1. Kumamoto: Kumamoto ken, 1961.

Kurihara Ryōichi. *Bakumatsu shotai hyakusen*. Tokyo: Akita shoten, 1974.

Lockwood, William W. *Economic Development of Japan*, rev. ed. Princeton, N.J.: Princeton University Press, 1968.

——, ed. *The State and Economic Enterprise in Japan*. Princeton, N.J.: Princeton University Press, 1965.

McLaren, Walter W., ed. "Japanese Government Documents." *Transactions of the Asiatic Society of Japan* 42, pt. 1 (1914).

Maruyama Masao. "Meiji kokka no shisō," in Rekishi gakkai, ed., *Nihon shakai no shiteki kyūmei*, pp. 181–236. Tokyo: Iwanami shoten, 1949.

———. *Thought and Behavior in Modern Japanese Politics.* Oxford: Oxford University Press, 1963.

Masumi Junnosuke, *Nihon seitōshiron*, vol. 1. Tokyo: Tokyo daigaku shuppankai, 1965.

Matono Hansuke. *Etō Nampaku*, 2 vols. Tokyo: Nampaku kenshōkai, 1915.

Matsumoto Sannosuke. "Keimō shisō no tenkai," in Hashikawa and Matsumoto, eds. *Kindai Nihon shisōshi*, vol. 1, pp. 151–79. Tokyo: Yūhikaku, 1971.

Matsuo Shōichi. *Jiyū minken shisō no kenkyū.* Tokyo: Kashiwa shobō, 1965.

Mayo, Marlene J. "The Iwakura Embassy and the Unequal Treaties, 1871–1873," Ph.D dissertation, Columbia University, 1961.

———. "Rationality in the Meiji Restoration: the Iwakura Embassy," in Harootunian and Silberman, eds., *Modern Japanese Leadership: Transition and Change*, pp. 323–69. Tucson, University of Arizona Press, 1966.

Meiji shiryō kenkyū renrakukai, ed. *Kindai shisō no keisei.* Tokyo: Ochanomizu shobō, 1959.

Mioka Takeo. *Yuri Kimimasa den.* Tokyo: Kōyūkan, 1917.

Miyake Setsurei. *Dōjidaishi*, vol. 1. Tokyo: Iwanami shoten, 1949.

Miyamoto Mataji, ed. *Osaka no kenkyū.* Osaka: Seibundō, 1967.

Miyatake Gaikotsu. *Fuhankenseishi.* Tokyo: Natori shoten, 1942.

Moore, Barrington, Jr. *Social Origins of Dictatorship and Democracy: Lord and Peasant in the Making of the Modern World.* Boston: Beacon, 1966.

Mōri Toshihiko. *Meiji rokunen seihen.* Tokyo: Chuō kōronsha, 1979.

*Nagasaki kenshi*, vols. 2, 3, and 4. Tokyo: Yoshikawa kōbunkan, 1973–76.

Naikaku kanbō. *Naikakuseido nanajūnenshi.* Tokyo: Ōkurashō insatsukyoku, 1955.

Najita, Tetsuo. *Hara Kei in the Politics of Compromise, 1905–1915.* Cambridge, Mass.: Harvard University Press, 1967.

Nakamura, James I. *Agricultural Production and the Economic Development of Japan, 1873–1922.* Princeton, N.J.: Princeton University Press, 1965.

Nakane, Chie. *Japanese Society*. Berkeley and Los Angeles: University of California Press, 1970.

Nihon keizai kenkyūjo, ed. *Kinsei Nihon no sandai kaikaku*. Tokyo: Ryuginsha, 1944.

Niwa Kunio. *Meiji ishin no tochihenkaku*. Tokyo: Ochanomizu shobō, 1962.

Norman, E. Herbert. "Feudal Background of Japanese Politics," in Dower, ed., *Origins of the Modern Japanese State*, pp. 317–464. New York: Pantheon Books, 1975.

——."Japan's Emergence as a Modern State," in Dower, ed., *Origins of the Modern Japanese State*, pp. 109–316. New York: Pantheon Books, 1975.

Ōe Shinobu. "Kumamotohan ni okeru hansei kaikaku," in Horie, ed., *Hansei kaikaku no kenkyū*, pp. 15–60. Tokyo: Ochanomizu shobō, 1955.

——. *Meiji kokka no seiritsu, tennōsei seiritsushi kenkyū*. Tokyo: Mineruba shobō, 1959.

Ogata Hiroyasu. "Kōshisci no kōsatsu." *Shakaikagaku tōkyū* 2, no. 2 (1957). 301–34.

Ōishi Kaichirō. *Nihon chihō zaigyōseishi josetsu*. Tokyo: Ochanomizu shobō, 1961.

Oka Yoshitake. *Kindai Nihon seijishi*, vol. 1. Tokyo: Sōbunsha, 1947.

——. *Reimeiki no Meiji Nihon: Nichi-Bei kōshōshi no shikaku ni oite*. Tokyo: Miraisha, 1964.

*Okayama kenseishi*, vol. 1. Okayama: Okayamaken, 1967.

Ōkubo Toshiaki. "Gokajō no seimon ni kansuru kōsatsu." *Rekishi chiri* 88 (1957): 1–27.

——. *Iwakura shisetsu no kenkyū*. Tokyo: Munetaka shobō, 1976.

——. *Meiji kempō no dekirumade*. Tokyo: Shibundō, 1956.

——. "Meiji shinseikenka no Kyūshū," in Ōkubo ed., *Meiji ishin to Kyūshū*, pp. 367–530. Tokyo: Heibonsha, 1973.

*Ōkumakō hachijūgonenshi*, 2 vols. Tokyo: Ōkumakō hachijūgonenshi hensankai, 1925.

Osatake Takeki. *Ishin zengo ni okeru rikkenshisō*. Tokyo: Jitsugyō no Nihonsha, 1948.

——. *Nihon kenseishi taikō*, 2 vols. Tokyo: Nihon hyōronsha, 1938.

Ōshima Tarō. *Nihon chihō gyōzaiseishi josetsu*. Tokyo: Miraisha, 1968.

Ōtsu Junichirō. *Dai Nihon kenseishi*, vol. 1. Tokyo: Hōbunkan, 1927.

Pittau, Joseph S. J. *Political Thought in Early Meiji Japan, 1869–1889*. Cambridge, Mass.: Harvard University Press, 1967.

Reischauer, Edwin O. *Japan, Past and Present*. New York: Knopf, 1964.

Rekishigaku kenkyūkai, ed. *Meiji ishin to jinushisei.* Tokyo: Iwanami shoten, 1956.

——. *Nihon shakai no shiteki kyūmei.* Tokyo: Iwanami shoten, 1949.

Sakata Yoshio, ed. *Meiji ishin no mondaiten.* Tokyo: Miraisha, 1962.

Sansom, George B. *The Western World and Japan: A Study in the Interaction of European and Asiatic Cultures.* New York: Knopf, 1950.

Sashihara Yasuzō. *Meiji seishi,* in *MBZ,* vol. 2, 1929.

Satō Seizaburō. "Ōkubo Toshimichi," in Kamishima, ed., *Kenryoku no shisō,* pp. 35–37. Tokyo: Chikuma shobō, 1965.

Sawada Akira. *Meiji zaisei no kiso kenkyū.* Tokyo: Kashiwa shobō, 1966.

Scalapino, Robert. *Democracy and the Party Movement in Prewar Japan.* Berkeley and Los Angeles: University of California Press, 1962.

Seki Junya. *Hansei kaikaku to Meiji ishin.* Tokyo: Yūhikaku, 1956.

——. *Meiji ishin to chiso kaisei.* Tokyo: Mineruba shobō, 1967.

Shibahara Takuji. *Meiji ishin no kenryoku kiban.* Tokyo: Ochanomizu shobō, 1965.

Shimoyama Saburō. *Kindai tennōsei kenkyū josetsu.* Tokyo: Iwanami shoten, 1975.

*Shinshū Shimanekenshi,* vols. 2 and 7. Shimane: Shimane ken, 1965 and 1967.

Shōji Kichinosuke. *Nihon seisha seitō hattatsushi.* Tokyo: Ochanomizu shobō, 1959.

Shumpokō tsuishōkai, ed., *Itō Hirobumi den,* vol. 1. Tokyo: Shumpokō tsuishōkai, 1940.

Smith, Thomas C. *The Agrarian Origins of Modern Japan.* Stanford, Cal.: Stanford University Press, 1959.

——. "Japan's Aristocratic Revolution," in Reinhard Bendix and Seymour M. Lipset, eds., *Class, Status and Power,* pp. 135–40. New York: The Free Press, 1966.

——. *Political Change and Industrial Development in Japan: Government Enterprise, 1868–1880.* Stanford, Cal.: Stanford University Press, 1955.

Soejima Yasoroku. *Kaikoku gojūnenshi,* vol. 1. Tokyo: Kaikoku gojūnenshi hakkōjo, 1900.

Someno Yoshinobu. "Saiban seido," in *Kōza Nihon kindaihō hattatsushi.* vol. 6, pp. 60–76. Tokyo: Keisō shobō, 1967.

Steiner, Kurt. "Popular Political Participation and Political Development in Japan: The Rural Level," in Ward, ed., *Political Development in Modern Japan,* pp. 213–47. Princeton, N.J.: Princeton University Press, 1968.

Suzuki Takashige, *Daikeishi Kawaji Toshiyoshikun den.* Tokyo: Tō-yōdō, 1912.

Suzuki Yasuzō. *Jiyū minken.* Tokyo: Hakuyōsha, 1948.

———. *Jiyū minken, kempō happu.* Tokyo: Hakuyōsha, 1949.

Tamamuro Taijō. *Saigō Takamori.* Tokyo: Iwanami shoten, 1960.

Tanaka Akira. *Kindai tennōsei e no dōtei.* Tokyo: Yoshikawa kōbundō, 1979.

———. *Meiji ishin seijishi kenkyū.* Tokyo: Aoki shoten, 1963.

Tokutomi Iichirō. *Kinsei Nihon kokuminshi,* vols. 86, 87, 100. Tokyo: Minyūsha, 1962.

———. *Kōshaku Matsukata Masayoshi den,* 2 vols. Tokyo: Matsukata Masayoshi denki hakkōjo, 1935.

———. *Kōshaku Yamagata Aritomo den,* 3 vols. Tokyo: Yamagata Aritomokō kinen jigyōkai, 1933.

———. *Ōkubo Kōtō sensei.* Tokyo: Minyūsha, 1927.

Tokyo shisei chōsakai. *Jichi gojūnenshi.* Tokyo: Tokyo shisei chōsakai, 1940.

Totman, Conrad. *The Collapse of the Tokugawa Bakufu, 1862–1868.* Honolulu, Hawaii: University of Hawaii Press, 1980.

———. *Politics in the Tokugawa Bakufu, 1600–1843.* Cambridge, Mass.: Harvard University Press, 1967.

Tōyama Shigeki. *Meiji ishin.* Tokyo: Iwanami shoten, 1951 and 1972.

———. "Seikanron, jiyūminkenron, hōkenron," in Meiji shiryō kenkyū renrakukai, ed., *Kindai shisō no keisei,* pp. 35–119. Tokyo: Ochanomizu shobō, 1959.

———. "Yūshi sensei no seiritsu," in Horie and Tōyama, eds., *Jiyū minkenki no kenkyū,* vol. 1, pp. 1–44. Tokyo: Yūhikaku, 1959.

Tōyama Shigeki and Adachi Shizuko, eds. *Kindai Nihon seijishi hikkei.* Tokyo: Iwanami shoten, 1961.

Tsuchiya Takao. *Hōkenshakai hōkai katei no kenkyū.* Tokyo: Kōbunkan, 1927.

Tsuchiya Takao and Ono Michio, comps. and eds. *Meiji shonen nōmin sōjōroku.* Tokyo: Keisō shobō, 1953.

Tsuda Shigemaro. *Meiji seijō to shin Takayuki.* Tokyo: Joshokai, 1928.

Tsukahira, Toshio G. *Feudal Control in Tokugawa Japan: the Sankin Kōtai System.* Cambridge, Mass.: Harvard University Press, 1966.

Tsumaki Chūta. *Shōgiku Kidokō den,* 2 vols. Tokyo: Meiji shoin, 1927.

Uete Michiari. *Nihon kindai shisō no keisei.* Tokyo: Iwanami shoten, 1974.

Ukita Kazutami. "Seitōshi," in Soejima Yasoroku, ed., *Kaikoku gojū-nenshi*, vol. 1. Tokyo: Kaikoku gojūnenshi hakkōjo, 1900.

Umegaki, Michio. "From Domain to Prefecture," in Jansen and Rozman, eds. *Japan in Transition: From Tokugawa to Meiji*, pp. 91–110. Princeton, N.J.: Princeton University Press, 1986.

Unno Fukuju and Watanabe Takaki. "Meiji kokka to chihōjichi," in Hara et al., eds., *Taikei Nihon kokkashi*, vol. 4, pp. 207–26. Tokyo: Tokyo daigaku shuppankai, 1975.

Wagatsuma Sakae, ed. *Nihon seiji saibanshiroku, Meiji zenki.* Tokyo: Daiichi hōki shuppan, 1962.

Ward, Robert E., ed. *Political Development in Modern Japan.* Princeton, N.J.: Princeton University Press, 1968.

Watanabe Takaki. "Chihō minkai no seiritsu katei." *Chihōshi kenkyū* 19, no. 1 (1969): 21–39.

Wilson, Robert A. "Genesis of the Meiji Government in Japan, 1868–1871," *University of California Publications in History* 56 (1957).

Yamanaka Einosuke. "Meiji shoki kanryōsei no keisei to Sakai kenchiji Ogō Kazutoshi," in Miyamoto Mataji, ed., *Osaka no kenkyū*, pp. 73–112. Osaka, Seibundō, 1967.

——. *Nihon kindai kokka no keisei to kanryōsei.* Tokyo: Kōbundō, 1974.

Yuri Masamichi. *Shishaku Yuri Kimimasa den.* Tokyo: Iwanami shoten, 1940.

# Index

Abolition of the feudal domains and the creation of the prefectures. *See Haihan chiken*

Absolutism, 11; in the Meiji histories, 8–13; and the fall of the Tokugawa, 9, 10–11, 20

Aichi (ken), 147–48

*Aikoku kōtō* (Public Party of the Patriots), 161, 195, 200

*Aikokusha* (Society of Patriots), 192; and the Osaka Conference, 202–4; as a national version of *Risshisha*, 204; and the popular rights movement, 207–11. *See also* Itagaki Taisuke; *Risshisha*

Aizu (han), 26, 37, 72, 97; and the Boshin War, 39, 50–52

Aomori (ken), 107

Asano Nagakoto, 42

Ayakōji (Ōhara) Toshizane, 41

Bakufu. *See* Tokugawa bakufu

Bakumatsu: in the Meiji histories, 19–20; and the nature of political competition, 20, 23–30, 179; and the rise of the Restoration activists, 23–24, 179–280; and daimyo, 24–26; the Tokugawa adaptation to, 26–30

Battle of Toba and Fushimi, 35, 36, 56, 83, 94, 124; and Hamada han, 37–38; and the Oath, 55

Bōjō Toshiakira, 125, 231 n. 25

Boshin War (War of the Restoration), 4, 5, 11, 17, 35, 50, 64, 90, 95, 96, 111; and the feudal domains, 35–39, 51–52, 61, 63, 65, 77, 92, 97; and the resurrection of feudal loyalism, 38–39, 40, 63, 81, 94; and the Tokugawa mainhouse, 39–40; and the Tokugawa territories, 40–43; and the Oath, 51–52, 55–56; in the Meiji histories, 52; and the financial burden, 62, 79–80, 100

*Bugyō*, 41

"Centralized feudalism," 3, 48; and the Tokugawa bakufu, 20–22; and the feudal domains, 20–23

*Chihōkan kaigi* (Prefectural Governors' Conference), 150, 153, 191;